ETHNO-CULTURAL GROUPS AND VISIBLE MINORITIES IN CANADIAN POLITICS

*This is Volume 7 in a series of studies
commissioned as part of the research program
of the Royal Commission on Electoral Reform
and Party Financing*

ETHNO-CULTURAL GROUPS AND VISIBLE MINORITIES IN CANADIAN POLITICS
THE QUESTION OF ACCESS

Kathy Megyery
Editor

Volume 7 of the Research Studies

ROYAL COMMISSION ON ELECTORAL REFORM
AND PARTY FINANCING
AND CANADA COMMUNICATION GROUP –
PUBLISHING, SUPPLY AND SERVICES CANADA

DUNDURN PRESS
TORONTO AND OXFORD

© Minister of Supply and Services Canada, 1991
Printed and bound in Canada
ISBN 1-55002-103-6
ISSN 1188-2743
Catalogue No. Z1-1989/2-41-7E

Published by Dundurn Press Limited in cooperation with the Royal
Commission on Electoral Reform and Party Financing and Canada
Communication Group – Publishing, Supply and Services Canada.

Canadian Cataloguing in Publication Data

Main entry under title:
Ethno-cultural groups and visible minorities in Canadian politics

(Research studies ; 7)
Issued also in French under title: Minorités visibles, communautés ethno-
  culturelles et politique canadienne.
ISBN 1-55002-103-6

  1. Minorities – Canada – Political activity. 2. Ethnic groups – Canada –
Political activity. I. Megyery, Kathy, 1962– . II. Canada. Royal Commission
on Electoral Reform and Party Financing. III. Series: Research studies
(Canada. Royal Commission on Electoral Reform and Party Financing) ; 7.

FC104.E84 1991   323.1'71   C91-090519-3   F1035.A1E84 1991

Dundurn Press Limited
2181 Queen Street East
Suite 301
Toronto, Canada
M4E 1E5

Dundurn Distribution
73 Lime Walk
Headington
Oxford, England
OX3 7AD

CONTENTS

TABLES

1. THE HOUSE THE PARTIES BUILT: (RE)CONSTRUCTING ETHNIC REPRESENTATION IN CANADIAN POLITICS

2. POLITICS AND ETHNICITY: REPRESENTATION OF ETHNIC AND VISIBLE-MINORITY GROUPS IN THE HOUSE OF COMMONS

3. VISIBLE MINORITIES AND THE CANADIAN POLITICAL SYSTEM

FOREWORD

THE ROYAL COMMISSION on Electoral Reform and Party Financing was established in November 1989. Our mandate was to inquire into and report on the appropriate principles and process that should govern the election of members of the House of Commons and the financing of political parties and candidates' campaigns. To conduct such a comprehensive examination of Canada's electoral system, we held extensive public consultations and developed a research program designed to ensure that our recommendations would be guided by an independent foundation of empirical inquiry and analysis.

The Commission's in-depth review of the electoral system was the first of its kind in Canada's history of electoral democracy. It was dictated largely by the major constitutional, social and technological changes of the past several decades, which have transformed Canadian society, and their concomitant influence on Canadians' expectations of the political process itself. In particular, the adoption in 1982 of the *Canadian Charter of Rights and Freedoms* has heightened Canadians' awareness of their democratic and political rights and of the way they are served by the electoral system.

The importance of electoral reform cannot be overemphasized. As the Commission's work proceeded, Canadians became increasingly preoccupied with constitutional issues that have the potential to change the nature of Confederation. No matter what their beliefs or political allegiances in this continuing debate, Canadians agree that constitutional change must be achieved in the context of fair and democratic processes. We cannot complacently assume that our current electoral process will always meet this standard or that it leaves no room for improvement. Parliament and the national government must be seen as legitimate; electoral reform can both enhance the stature of national political institutions and reinforce their ability to define the future of our country in ways that command Canadians' respect and confidence and promote the national interest.

In carrying out our mandate, we remained mindful of the importance of protecting our democratic heritage, while at the same time balancing it against the emerging values that are injecting a new dynamic into the electoral system. If our system is to reflect the realities of Canadian political life, then reform requires more than mere tinkering with electoral laws and practices.

Our broad mandate challenged us to explore a full range of options. We commissioned more than 100 research studies, to be published in a 23-volume collection. In the belief that our electoral laws must measure up to the very best contemporary practice, we examined election-related laws and processes in all of our provinces and territories and studied comparable legislation and processes in established democracies around the world. This unprecedented array of empirical study and expert opinion made a vital contribution to our deliberations. We made every effort to ensure that the research was both intellectually rigorous and of practical value. All studies were subjected to peer review, and many of the authors discussed their preliminary findings with members of the political and academic communities at national symposiums on major aspects of the electoral system.

The Commission placed the research program under the able and inspired direction of Dr. Peter Aucoin, Professor of Political Science and Public Administration at Dalhousie University. We are confident that the efforts of Dr. Aucoin, together with those of the research coordinators and scholars whose work appears in this and other volumes, will continue to be of value to historians, political scientists, parliamentarians and policy makers, as well as to thoughtful Canadians and the international community.

Along with the other Commissioners, I extend my sincere gratitude to the entire Commission staff for their dedication and commitment. I also wish to thank the many people who participated in our symposiums for their valuable contributions, as well as the members of the research and practitioners' advisory groups whose counsel significantly aided our undertaking.

Pierre Lortie
Chairman

INTRODUCTION

THE ROYAL COMMISSION'S research program constituted a comprehensive and detailed examination of the Canadian electoral process. The scope of the research, undertaken to assist Commissioners in their deliberations, was dictated by the broad mandate given to the Commission.

The objective of the research program was to provide Commissioners with a full account of the factors that have shaped our electoral democracy. This dictated, first and foremost, a focus on federal electoral law, but our inquiries also extended to the Canadian constitution, including the institutions of parliamentary government, the practices of political parties, the mass media and nonpartisan political organizations, as well as the decision-making role of the courts with respect to the constitutional rights of citizens. Throughout, our research sought to introduce a historical perspective in order to place the contemporary experience within the Canadian political tradition.

We recognized that neither our consideration of the factors shaping Canadian electoral democracy nor our assessment of reform proposals would be as complete as necessary if we failed to examine the experiences of Canadian provinces and territories and of other democracies. Our research program thus emphasized comparative dimensions in relation to the major subjects of inquiry.

Our research program involved, in addition to the work of the Commission's research coordinators, analysts and support staff, over 200 specialists from 28 universities in Canada, from the private sector and, in a number of cases, from abroad. Specialists in political science constituted the majority of our researchers, but specialists in law, economics, management, computer sciences, ethics, sociology and communications, among other disciplines, were also involved.

In addition to the preparation of research studies for the Commission, our research program included a series of research seminars, symposiums and workshops. These meetings brought together the Commissioners, researchers, representatives from the political parties, media personnel and others with practical experience in political parties, electoral politics and public affairs. These meetings provided not only a forum for discussion of the various subjects of the Commission's mandate, but also an opportunity for our research to be assessed by those with an intimate knowledge of the world of political practice.

These public reviews of our research were complemented by internal and external assessments of each research report by persons qualified in the area; such assessments were completed prior to our decision to publish any study in the series of research volumes.

The Research Branch of the Commission was divided into several areas, with the individual research projects in each area assigned to the research coordinators as follows:

F. Leslie Seidle   Political Party and Election Finance
Herman Bakvis   Political Parties
Kathy Megyery   Women, Ethno-Cultural Groups
                                   and Youth
David Small   Redistribution; Electoral Boundaries;
                                   Voter Registration
Janet Hiebert   Party Ethics
Michael Cassidy   Democratic Rights; Election
                                   Administration
Robert A. Milen   Aboriginal Electoral Participation
                                   and Representation
Frederick J. Fletcher   Mass Media and Broadcasting in
                                   Elections
David Mac Donald   Direct Democracy
(Assistant Research
Coordinator)

These coordinators identified appropriate specialists to undertake research, managed the projects and prepared them for publication. They also organized the seminars, symposiums and workshops in their research areas and were responsible for preparing presentations and briefings to help the Commission in its deliberations and decision making. Finally, they participated in drafting the Final Report of the Commission.

On behalf of the Commission, I welcome the opportunity to thank the following for their generous assistance in producing these research studies – a project that required the talents of many individuals.

In performing their duties, the research coordinators made a notable contribution to the work of the Commission. Despite the pressures of tight deadlines, they worked with unfailing good humour and the utmost congeniality. I thank all of them for their consistent support and cooperation.

In particular, I wish to express my gratitude to Leslie Seidle, senior research coordinator, who supervised our research analysts and support staff in Ottawa. His diligence, commitment and professionalism not only set high standards, but also proved contagious. I am grateful to Kathy Megyery, who performed a similar function in Montreal with equal aplomb and skill. Her enthusiasm and dedication inspired us all.

On behalf of the research coordinators and myself, I wish to thank our research analysts: Daniel Arsenault, Eric Bertram, Cécile Boucher, Peter Constantinou, Yves Denoncourt, David Docherty, Luc Dumont, Jane Dunlop, Scott Evans, Véronique Garneau, Keith Heintzman, Paul Holmes, Hugh Mellon, Cheryl D. Mitchell, Donald Padget, Alain Pelletier, Dominique Tremblay and Lisa Young. The Research Branch was strengthened by their ability to carry out research in a wide variety of areas, their intellectual curiosity and their team spirit.

The work of the research coordinators and analysts was greatly facilitated by the professional skills and invaluable cooperation of Research Branch staff members: Paulette LeBlanc, who, as administrative assistant, managed the flow of research projects; Hélène Leroux, secretary to the research coordinators, who produced briefing material for the Commissioners and who, with Lori Nazar, assumed responsibility for monitoring the progress of research projects in the latter stages of our work; Kathleen McBride and her assistant Natalie Brose, who created and maintained the database of briefs and hearings transcripts; and Richard Herold and his assistant Susan Dancause, who were responsible for our research library. Jacinthe Séguin and Cathy Tucker also deserve thanks – in addition to their duties as receptionists, they assisted in a variety of ways to help us meet deadlines.

We were extremely fortunate to obtain the research services of first-class specialists from the academic and private sectors. Their contributions are found in this and the other 22 published research volumes. We thank them for the quality of their work and for their willingness to contribute and to meet our tight deadlines.

Our research program also benefited from the counsel of Jean-Marc Hamel, Special Adviser to the Chairman of the Commission and former

Chief Electoral Officer of Canada, whose knowledge and experience proved invaluable.

In addition, numerous specialists assessed our research studies. Their assessments not only improved the quality of our published studies, but also provided us with much-needed advice on many issues. In particular, we wish to single out professors Donald Blake, Janine Brodie, Alan Cairns, Kenneth Carty, John Courtney, Peter Desbarats, Jane Jenson, Richard Johnston, Vincent Lemieux, Terry Morley and Joseph Wearing, as well as Ms. Beth Symes.

Producing such a large number of studies in less than a year requires a mastery of the skills and logistics of publishing. We were fortunate to be able to count on the Commission's Director of Communications, Richard Rochefort, and Assistant Director, Hélène Papineau. They were ably supported by the Communications staff: Patricia Burden, Louise Dagenais, Caroline Field, Claudine Labelle, France Langlois, Lorraine Maheux, Ruth McVeigh, Chantal Morissette, Sylvie Patry, Jacques Poitras and Claudette Rouleau-O'Toole.

To bring the project to fruition, the Commission also called on specialized contractors. We are deeply grateful for the services of Ann McCoomb (references and fact checking); Marthe Lemery, Pierre Chagnon and the staff of Communications Com'ça (French quality control); Norman Bloom, Pamela Riseborough and associates of B&B Editorial Consulting (English adaptation and quality control); and Mado Reid (French production). Al Albania and his staff at Acart Graphics designed the studies and produced some 2 400 tables and figures.

The Commission's research reports constitute Canada's largest publishing project of 1991. Successful completion of the project required close cooperation between the public and private sectors. In the public sector, we especially acknowledge the excellent service of the Privy Council unit of the Translation Bureau, Department of the Secretary of State of Canada, under the direction of Michel Parent, and our contacts Ruth Steele and Terry Denovan of the Canada Communication Group, Department of Supply and Services.

The Commission's co-publisher for the research studies was Dundurn Press of Toronto, whose exceptional service is gratefully acknowledged. Wilson & Lafleur of Montreal, working with the Centre de Documentation Juridique du Québec, did equally admirable work in preparing the French version of the studies.

Teams of editors, copy editors and proofreaders worked diligently under stringent deadlines with the Commission and the publishers to prepare some 20 000 pages of manuscript for design, typesetting and printing. The work of these individuals, whose names are listed elsewhere in this volume, was greatly appreciated.

Our acknowledgements extend to the contributions of the Commission's Executive Director, Guy Goulard, and the administration and executive support teams: Maurice Lacasse, Denis Lafrance and Steve Tremblay (finance); Thérèse Lacasse and Mary Guy-Shea (personnel); Cécile Desforges (assistant to the Executive Director); Marie Dionne (administration); Anna Bevilacqua (records); and support staff members Michelle Bélanger, Roch Langlois, Michel Lauzon, Jean Mathieu, David McKay and Pierrette McMurtie, as well as Denise Miquelon and Christiane Séguin of the Montreal office.

A special debt of gratitude is owed to Marlène Girard, assistant to the Chairman. Her ability to supervise the logistics of the Commission's work amid the tight schedules of the Chairman and Commissioners contributed greatly to the completion of our task.

I also wish to express my deep gratitude to my own secretary, Liette Simard. Her superb administrative skills and great patience brought much-appreciated order to my penchant for the chaotic workstyle of academe. She also assumed responsibility for the administrative coordination of revisions to the final drafts of volumes 1 and 2 of the Commission's Final Report. I owe much to her efforts and assistance.

Finally, on behalf of the research coordinators and myself, I wish to thank the Chairman, Pierre Lortie, the members of the Commission, Pierre Fortier, Robert Gabor, William Knight and Lucie Pépin, and former members Elwood Cowley and Senator Donald Oliver. We are honoured to have worked with such an eminent and thoughtful group of Canadians, and we have benefited immensely from their knowledge and experience. In particular, we wish to acknowledge the creativity, intellectual rigour and energy our Chairman brought to our task. His unparalleled capacity to challenge, to bring out the best in us, was indeed inspiring.

Peter Aucoin
Director of Research

PREFACE

THIS VOLUME EXAMINES the participation of ethno-cultural groups in Canada's electoral system. The underlying objective of this research is to determine the extent to which these groups are represented in the political system in order to provide a picture of the obstacles they may be facing and thus find ways of maximizing their participation and representation in the electoral process.

The study of ethno-cultural groups, and visible minorities in particular, is especially important given they make up a growing portion of the Canadian population. Canadian society has become increasingly open to ethnic pluralism since the 1960s – with the Canadian Bill of Rights, multiculturalism policy and, most recently, the *Canadian Charter of Rights and Freedoms* being the most notable expressions of that openness.

The analysis is carried out using three approaches. The first, adopted by Daiva Stasiulis and Yasmeen Abu-Laban, concentrates on political parties. The authors analyse the strategies political parties used to encourage participation of ethno-cultural groups and visible minorities during the 1984 and 1988 elections and the 1990 Liberal leadership convention. They conclude that the underrepresentation of ethno-cultural groups and visible minorities in political parties is the result of structural, cultural and organizational obstacles. According to Stasiulis and Abu-Laban, language barriers help to explain the lack of familiarity with Canada's political culture. Nor do visible minorities in general receive support from the political parties. The authors analyse a number of factors that reinforce the exclusion of ethnic groups, including the bicultural tradition in Canadian politics and procedures for recruiting candidates, which are based for the most part on traditional networks.

The second study, by Alain Pelletier, assesses changes in the representation of ethno-cultural groups, and visible minorities in particular, in the House of Commons since 1965. The author notes that in both cases there has been a significant and constant increase in the representation of these groups. However, visible minorities lag well behind other ethno-cultural groups in their efforts to achieve equitable representation. The author also considers the likelihood of electoral success of a candidate who is a member of one of these groups. Based on the results of the 1988 election, Pelletier shows that although candidates from ethno-cultural groups usually ran in constituencies where ethno-cultural groups made up at least 10 percent of the population, they seldom ran in constituencies where the party they represented had won in 1984 or 1980. Here again, visible minorities are in a less favourable situation than ethno-cultural groups as a whole.

The third approach, adopted by Carolle Simard, examines attitudes toward and perceptions of the Canadian political system by these groups in order to see how they can be integrated into that system. Simard bases her analysis in part on semi-structured interviews with the leaders of six visible minority communities. She concludes that there is an internal dynamic within each community that is determined by cultural, religious, historical, generational, personal and migrational factors. Nevertheless, the interviews reveal that members of visible minorities are clearly interested in Canadian politics and want to participate and play an increased role. The interviewees did not always feel that Canadian society was as open as they would like, however; ethnic concerns tend to be marginalized. Although they firmly believe Canada is free, democratic and egalitarian, they would also like to see it become a multi-ethnic democracy. Simard also discovered that members of these communities detect a gap between the rights that accompany citizenship and the real opportunities to exercise these rights. They feel excluded from the decision-making process and from the networks of influence within political parties, and they point out the system's lack of balanced representation. These communities see this concept of representativeness as a way of protecting their specific interests.

These studies reveal the nature of the underrepresentation of ethno-cultural groups, and visible minorities in particular, in both the House of Commons and political parties. These studies also underline the progress that has been made in recent years, attributable in large part to the greater acceptance of ethnic pluralism in Canadian society and to the desire of members of ethno-cultural communities to integrate into the Canadian political system.

I want to thank Alain Pelletier, researcher with the Commission, for his valuable assistance and expertise in this area, and Peter Aucoin, Director of Research, for his guidance and unfailingly cheerful support.

Kathy Megyery
Research Coordinator

ETHNO-CULTURAL GROUPS AND VISIBLE MINORITIES IN CANADIAN POLITICS

1

THE HOUSE THE PARTIES BUILT
(Re)constructing Ethnic Representation in Canadian Politics

Daiva K. Stasiulis
Yasmeen Abu-Laban

D URING BOTH THE 1988 federal election and the 1990 Liberal leadership convention, "ethnic politics" captured media attention. The constituency nomination meetings preceding the federal election in many Toronto-area and other urban ridings were hotly contested by "ethnic" (chiefly visible minority and Southern European) candidates. Similarly, the campaign for a new national Liberal leader saw organizers for contending leadership candidates filling delegate-selection meetings with newly recruited ethnic minority supporters.

Divergent interpretations have accompanied the increased visibility of members of non-Anglo, non-French communities in candidate and leadership selection processes within the three major political parties. Where some observers have seen manipulation of networks of uninformed immigrants and abuse of established liberal democratic processes by "ethnic brokers," others have discerned the efflorescence of democracy and the rejuvenating potential of the integration of politically astute ethnocultural minorities within parties that have historically been the preserve of white British and French interests. Still others have focused on what the candidate and leadership selection processes reveal about the limitations of the political parties themselves as democratic, accessible and accountable organizations.

This study investigates the ethnic activism reflected within these and other processes, and the responses of the parties to increased minority participation, in order to explore and illuminate the contemporary relationship between the three major national political parties and non-dominant ethnocultural groups. While in the past the major federal political parties have shown interest in ethnic minorities primarily as potential voters, more recently they have shown awareness, albeit unevenly across parties, regarding the issue of ethnic and visible minority representation within party organizations – as candidates for legislative office, and in positions of leadership. In large part, this new awareness is attributable to the pressures and proposals put forward by minorities active within the parties. Clearly, however, minorities within the parties express different perspectives on political action, including views on the most effective means of facilitating increased minority representation.

Although parties have begun to respond to ethnic diversity through both formal policies and informal liaison structures, our general assessment is that such responses have not gone far enough in redressing inequitable representation of ethnic – and particularly visible – minorities. More attention needs to be directed at the many obstacles pertaining to the traditional organizational culture and practices of the political parties that inhibit the participation and integration of new Canadians, ethnocultural minorities and visible minorities.

The existence of a federal policy on multiculturalism since 1972, endorsed by all three national parties, suggests the need to examine ethnicity in relation to party politics beyond Canada's historic French–British schism. Yet, for the most part, Canadian political science has been silent on the relationship between the political parties and minorities of non-Anglo, non-French, non-Aboriginal origins. This silence makes it difficult to account for emergent forms of ethnic politics that have characterized the constituency nominations during recent federal elections and delegate selection meetings. It also leaves unaccounted the minority strategies aimed at ameliorating the underrepresentation of ethnic and racial minorities within the major parties, particularly at higher levels, and the responses from party leaders and party organizations to such strategies.

Generally speaking, the representativeness of key political institutions, such as political parties, is considered to be the defining feature of democratic government (Bashevkin 1985, 80). Indeed, questions concerning representation within the parties invariably concern the nature of democracy in Canada, and they thus warrant serious attention. Underlying the heightened party involvement of minority groups is a strong belief among members of these groups in the need to redress statistical underrepresentation of ethnic and visible minorities – within elected and appointed party positions, within the party leadership, and within the federal House of Commons and the Cabinet. Such activism also challenges the manner in which the policy-related interests of minority groups are represented within the parties. The quality of interest or substantive representation of ethnic minorities is most evident in policy areas such as immigration, human rights, multiculturalism and external affairs, but it is not confined to policies with an obvious "ethnic" content or component.

Given the dearth of Canadian studies on the activities and representation of ethnic minorities in the major political parties, this research study is necessarily exploratory in nature and is heavily dependent upon the views, perceptions and interpretations of party activists and party officials. In exploring the activities of minorities in the Progressive Conservative, Liberal and New Democratic parties during candidate selection processes, this study is examining only a small segment of the political and party-based activities of ethnocultural minorities, albeit one that has received considerable attention within the media and within the parties themselves. A complete analysis of the efforts of ethnic minorities to exercise political influence would also investigate and account for the full range of "pressure group" activities through ethnic associations, through the "ethnic press," and through issue-specific organizations and coalitions, as well as other forms of protest and collective action directed at local, provincial and federal levels of government.

Such an analysis would also have to explain why ethnic minorities have made comparatively more significant advances in municipal and provincial politics than they have in the federal arena. Access to elected office for individuals of non-British, non-French origin has been greatest at the municipal level, where the financial costs incurred by candidates tend to be lower and the impediment of political party structures is less important. At provincial levels of leadership, recent instances of ethnic minority success include Premiers Joseph Ghiz of Prince Edward Island (Lebanese-Canadian, 1986) and Gary Filmon of Manitoba (Rumanian descent, 1988) and former Premiers Edward Schreyer of Manitoba (German descent, 1969–77; governor-general, 1979–84) and William Vander Zalm of British Columbia (Dutch-born, 1986–91). A comprehensive accounting of ethnic minority representation in Canadian political institutions would need to include consideration of the relatively greater visibility of minorities within the provincial party systems, as well as within municipal politics.

In focusing on the contemporary relationship between ethnocultural minorities and the federal Progressive Conservative, Liberal and New Democratic parties, it becomes clear that this relationship is complex and evades simplistic generalizations. For example, to the extent that social scientists have reflected on ethnic minorities in the electoral process, there has been a tendency to portray multiculturalism in terms of its utility as an electoral ploy designed to capture the so-called ethnic vote (Breton 1986, 53; Burnet 1978, 107). There are two related and problematic assumptions inherent in this generalization. The first is that minority ethnic groups are passive, that they merely respond to whatever pre-election promises the parties hold out, rather than engaging as active participants within party and electoral politics. The second is that the roughly one-third of the population comprising people of non-Aboriginal, non-French, and non-British origin is politically homogeneous, cohesive and like-minded, as reflected in the notion of the "third force."

However, the active participation of members of non-Anglo, non-French communities in recent candidate and leadership selection processes within the major parties undermines the notion that these communities are politically passive. Furthermore, while ethnocultural minorities may be seen as collectively contesting the hegemony of biculturalism and of racial and ethnic exclusivity within the federal party system, they are otherwise socially and politically diverse. For example, differences exist both between and within ethnic groups relating to such factors as their migration and settlement histories, generational composition, socio-economic status, official language competence, and, in comparison with white British and French populations, "racial" and cultural distinctiveness. In the Canadian context, these differences are compounded by the uneven geographical distribution of minority ethnic groups, rendering highly variable the relationship between the federal parties and minority ethnic groups, and accounting for the largely urban character of present-day "ethnic" electoral politics.

Ironically, it is only by keeping in mind the considerable heterogeneity of minority ethnic groups that the relationship between ethnocultural minorities and the three major parties can be understood. Ethnocultural minorities are here defined as non-British, non-French immigrants and their descendants. This collectivity excludes Aboriginal peoples but includes "visible minorities," which according to the federal government's employment equity definition are "persons, other than aboriginal peoples, who are ... non-white in colour or non-Caucasian in race."[1] What becomes clear in the political parties' efforts to contend with the multicultural, multiracial diversity of Canadian voters, and of their own party memberships, is that differences exist over the ranking of minority groups deemed most in need of special or enhanced means of representation. For instance, as will be elaborated in this study, tension exists within the Ontario New Democratic Party's affirmative action policy for electoral candidates between the promotion of "ethnic" candidates and affirmative action for visible minorities.

Indeed, within the everyday politics of parties, different definitions of the "excluded other" arise, vacillating between "visible minorities," "ethnic minorities" and "immigrants." Consensus is hindered by the fact that these concepts are socially constructed and are impregnated with common-sense forms of ideology and stereotyping. For example, while the concept of "immigrant" has a particular legal definition under Canadian law, in popular usage it takes on meaning that extends well beyond the legal definition. Thus, "immigrant" is popularly used to refer to people of colour, people from Third World countries, people who do not speak English or French well and who may hold menial jobs. Given the confusion and conflation in popular discourse over terms such as "ethnic," "visible minority" and "immigrant," it is understandable that there is considerable confusion and dissension within the parties about the definition of equity issues and associated target groups that need to be addressed in policy terms. These equity issues pertain to racism and the stigma attached to skin colour, and the disabling effects of a lack of competence in the official languages, or indeed the possession of a non-Anglo, non-French surname. In this, the necessity for special means of minority representation and the appropriate target groups for affirmative action or other ameliorative measures become issues infused with a great deal of controversy.

This study explores some of the debates taking place both within and between the major parties concerning ethnic minority representation. Its focus is twofold. First, it examines the activities of members of ethnocultural minorities in seeking more direct exercise of power within the federal parties as candidates for federal election, as convention delegates and as members of riding executives, and the perceptions of minority party activists regarding ethnic minority electoral strategies and their party's openness, accessibility and legitimacy.[2] Second, it surveys the responses of parties to the changing ethnocultural and racial composition of party activists, and the measures taken by the three major parties (at both the federal and Ontario provincial levels) to garner the support of ethnocultural minorities and to encourage the participation of minority group members within different levels of party organization and decision making. The guiding concerns of this study centre on issues of representation – for both the statistical

and substantive representation of minority groups within party organizations and the means to enhance such representation.

The study is divided into four sections. The first section offers a
historical perspective on the relationship between ethnocultural minorities and the three national parties. It examines barriers to participation
of ethnic minorities within the traditional parties and the limited historical representation afforded by these parties to non-British, non-
French groups. This section also discusses the current composition of
the House of Commons by ethnic origin. Efforts to draw from official
ethnic origin statistics poignantly illustrate how contested and variable the concept of ethnicity is, posing difficulties for the gathering and
interpretation of such vital information as the number of ethnic minorities within the political parties and the House of Commons. This poses
major challenges, both for researchers of "ethnic politics" and for party
organizations, where ethnicity is increasingly being recognized as something to be addressed by policies such as affirmative action and by liaison structures with ethnic communities.

The second and third sections explore the contemporary relationship
of ethnocultural minorities to the three parties and to their counterparts
at the provincial level in Ontario. Much of the information for these two
sections derives from a series of open-ended interviews with members
of Parliament, national and Ontario party staff, and party activists.[3]

The second section begins by drawing on census data to discuss
the demographic distribution of immigrants and ethnic minorities
across the 295 federal electoral constituencies in Canada. Ontario is
unique in having both the greatest proportion of recent immigrants in
its total population and the largest number of urban ridings with concentrations of minority ethnic groups. Given these patterns of concentration, Toronto-area ridings are particularly fertile ground for minority
ethnic party activism.

The second section also examines the avenues by which members
of ethnocultural minorities are seeking power within the parties, focusing on candidate and leadership selection. As is apparent in media
accounts, the increased activism of ethnic minorities has frequently
been sensationalized and has been portrayed in terms of the manipu-
lative tactics of ethnic brokers in relation to unruly and ill-informed
mobs recruited from ethnic minority communities. Our position is that
there is a need to separate the problems with rules and procedures governing candidate and leadership selection processes from the individuals and groups who have become recent participants in these processes.
All too often, responses from the parties' more established interests
have conflated the types of practices that accompany hotly contested

nomination battles with the ethnicity and "race" of those who have become actors and supporting casts in these processes. Such conflation reflects ethnic and racial biases, and also runs the risk of relieving parties of the responsibility of redressing biases within their own organizations and processes of recruitment. It is only by addressing these biases that the parties may become more representative and thus more democratic bodies.

The third section reviews the organizational structures developed to liaise with ethnic minority communities and looks at formal and informal affirmative measures developed within the three parties vis-à-vis ethnocultural minorities. Such policies and structures have been developed most extensively at the provincial level of the parties in Ontario, reflecting the high levels of ethnic diversity within that province. One major question examined here is to what extent such organizational structures are integrating – or ghettoizing – minority participation. This section also addresses matters such as the character and basis of support among ethnic minorities for the three national parties, minority perceptions of barriers to participation and influence within the parties, and the contested definitions of "disadvantaged minority" (such as visible minority versus ethnic minority).

The fourth section concludes the study with a discussion of suggested reforms in party politics to further the integration into and representation of various categories of ethnic minorities (such as visible minorities and immigrant groups that lack competence in the official languages) in the party system. The concerns expressed by MPs and by members and staff in all three parties speak to the need to balance accessibility, representativeness and democratic growth of the parties on the one hand, and their impartial, efficient and accountable operation on the other. Our recommendations focus on issues of accessibility and representativeness. We take the view that to maximize sensitivity to ethnocultural interests (such as human rights and antiracist issues, and immigration and refugee policies) within party organizations and the Canadian House of Commons, political parties must take responsibility for promoting greater accessibility to ethnic and racial minorities. Measures should be adopted to encourage and facilitate the greater involvement of minorities, not only as voters, but also as participants in the upper echelons of power and influence within the parties and within the government.

HISTORICAL PERSPECTIVES

The political representation of any group involves both numerical (or statistical) and substantive representation (or the representation of interests). While the relationship between these two dimensions of representation is complex (raising questions about the necessary connection or identity of an individual with his or her gender, class or ethnic group), we contend it is nonetheless important. As argued by several researchers who have charted the political participation of women, statistical representation of a given group in the House of Commons facilitates the articulation of views on issues and policies that are important to that group (Bashevkin 1985; Maillé 1990). Thus, in interviews with several ethnic minority MPs conducted in the current study, it was frequently suggested that their election fostered or strengthened sensitivity to particular issues, such as immigration and refugee policies, antiracism and human rights. Similarly, in addressing the impact of Blacks in American politics, Thernstrom notes the substantive difference made by increasing the presence of Blacks in positions of influence:

> Pulling blacks into the political process where they have been excluded serves ends other than holding racists in check and heightening confidence in black political competence. Whether on a city council, on a county commission, or in the state legislature, blacks inhibit the expression of prejudice, act as spokesmen for black interests, dispense patronage, and often facilitate the discussion of topics (such as black crime) that whites are reluctant to raise. That is, governing bodies function differently when they are racially mixed, particularly where blacks are new to politics and where racially insensitive language and discrimination in the provision of services are long-established political habits. (Thernstrom 1987, 239)

Writing on ethnic minorities in the British political system, Muhammed Anwar further highlights the connection between statistical representation and the representation of interests:

> One way to achieve political action [in implementing anti-racist policies] by the political parties is to increase the number of members of ethnic minorities who are active in the decision-making process. This will help to achieve equal opportunity not only within the political parties but also outside them. As the white members of the political parties become more aware of the issues and needs of ethnic minorities they will thus formulate and implement relevant policies. (Anwar 1986, 3)

Anwar's depiction of the relationship between statistical representation and social equity may be too simplistic. For instance, it is unmindful of the political sanctions and party discipline that restrict the attention paid to minority issues by ethnic minority politicians, the complexity of forces that determine state policies, and the strength of racist ideologies that are not simply dismantled through exposure to rational argumentation (see Albo and Jenson 1989; Stasiulis 1988a). Nonetheless, Anwar raises a legitimate point when he argues for the necessity – on social justice and democratic grounds – for the parties to reflect, within their decision-making structures, the ethnic diversity that exists within the larger society.

Viewed historically, the major political parties in Canada have not been representative of ethnic minorities. A large number of institutional and cultural barriers blocked access to the equitable participation of non-British, non-French minority groups within the traditional parties and the electoral system. Until recently, the House of Commons has had a limited number of MPs from minority backgrounds, and ethnic minorities have not had the same opportunity to organize their interests through the political parties that the French and British have enjoyed. Clearly, the nature of the relationship between Canada's major political parties and minority ethnic groups depends on the time period being addressed and on the ethnic group under examination. However, in general, the historical record suggests that all three parties have not fared well in statistically representing ethnocultural minorities within their ranks or in representing these minorities' interests in party and state policies. The following discussion suggests some reasons for this general pattern of minority exclusion, as well as providing some empirical evidence of minority underrepresentation.

Barriers to Participation and British–French Domination
Many obstacles, both within and external to the party system, have contributed to a pattern of neglect and exclusion of ethnocultural minorities and their concerns within the major parties. An explicitly racist and restrictive immigration policy prevailed from the 1880s until the 1960s, signalling the intentions of colonial authorities to develop Canada as a "white settler colony." The desirability of immigrants was judged according to a racial and ethnic pecking order, with the white Protestant British standing at the pinnacle as the model of cultural and physical acceptability (Palmer 1976, 85). It was against this model that all other potential immigrants were judged. For Asians and Blacks in particular, a marginal political status was linked to severe curtailment of the growth of their communities through restrictive immigration policies.

Denial of the franchise through provincial and federal legislation further secured this position of political marginality and subordination for Asians, and limited the chances of these groups to build links to, and have their interests met through, the party and electoral systems (Ward 1950, 235–37). In fact, in British Columbia, where the majority of Asians resided, politicians tried to outdo one another in promises and policies aimed at limiting the economic and political involvement of Asians in Canada (Burnet and Palmer 1988, 61).[4] Other groups, such as Central and Eastern Europeans labelled "enemy aliens" during the First World War, also faced periods of disenfranchisement and isolation from party and electoral politics.

While restrictions on immigration and denial of the franchise affected some minority ethnic groups more harshly and for longer periods of time than others, one feature of the Canadian party system that has affected all minority ethnic groups has been the pre-eminence given to the French–English question by all three major parties. The hegemonic vision of Canadian society reflected within party discourse has at best reflected biculturalism and at worst Anglo-conformity (Brodie and Jenson 1988; Peter 1981). This has meant that the collective identities and aspirations of the British, and to a lesser extent the French, have been legitimized within party and state discourse and agendas, whereas those of non-British, non-French groups have been suppressed.

More recently, multiculturalism has been added to the recipe of ethnic policies ascribed to by the parties as a means of accommodating the symbolic aspirations of non-British, non-French communities (Stasiulis 1988b). Nevertheless, as signified by the ancillary position of multicultural rights within the *Canadian Charter of Rights and Freedoms* and by the low status of the federal multiculturalism bureaucracy, multiculturalism has never seriously challenged the pre-eminent position of a national politics centred around the French–English question (Kallen 1987; Stasiulis 1988b, 1991).

No simple or automatic link exists between the official discourse on ethnicity of the parties, on the one hand, and on the statistical and substantive representation of ethnic minorities within the parties, on the other. Nonetheless, we maintain that the legitimacy given to the claims of particular groups, and the silence with which other claims have been received, have had an important influence in limiting access to the equitable participation and representation of ethnocultural minorities. Thus, themes such as biculturalism, two-nation society, Charter groups and founding peoples reflected in the early history of Canada's political parties signified that the British–French division was "the significant political cleavage" in Canadian society and politics (Peter 1981; Brodie and Jenson 1988). Obversely, the non-British, non-French were defined as second-class citizens and as marginal to these nation-building and party-building images (Breton 1984, 134). The early discourse on ethnicity and ethnic politics of the three major parties has thus not been conducive to the incorporation of minority ethnic groups as candidates in these parties and as MPs in the federal House of Commons.

Early Representation of Minorities in the Major Parties

In spite of the historically bicultural character of federal politics, by the close of the first decade of this century the voting potential of ethnic minorities could not be ignored by political parties. This was largely because of their growing numerical significance within rural Prairie ridings and within cities in central and western Canada.[5] Often, parties would try to court the "ethnic vote," and at times ethnic minorities were even nominated as candidates. However, those few elected MPs from non-British, non-French backgrounds typically represented heavily "ethnic constituencies" – such as the predominantly Ukrainian riding of Vegreville in Alberta or heavily Jewish ridings in cities such as Montreal, Toronto and Winnipeg (Burnet and Palmer 1988, 162). Even when ethnic minorities attained office in the House of Commons, they had limited impact in shaping policies in a manner favourable to the ethnic groups they represented, especially when the prevailing party policy orientation clashed with those interests. For example, in 1926 Michael Luchkovich of the United Farmers of Alberta was the first Ukrainian-origin MP in the House of Commons. However, while Luchkovich favoured a liberal immigration policy, his own party advocated a closed-door, restrictive policy (ibid.).

The limited influence of ethnic MPs was further underscored during the 1930s in a poignant and tragic fashion. While two Liberal Jewish MPs, Samuel Jacobs (from Montreal) and Sam Factor (from Toronto), worked to allow the entry of Jewish refugees who had been uprooted as a result of Nazi atrocities, the King Liberal government resolutely ignored their requests (Abella and Troper 1982, 14–15).[6] Hence, even when interests of concern to minority ethnic groups were provided with a platform in Parliament or even within the governing party, these interests could be dealt with in a dismissive manner.

Thus, for most of their early history, political parties responded in two ways to minority ethnic groups and their interests. The first was to ignore these interests and prevent groups from entering into Canadian political life by applying nativist doctrines and racist policies of exclusion. At times, these exclusionary policies could even provide the fuel for an election appeal to the wider electorate, which was receptive to racist platforms. The second response was to appeal to the ethnic vote and even to incorporate some members of minority groups as candidates. However, the evidence suggests that even when ethnic minorities were represented in the parliamentary wing of the party, their numbers were small. Lacking a "critical mass" in the House of Commons, minority politicians had limited power to shape party or government policy in directions favourable to the interests of their communities.

As will be elaborated below, the limited influence of minority ethnic MPs was likely related to their small numbers within the major parties and the House of Commons. But, in addition, the substantive or policy-making influence of minority MPs is constrained by party discipline, which according to parliamentary convention in Canada, obliges members of Parliament to vote according to the party line. The positions of party leaders form another barrier to the influence of minority MPs on party policy. Party leaders can claim to be accountable not only to minority interests but also to more broadly defined party and societal interests. In a social climate of racism, such as that which prevailed in Canada before the Second World War, this factor would have imposed a major constraint on the potential policy influence of minority MPs in directions favourable to enhancing the interests of their ethnic communities.[7]

Between the years 1867 and 1964, a total of only 97 individuals of non-British, non-French origin were members in the House of Commons (Canada, Royal Commission 1970, 272; Manzer 1974). Among the minority communities, Germans[8] and, to a lesser extent, Ukrainians and Jews, had the largest number of MPs. Other groups (such as the Chinese, with a long history in Canada but subjected to severe legal constraints on political participation) had weaker or negligible membership in the federal legislature. In fact, it is striking that from Confederation until the mid-1960s the non-British, non-French groups became increasingly underrepresented in the Canadian House of Commons in comparison with their growing proportions in the Canadian population (Manzer 1974, 251). Moreover, during this period, members of non-British, non-French communities were virtually absent from the Canadian Cabinet and were also underrepresented as judges, senators and in the highest ranks of the civil service (Burnet and Palmer 1988, 173–74).[9]

The proportion of MPs whose origins are neither British nor French clearly increased in the 1980s in comparison with the 100 years since Confederation. Following the 1984 federal election, the Canadian Ethnocultural Council (CEC) reported that 51 members (out of 282) had origins other than British or French – about 18 percent of all MPs (Canadian Ethnocultural Council 1989, 7). In 1988 the total number of MPs of non-British, non-French origin had dropped to 49 (out of 295 constituencies), forming 16.6 percent of the House of Commons (ibid.).[10] The vast majority of ethnic minority MPs were of European origin. North and East European MPs tended to be elected as Conservatives in Prairie ridings. South European (primarily Italian) MPs tended to be Liberals and represent ridings in southern Ontario and Quebec (Pelletier 1991).

It is important to note that an assessment of the degree to which non-British, non-French groups continue to be underrepresented in the House of Commons depends on the definition and measurement of the ethnic origins of MPs and of Canadians as a whole. At present, the Canadian census allows respondents to indicate up to three ethnic origins based on the question, "To which ethnic or cultural group(s) do you or did your ancestors belong?" (Canada, Statistics Canada 1988, xxxvi). As a result, approximately 28 percent of Canadians nationally claimed in 1986 to have multiple ethnic origins, although there was considerable provincial variation in the distribution of multiple origins, with Quebec residents giving a particularly small proportion of multiple responses (see appendix A, table 1.A1). Despite the large proportion of Canadians who claimed to have more than one ethnic origin, the ethnicity of this group of people is difficult to assess, as a discussion of the question of ethnic representation in the House of Commons will show.

At present, according to the CEC data, MPs of French or British origin account for more than 83 percent of the House of Commons. If this is compared with the 50 percent of the national population who in the 1986 census claimed a single origin, either British or French, then this would suggest that the British and French remain substantially over-represented in the House of Commons. However, if the single-origin British and French figures are combined with the figures of those claiming multiple origins (British, French and other), the proportion rises to approximately 75 percent of the population. Thus, the British and French MPs would still be overrepresented, but to a much lesser degree. The substantially different assessments of ethnic representation illustrate the difficulty in measuring and inferring meaning from measurement of ethnic origin, particularly in the case of respondents who give more than one origin.[11]

Far less ambiguity currently exists in assessing the degree of under-representation of visible minorities. It is clear that the House of Commons remains a "very white" institution, with only six visible minority MPs (or 2 percent of the total number) elected in 1988, an increase from three in 1984 (Pelletier 1991).[12] This compares poorly with the 6.1 percent of visible minorities in the Canadian population in 1986. If their numbers in the population at large were represented in Parliament, there would be approximately 18 visible minority MPs.

The facts that data on the ethnicity of MPs are not collected systematically and that "ethnicity" can be defined and measured in different ways make it difficult to form judgements about the representation or underrepresentation of ethnocultural minorities in general, and of specific groups. (See Pelletier 1991 for the different criteria used to determine the ethnicity of MPs.) This in itself militates against formulas that suggest that the House of Commons should simply mirror census statistics on ethnicity in order to be statistically representative of ethnic minority groups. Given that the census does not have a question on "race" or on "being in a visible minority," and that the visible minority count is derived chiefly from responses to the "ethnic origin" question, it would also be prudent not to be mesmerized by statistical counts of visible minorities in redressing the latter's underrepresentation (see Stasiulis 1991). Nonetheless, reference to census data does suggest that the House of Commons remains far from representative of the ethnocultural and racial diversity that exists within Canadian society, with visible minorities being particularly underrepresented.

Ethnicity, as it expresses itself both in everyday life and in politics, is a variable phenomenon, possessing structural, subjective and situational dimensions. Thus, both for certain culturally assimilated politicians or those who still retain some ties to their ethnic communities, their ethnicity may be neither a public liability nor an asset, except for occasional circumstances, e.g., when campaigning in heavily "ethnic" ridings or during holidays celebrated by the communities linked to their ancestry. On the other hand, for recent immigrants who lack full competence in one of the official languages or who have discernible accents, their ethnicity may be more of a liability for participation within the political parties. For visible minorities, their "race" or perceived visible differences may evoke racism and resistance to equal participation from voters, from the party rank and file or from party leaders. It is with these differences in mind that the next two sections of this study deal with the contemporary relationship between minority ethnic groups and the three major parties.

PARTY POLITICS AND ETHNIC MINORITY ACTIVISM

The 1984 and 1988 federal elections and the 1990 Liberal leadership convention were notable for the increased involvement of ethnic minorities. Unprecedented numbers of minority group members ran as candidates and delegates, and provided high-profile leadership, back-room organizing and mass support for electoral and leadership candidacies. An important observation that arises from analyses of this recent party involvement of minorities is the complex face of "third force" politics within the Canadian party system and the electoral process.

Surveys before federal elections confirmed a growing trend toward a weakening of traditional party loyalties among ethnic minorities, thus undermining any simplistic notion of "the ethnic vote." Members of nondominant ethnic communities supported parties and candidates for the same general policy-related reasons as Canadians of British and French origin, rather than solely on the basis of specifically "ethnic" appeal. Similarly, members of the same ethnic communities were split when it came to organizing and supporting campaigns for competing candidates for federal elections and for leadership of the Liberal party. Thus, in terms of partisan voting preferences, membership and active participation within political parties, political ideologies, and perspectives on political participation, it is clear that diversity rather than homogeneity characterizes the contemporary relationship of ethnic minorities to the major parties.

Nonetheless, despite the differences between ethnic groups in the level and type of involvement, such notions as "packing" and "instant" Liberal (Tory, NDPer) have emerged in recent federal elections as pejorative terms to stereotype the involvement of minority ethnic groups in party and electoral politics. Indeed, the frequency with which these terms have been associated with ethnic and visible minorities has meant that they now carry connotations of illegitimate political involvement by ethnic and racial minorities.

As suggested here, such stereotypes fail to separate the characteristics of party functioning, such as certain unwritten but well-established party traditions, from the groups that are the most recent or visible participants (by virtue of their cultural or "racial" characteristics) in party activities. As such, these stereotypes form part of the contemporary culture of exclusion of ethnic minorities from politics, contributing to and reinforcing their underrepresentation within party structures and as candidates in "winnable" ridings.

This conflation of party rules and operations with minority party players has two unfortunate consequences. First, it misleadingly deflects recommendations for reform away from the general party structures (such as local party constituency associations) and practices, and diverts it to "ethnic politics." Second, it detracts attention from the barriers remaining within the parties to the incorporation of members of minority groups within all levels of party organization and leadership. Although MPs and party officials expressed diverse views about reforms required to regulate the candidate and leadership selection processes, they were adamant in their belief that abuses of these processes were not attributable to the minority ethnic status of participants but were features of party traditions and organizations. Further, and more importantly, they agreed on the need to balance such regulation with mechanisms ensuring access and party renewal.

Before reviewing the party involvement of ethnocultural minorities in recent federal elections and in the Liberal leadership convention, and before addressing the issues raised by contemporary ethnic activism, it is necessary to examine some demographic features of contemporary ethnic politics. A brief consideration of the factors accounting for differences in party participation among minority groups will also be provided.

The Demography of Contemporary Ethnic Politics

Non-British and non-French immigrants and their descendants are unevenly distributed across Canada. Numbers of immigrants, their representation within the total provincial population, and their source countries all vary considerably from province to province. Ontario stands out as unique in terms of having the greatest proportion of recent immigrants in its total population (Canada, Statistics Canada 1988).

An overview of the demographic characteristics of the ridings in Canada suggests that the number of ridings with a majority of ethnic minorities (50 percent or more, as based on single origin) is significantly higher in Ontario and western Canada, as compared with Quebec, eastern Canada and the territories (see appendix A, table 1.A2). Using this rigorous standard of 50 percent or more ethnic minorities across the 295 federal ridings in Canada, only about one in five can be considered to be significantly populated with people of non-British, non-French origin. The striking feature of the majority of "ethnic ridings" is their location in urban centres, with the Metropolitan Toronto area having the largest number (see appendix A, table 1.A3).

Nonetheless, "ethnic politics" are not confined to the Toronto area, given that other regions, cities and constituencies are also ethnically diverse and contain concentrations of recent immigrants. For example, within Montreal, Edmonton and Vancouver, the potential for politics to venture beyond the traditional French–British cleavage is high.[13] Nonetheless, the virtual absence of constituency-level concentrations of non-British, non-French minorities in the Maritimes make federal Atlantic-region ridings less fertile ground for ethnic mobilization.

Another demographic feature with important regional implications pertains to the shift that has occurred in immigration from European to non-European sources following changes in immigration policy during the 1960s. This shift has ensured that Canadian society has increasingly become not only ethnically but also racially diverse, a trend that is not likely to alter in this century. Whereas 30 years ago more than 80 percent of Canada's immigrants came from Europe or were of European heritage, currently 70 percent come from Asia, Africa and Latin America, with 43 percent coming from Asia alone (Canada, Employment and Immigration Canada 1989, 8). Racial diversity is most salient in urban centres that serve as magnets for recent immigration. Thus, whereas visible minorities made up an estimated 6.1 percent of the Canadian population in 1986, almost 17 percent of both Torontonians and Vancouverites were visible minorities. In fact, in 1986 almost three-quarters of the visible minority population in Canada resided in five major cities: Toronto, Vancouver, Montreal, Calgary and Edmonton (Pendakur 1990). As will be addressed in the third section of this study, the recent immigration, the growing numbers and the regional concentration of visible minorities in Canada all have important implications for the choice of target groups for affirmative measures within parties.

Kinnear (1984) is one of the few political analysts to focus on the political ecology of federal constituencies as a means of analysing federal electoral behaviour. He isolates three major influences as the key to understanding variations between constituencies: the ethnic composition of each seat, its economic condition and the individual candidates. With respect to ethnicity, he highlights the importance of changes in the alignment of minority groups in some constituencies, even if the latter compose far less than 50 percent of the population. Certainly, in the 1984 and 1988 federal elections, strategists within the major political parties and candidates from both the established (British, French) and minority groups recognized the significance of the "ethnic" factor in particular areas across the country and in particular ridings.

One conclusion that can be drawn by shifting focus from the macro level of the nation or province to the micro level of the federal riding is that the latter can provide a far more useful and appropriate geographical unit in analysing electoral-focused ethnic politics. A variety of ecological factors pertaining to the attributes of the constituency may affect the political behaviour of members of a single ethnic group across the country (Eagles 1990, 292). Therefore, Italians, Sikhs, Macedonians, Koreans and so on (even of the same age, social class and other characteristics) may not behave in the same way toward the Liberal, Conservative or New Democratic parties in Halifax or Vancouver – or indeed in rural Ontario ridings – as they might in Toronto.

In addition to differences across constituencies in ethnic party and electoral politics, there are also clear differences in the relative involvement of different minority ethnic groups. These differences are in part attributable to "community maturation." Thus, many new immigrants to Canada have concerns that take precedence over involvement in the political process. It can take several years for the newly arrived to establish a new home, learn a new language and become accustomed to a new culture, including its political traditions. Economic considerations, especially purchasing a home and educating children, are often higher priorities than participation within party and electoral politics. Participation usually comes from the ranks of those immigrants who have attained some degree of social and economic security, or from their Canadian-educated children (first or second generation), who have the interest and resources to become active in party and electoral politics.

Several MPs and electoral candidates who themselves are from minority ethnic backgrounds spoke of the different steps in the political maturation of ethnic communities: from voting, to putting up lawn signs, to demanding a say in who will be the candidate or leader, to pursuing nomination as a candidate for office (first in unwinnable and then in winnable ridings) and, once elected, to demanding a share in power at high levels of the party and government.[14] The Ontario director of operations for the Progressive Conservative party, Susan Warren, observed that "it takes thirty years to get involved in politics as a community. Look at the Italians."[15]

The degree and speed of involvement in the political system by different immigrant communities, however, depends on a variety of factors: traditions of involvement in homeland politics, knowledge of the official languages, exposure to the Canadian educational system, social class and occupation. Several of the "ethnic" MPs were either second generation (i.e., Canadian-born) or had immigrated to Canada in their youth.

Clearly, a multitude of factors must be considered in accounting for minority participation. Thus, such concepts as the "ethnic vote" and the "third force" should be treated with caution insofar as they mask considerable variations in political behaviour and "community maturation," both between and within ethnic groups, as well as variations in regional and constituency concentration. Some of these variations are revealed in an examination of minority community involvement in the 1984 and 1988 federal elections and in the 1990 Liberal leadership convention.

The 1984 Federal Campaign
During the 1984 federal election, the impact of ethnic heterogeneity on the parties in Metro Toronto was demonstrated by the diversity of candidates. At least 20 of the candidates fielded by the three main parties in 1984 were from minority ethnic backgrounds (Serge 1984). Indeed,

Canadians of Italian, Ukrainian, Portuguese, West Indian and other backgrounds were reported to be increasingly active in the riding associations of all three parties, with new members being recruited by the hundreds. That the integration of ethnic minorities into the traditional parties was a gradual process is evident from the fact that in 1980 about 16 candidates for the three parties had non-British, non-French origins (ibid.).

Also during 1984, four Liberal party activists from the Italian, Portuguese and Sikh communities came together with the objective of pushing for a more prominent role for Canadians of non-Charter group origin to "expand their roles beyond simply licking envelopes for the WASP candidates" (Johnson 1988; Dewar 1988).[16] The four activists decided to throw the weight of the combined forces of their recruited memberships behind the bid for Liberal party leadership by John Roberts,[17] after Roberts had promised to deliver their message to the 1984 Liberal leadership convention. That message, conveyed in a speech to the convention floor, was to the effect that "Canada is a changing reality. In the future, an Ianno, a Singh could be a leader" (interview with Tony Ianno).

Given the visible involvement of individuals of diverse origins as members of riding executives, as organizers and as candidates, it is not surprising that during the 1984 election campaign articles in the print media highlighted the significance of the so-called ethnic vote in several ridings (Kinnear 1984). However, on close examination of some of these ridings, it becomes clear that the ethnic vote did not mean the same thing in every constituency.

For instance, in the Toronto riding of Eglinton–Lawrence, Liberal incumbent Roland de Corneille seemed to face a challenge to the tradition of Italian support for the Liberal party when Dan LaCapara, an Italian-Canadian, ran for the Conservatives. To help garner the support of the Italian community, de Corneille stressed his involvement in the multicultural field, including his role as chairperson of the Canada–Italy Parliamentary Friendship Group. Although LaCapara's campaign manager banked on the "new recognition that the Liberals aren't the only party that supports multiculturalism," de Corneille won the seat in the riding (*Globe and Mail* 1984).

It is not known with certainty how the "Italian vote" (an estimated 19 percent of the riding) was registered in the 1984 Eglinton–Lawrence race. Nonetheless, there continues to be a perception, based partially on party and independent polls, that immigrant groups such as the Italians maintain voter loyalty to the Liberal party even when members of their own community are candidates for the other parties. Thus, regardless of their ethnic background, candidates from these groups running for the Conservatives within constituencies that are "heavily Mediterranean" are running in unwinnable ridings that are referred to by Tory organizers as part of the "dead zone."[18] Overall, however, many minority candidates in all three parties entered the race with the almost certain knowledge of losing. The reasons conveyed by candidates contesting elections in unwinnable ridings include the benefits of campaigning experience gained by the candidates themselves and the role model and political education provided to the candidate's community.[19]

Analysis of other constituency results during the 1984 election further suggests that candidates do not always get support from their ethnic community. In the Toronto riding of Parkdale–High Park, long-time Liberal incumbent Jesse Flis was beaten by Conservative Andrew Witer. Witer's success was linked to his ability to capture the support of the riding's heavily Eastern European communities, including the Polish community of which his Liberal opponent was a member (Harrington 1984b).[20] Moreover, Witer's campaign (echoing his leader's 1984 promise of "jobs, jobs, jobs!") had emphasized employment and tenant issues – issues that are difficult to categorize as "ethnic concerns" but that can be as important to voters from ethnic minority communities as to Anglo-Canadian voters (Harrington 1984a).

Another instance where the notion of the ethnic voting bloc is problematic is in races for candidate selection or general election that pit two or several candidates from the same ethnic community against each other. The situation wherein several candidates from the same community ran for nomination was a feature of several ridings preceding the 1988 federal election.[21]

In 1984, in the riding of York West, Sergio Marchi won the Liberal nomination in a hotly contested battle that included three others of Italian background, making four of the five candidates Italian in origin (Serge 1984).[22] In the election, the NDP fielded Italian-Canadian Bruno Pasquantonio; Frank Di Giorgio ran for the Tories in York West. Thus, all three parties had Italian-Canadian candidates in this riding, which was ultimately won by Sergio Marchi. Marchi's success clearly must be accounted for by factors beyond his ethnic origin.[23]

While the lion's share of media focus on ethnic mobilization in 1984 addressed the politics of Toronto ridings, the "ethnic vote" was deemed to play a significant role in the electoral outcome in other areas. For example, in Calgary East, both the winning Conservative candidate, Alex Kindy, and the Liberal candidate, Rod Sykes, worked hard to recruit the support of different ethnic communities in a riding that is heavily non-British and non-French. Thus, Kindy was supported in his nomination by hundreds of East Indians, while Sykes was popular with Italian-Canadians. In this context, the NDP candidate, Barry Pashak, argued that as the representative of the social democratic party, he was "unable to gain much of the ethnic support because of the connection between social democracy and repressive regimes" from which many immigrants came (Sarjeant 1984).

There were signs in 1984 that the leadership of the Liberal party was intervening in, and in some cases blocking, the quest for nomination by ethnic minority candidates, and in particular candidates from visible minorities. Jean Gammage, a long-time Liberal Toronto West Indian who sought the nomination for Don Valley West, alleged that she was "encouraged" by the Liberal party brass not to go after the nomination. Similarly, Jamaican-born Alvin Curling, an established resident of York–Scarborough, declared that he was not favoured to run by party leader John Turner. Instead, Turner supported the candidacy of June Rowlands, a high-profile Toronto alderperson, who was "parachuted" into the riding (Serge 1984).

The efforts to promote visible minority candidates within the Liberal party were supported organizationally by Political Awareness of Visible Minorities (PAVE), which was started in 1983 by Murad Velshi (later the first South Asian MPP in Ontario, elected during the rule of the Peterson government). According to Velshi:

> Turner rejected us and refused to meet with us. We sought out four visible minority candidates [for the 1984 federal election]: Alvin Curling in York–Scarborough, Jean Gammage in Eglinton, Len Brathwaite in Etobicoke and Jean Frederic Cameron in Woodbine. The party opposed us in all four ridings. (Interview)

Black community spokespersons were critical of the contradiction that existed between Turner's promises during the Liberal leadership campaign to involve visible minorities at all levels of the party, and the absence of high-level involvement of visible minorities in the 1984 election campaign (Serge 1984).

From a review of the involvement of ethnic minorities within the party system and the federal campaign in 1984, it is possible to see particular patterns and issues that took more definite form and gained greater media attention during the 1988 federal election. First, all parties were sensitive to the ethnic vote, as manifested by their deliberate choice to field candidates whose ethnic origins matched those of some statistically significant community in local ridings. Moreover, while the national campaigns of the three parties did not address issues of specific concern to ethnic minorities (except for the vague endorsement of multiculturalism),[24] within local ridings the candidates' positions on issues such as racism and human rights in the homelands of particular communities did become an issue.[25]

Second, the relevance of ethnicity to the national parties and to electoral politics depended on characteristics at the local level of the constituency. Ethnic politics were more salient in Toronto-area ridings than in other areas of the country that had smaller concentrations of new Canadians of non-British, non-French origin. However, the settlement of recent immigrants in several cities, such as Calgary, Vancouver, Winnipeg and Montreal, meant that candidates in urban ridings across the country were sensitive to the ethnic vote.

Third, the concept of the ethnic vote – a problem revealed in the 1984 election – carried with it the assumption that minority ethnic groups voted as a bloc. Yet in the 1984 election results it was becoming evident that while traditional party loyalties continued to prevail, e.g., Italian and West Indian support for Liberals,[26] there was no such thing as monolithic minority support for any one party.[27] The very fact that all major parties were fielding minority candidates of the same ethnic origin in some Toronto ridings was itself a recognition (and perhaps a hope) by organizers within the three parties that ethnic minority support could be split.

Fourth, where candidates of the same ethnicity were contesting nomination for candidacy within parties or in general elections, members of their communities at times based their choice either on the candidates' attributes or on policy positions that transcended ethnic allegiances.[28] This underscores a second problem with the notion of the "ethnic vote" – it mistakenly assumes that minority ethnic groups are preoccupied with "ethnic" issues and are unconcerned with issues of more general concern, such as the state of the Canadian economy.

Fifth, in 1984 the new level of involvement of ethnic minorities as party activists was met, at least in the media, with curiosity, a sense of a new level of political awareness among ethnic minorities, rather than with disapprobation as was common four years later. In 1984 there was little overt mention of the "packing" of nomination meetings with "instant" party members and of riding association "take-overs," which became the conventional discourse of political journalists in 1988, leaving the impression that ethnic minorities were either disdainful or ignorant of the Canadian traditions of democracy.[29]

Finally, the difficulties faced by visible minorities in capturing nominations during the 1984 federal campaign suggested that there existed a gap between the rhetoric of openness expressed by the party leadership and its actual willingness to accept ethnic minority and especially visible minority candidates, particularly in winnable ridings. That the discussion of accessibility centred on the Liberal party also reflected the fact that the Liberals, long-time beneficiaries of minority ethnic support, were regarded as the most open of the three major parties to the active participation of minority individuals.[30] These themes were further developed within internal party discussions and political journalism during the 1988 federal campaign and in the months preceding the 1990 Liberal leadership convention.

The 1988 Federal Election: Increasing Minority Activism

If there was a question as to which party would receive ethnic minority support in 1984, by 1988 this question had been amplified. One Environics poll taken before the election showed that the Tories were favoured by 40 percent of people of non-British, non-French origins, compared with 28 percent for the NDP and 26 percent for the Liberals (Trickey 1988). A Gallup poll taken in Metro Toronto in the early weeks of the campaign suggested that different ethnic communities supported different parties. The Conservatives had a big lead among Northern Europeans, the Liberals among Southern Europeans, Africans and Asians, and the Eastern European votes were split among the three federal parties (Smith 1988).

The Canadian Ethnocultural Council attributed the overall weakening in Liberal party loyalties among minority ethnic voters to Brian Mulroney's appreciation of ethnic communities and his support of multiculturalism (Trickey 1988). Another interpretation of the shift toward Tory support emphasized that critical issues for ethnic voters might not necessarily differ from those of other voters. Indeed, the pitch by all three major parties, translated into several languages, was reported to have been focused on free trade (Smith 1988).

While the November 1988 federal election will be remembered primarily as the "free-trade election," the months preceding the election, especially in urban Ontario ridings, were also marked by the new muscle flexed by minority ethnic groups. Party activists, chiefly from Southern European and from visible minority groups, were recruiting record numbers of minority ethnic members to their parties to support nomination battles and were fielding record numbers of ethnic minority candidates. Within Canada as a whole, 36.6 percent (59/161) of Liberal candidates, 34.2 percent (55/161) of NDP candidates and 29.2 percent (47/161) Conservative candidates were of ethnic minority origin. The Liberals and the NDP each fielded 13 visible minority candidates, while the Conservatives ran only three visible minorities (Pelletier 1991).

Within the Metro Toronto area, of the 33 federal ridings, one-half of the Liberal candidates were of non-British, non-French origin. Ten, or one-third, of the NDP candidates were of ethnic minority origin. The Conservatives had the smallest number of ethnic minority candidates (eight) running in Metro Toronto.[31] Fierce nomination competitions, mostly within the Liberal party and often involving two or more minority candidates, were a feature of Toronto ridings such as Eglinton–Lawrence, Trinity–Spadina, Mississauga East, Etobicoke North, Scarborough–Rouge River, York West, York Simcoe and Davenport. The "packing" of constituency meetings with "instant" party members was a commonly reported feature of this phenomenon (see Stasiulis and Abu-Laban 1990, 585–88).

In Toronto, ethnic minority candidates were most commonly found within the Liberal party, and in Montreal it was the New Democrats that fielded the greatest number of ethnic minority candidates. This suggests that local party organizations within parties that have low expectations for success during elections offer the greatest opportunities for ethnic minority candidacy. The NDP candidates in Montreal included five Italians, one Russian-Canadian (in Duvernay), a Hungarian (in Lachine–Lac-Saint-Louis), a Pakistani (in Mount Royal), a Moroccan (in Pierrefonds–Dollard), a Chilean (in Saint-Denis) and a Palestinian (in Saint-Jean) (Parkes 1988; Bauch 1988).

The Montreal-area Liberal candidates were also diverse and included those of Italian, Jewish, Greek, Lebanese and Armenian origin.[32] As in Toronto, of the three major parties, the Conservatives in Montreal ran the fewest ethnic minority candidates (Cauchon 1988).

In a national survey of ethnic minority candidates, the Canadian Ethnocultural Council (CEC) found that candidates of Italian origin had the highest number (29), followed by Jewish (17), Polish (14) and Ukrainian (5) (*Toronto Star*, 20 November 1988). The CEC predicted that about 20 percent of the 295 House of Commons seats would be filled by MPs of non-British, non-French, non-Aboriginal origin. In actual fact, as mentioned in the first part of this study, successful candidates from ethnic minority backgrounds in the November 1988 election made up only 16.6 percent of the 295 MPs, a slight dip from 1984, when 51 of the 282 MPs were of ethnic minority origin (Montreal *Gazette*, 24 November 1988). Notwithstanding the relatively small number of "ethnic" MPs, "packing" had been raised as an issue both by the media and by some party activists.

The 1990 Liberal Leadership Race: "Packing" and the Third Force

The Liberal leadership convention on 23 June 1990 was preceded by months of recruitment of unprecedented numbers of members from several ethnic minority communities. The race between the two front runners (Jean Chrétien and Paul Martin) was called a "contest of numbers" played by organizers attempting to round up as many new recruits as possible (Speirs 1990). Frequently, the various leadership camps recruited new members from ethnic communities just hours before party deadlines for delegate-selection meetings (ibid.).

While ridings in the cities of Montreal, Calgary and Vancouver reported similar recruiting patterns, it was in Toronto that much of the pre-convention "ethno-politics" was played out.[33] In 20 of the Metro area's 33 ridings, groups such as the Sikhs, Italians, Macedonians, Croatians and Portuguese were portrayed as pawns in an "ethnic chess game" between different leadership contenders (Winsor 1990).

The Sikhs formed one of the most active communities; large numbers of Sikhs were present at delegate selection meetings in Toronto, southwestern Ontario, Calgary and Vancouver. Sergio Marchi, an organizer for Jean Chrétien, suggested that Sikhs were easy to organize because of their "tightly knit communities [which] have extensive networks centred around temples and religious/political groups," and because of their dissatisfaction with the Conservatives as a result of External Affairs Minister Joe Clark's unsympathetic handling of the issue of a Sikh state in the Punjab (Winsor 1990).

The distortion inherent in the notion of the ethnic vote was reflected in the splits within communities such as that of the Sikhs, who were recruited in support of both the Paul Martin campaign and the Jean Chrétien campaign. In Sergio Marchi's own riding, organizers of Paul Martin's campaign were able to bring 1 200 new recruits (almost half from the Sikh community). Marchi countered by drawing some 2 000 new recruits from the Italian-Canadian community (Howard 1990). The intraparty splits among the new members recruited from the "third force" also existed within the "ethnic party élite" (where Italian-Canadians predominate). For example, while MP Sergio Marchi worked for Jean Chrétien, fellow Italian-Canadian MPs Joseph Volpe and Albina Guarnieri supported Paul Martin, reportedly because of hostilities with Marchi (Speirs 1990).

Thus, both the 1988 nomination contests in several urban ridings and the Liberal leadership race brought the issue of packing to the forefront. Several Liberal party activists expressed concern about whether the packing of riding meetings with "instant Liberals" was an appropriate way to choose the leader of the party – and, potentially, of the country. Questions were asked as to whether policy or performance in the House of Commons and public debates were becoming less important in leadership races than the ability of brokers to attract new party members (Winsor 1990).

However, what was frequently ignored in these criticisms was that the nature of candidate and delegate selection that prevails in the Canadian party system actually encourages the practice of signing up large numbers of new members. Insofar as candidates and delegates are chosen by the membership of the riding association, the process is based on a "numbers game." The intensity of recruiting, the number of members recruited by competing camps, and the extent of packing all depend on how closely contested and how much of a "horse race" a given candidate or leadership contest is (Wearing 1988, 194; Guarnieri 1990, 9). Indeed, media and party criticisms of candidates and organizers in 1988 and 1990 made wider reference to problematic features of the candidate and leadership selection processes or "rules of the game" that were in need of reform, issues that were distinct from the ethnicity of the actors and collectivities involved. However, the unseemly stories in the media about "strong-arm tactics," recruitment of "instant Liberals," and charges of "slate packing" almost invariably stated or implied that the volume and nature of involvement by ethnic minorities were inherent features of the problem (Speirs 1990). The connections between candidate-selection processes and ethnic minority political mobilization are further explored below.

Packing and Instant Party Members

The most important functions of the parties' riding associations have traditionally been the selection of candidates for elections and the selection of delegates for party conventions, e.g., leadership conventions. The riding association chooses its candidate, its delegates and its riding executive at a general meeting of the whole membership. Thus, candidate selection in the Canadian party system is different from the British system, where election candidates are chosen by constituency committees rather than by the whole membership; it is also different from the American system, where candidates are chosen in primaries in which the whole electorate may participate, depending on individual state law (Wearing 1988, 192).

A new phenomenon in the 1983 and 1984 leadership conventions held by the Conservatives and Liberals respectively was the "contest for delegate positions between opposing *slates* pledged to particular leadership candidates" (Wearing 1988, 206). In the 1990 Liberal leadership convention, very few delegates were "free agents"; the vast majority formed part of delegate slates elected at local riding association meetings, which were often filled with supporters of contending leadership hopefuls.[34]

Within the three major parties, members eligible to vote (at candidate- and delegate-selection meetings for election of the riding executive, etc.) must be 14 years of age or older, must be landed immigrants or Canadian citizens, and must have held membership for a period (the "cut-off date") specified by the constitutions of riding associations before the relevant meeting. The federal New Democrats and Liberals (but not the Conservatives) also require that the party member should not be a member of another political party.[35]

The period preceding the cut-off is often marked by intense efforts to sign up new members before the nomination or delegate-selection meeting. Thus, the packing of constituency meetings with instant party members was part and parcel of the aggressive nomination and delegate-selection contests within Liberal riding associations. As Joseph Wearing observes of the process of signing up new members before significant votes: "Those who are doing it will justify the whole exercise by calling it 'recruiting'; their opponents will accuse them of 'packing.' It all depends on one's perspective" (Wearing 1988, 194).

Although both packing of nomination and delegate-selection meetings and instant party members have been most strongly associated with the involvement of ethnic minorities within Liberal riding associations, these are terms that appeared earlier in media descriptions of delegate-selection meetings for the 1983 Conservative leadership convention. Among the newly signed Conservative members to help elect delegates backing Joe Clark, Brian Mulroney and other candidates were "derelicts" recruited from Montreal's Old Brewery Mission and children under the age of 14 (Harris 1984; Wearing 1988, 194). Leadership hopeful John Crosbie was reported as defending a delegate-selection meeting in Kamloops, British Columbia that was packed with people recruited by Amway distributors (*Toronto Star* 1983).[36]

Indeed, in the 1984 Liberal leadership convention, Liberal organizer Marcel Lessard praised the party's ability to steer clear of instant Grits in Quebec; he contrasted this with the bussing in of instant Tories in the 1983 Conservative leadership convention (Harris 1984). Less than a month later, however, it was revealed that in both Kingston and Kitchener, Portuguese-Canadians had been rounded up by Liberal organizers and were packing delegate-selection meetings (Montreal *Gazette* 1984).

Thus, both packing and instant party members were not novel features of the 1988 Liberal nominations; nor were they particularly Liberal or ethnic in their genesis. However, the frequency with which political journalists employed these terms in 1988 and 1990 in association with the words "ethnic" and "Liberal" cemented an image in the public mind of instant Liberals as the duped or ignorant ethnic masses "speaking funny languages"[37] or wearing turbans.

Ethnic minority MPs, staff members and activists within the three parties have expressed strong feelings regarding packing and instant party members, which are revealing about issues of accessibility and democracy within the party system, and also about the racial and ethnic biases prevailing within the media, the party establishment and the public at large. Several MPs suggested that "nomination meetings and delegate selection are both based on a numbers game. They are no different than they were in the past" (interview with John Nunziata). The director of operations for the Ontario wing of the Conservative party illustrated the racial and ethnic biases inherent in the terms "instant Liberal" or "instant Tory" by drawing from the experience of the 1984 Conservative nomination contest within Broadview–Greenwood:

> Peter Worthington [former editor of the *Toronto Sun*] who lost the nomination in 1984 to a Greek candidate said, "How can we be supported by people who are obviously not Tories?" But Worthington also signed up 5 000 new members who I know were not Tories. The difference was that they were white. (Interview with Susan Warren)

Several ethnic minority party activists were unequivocal in their rejection of the notion of instant party member insofar as it was a term applied exclusively to members from ethnic and visible minorities, and because it made certain assumptions about ethnic minority communities. Jasbir Singh Mangat, who in 1988 had made a bid for the Liberal candidacy in Etobicoke North, criticized the media's use of the term "instant Liberal," which he said ignored the fact that many of the Sikhs so designated had worked for the party for several years. "When do you stop being 'instant'?" he asked (interview with Jasbir Singh Mangat). Similarly, Albina Guarnieri, Liberal MP for Mississauga East, stated:

> "Instant Liberal" is a term exclusively reserved for ethnics. When does one stop being an instant Liberal? The implication is that these people don't know what they're doing, but this isn't true. (Interview with Albina Guarnieri)

Other MPs and party activists from ethnic minority backgrounds also criticized the term because it implies that ethnocultural communities lack political sophistication and are easily manipulated by power brokers. Indeed, these MPs argued that the very fact that ethnic communities use their voting strength to take control of riding executives or to support particular candidates or delegate slates is itself a reflection of high levels of political awareness.[38] As expressed by Tony Ianno:

"The one thing that irks me is that people of non-Anglo, non-French origins are portrayed as if they don't know about politics. Often they are *more* knowledgeable than others" (interview).

The practice of utilizing ethnic community networks for the purpose of recruitment before nomination or delegate-selection meetings was also more often defended by minority activists than it was rejected. As stated simply by Ianno:

> We're not Rosedale [a wealthy neighbourhood in Toronto], homogeneous or Anglo, so there is recruiting along ethnic lines. In other ridings, you have cliques of other origins. In Rosedale, you have all the students from St. Martin's College. (Interview)

Joe Pantalone, an NDP Metro Toronto councillor of Italian background, expressed a similar sentiment:

> Those people who criticize this process are being intolerant of other peoples or other cultures. No one objects if recruitment occurs within an Anglican parish, and parishioners come out. The same should be true for the Sikhs, Italians. (Interview)

Several party activists also suggested that recruitment along ethnic lines only became a problem when it was done to support *ethnic minority* candidates. As Armindo Silva submitted, "Portuguese supporters are welcome if they support Anglos. They're only a problem if they support their own. There is also this bias within the [Liberal] party" (interview). Similarly, Jasbir Singh Mangat opined, "They apply a double standard to the recruiting of new members. As long as they're helping established candidates, then there's not a problem" (interview).

Raymond Cho, the NDP candidate in 1988 for Scarborough–Rouge River, echoed this sentiment:

> There is nothing wrong with this [recruiting new members of ethnic communities for nomination meetings]. The white recruit from the white community, Black community, Oriental community. *But if an Oriental candidate recruits from the Oriental community, then there's a problem. This is real prejudice and racism.* (Interview)[39]

As discussed earlier, candidate selection, and delegate selection for leadership contests, are based on a numbers game, which many party officials and MPs argue is *legitimately* played by "using one's personal following, drawing on loyalty and friendship," or "recruiting wherever you have a base" (interviews with Susan Warren and Albina Guarnieri). According to the Ontario director for the Conservative party, "Stacking a meeting is a time-honoured tradition. It's a numbers game. This is the bottom line for both nominations and leadership selection" (interview with Susan Warren).[40]

Derek Lee, the Liberal MP from Scarborough–Rouge River, had recruited support from many ethnic and linguistic communities to win the 1988 nomination in his ethnically diverse riding, which was contested by four other candidates, all members of visible minority communities. Lee, who is white and of British origin, emphasized the need to know the homeland politics of the many ethnic groups making up his constituency to garner their electoral support systematically through use of the "ethnic lever." "The ethnic lever exists," stated Lee, "but so does the gender lever, the blue suit lever" (interview).

At the same time that MPs, party activists and party staff rejected the pejorative connotations of the notion of instant member, they frequently expressed two concerns related to the process of mass recruitment and the subsequent tenor of ethnic relations within party ridings. The phenomenon of instant members was viewed as problematic in that it had encouraged the manipulation and "duping" of new members, as well as other nomination abuses. This led on the one hand to doubts among established party interests about the loyalty of the membership of ethnic minorities, and to doubts among ethnocultural communities about the legitimacy of the party system or particular parties, on the other. As well, mass recruitment of new members was perceived as having divisive, undemocratic and destructive consequences for riding-level party organization, and as encouraging an "us–them" mind-set about party members from dominant and nondominant ethnic groups.[41]

Manipulation of Ethnic Communities and Other Nomination Abuses

Supporters for competing candidates may use manipulation and misrepresentation in signing up members, practices that are more likely to occur with new Canadians whose official language skills and knowledge of the Canadian political system are poor. Howard Levitt, a Liberal party member, elaborates on how ethnic minorities are "used" by some candidates:

> The community leaders who sign them up and bring them to the meeting in turn are owed political debts by the candidate. Many of these voters, unable to read or write English, know nothing about the candidate. Unaware of even the name, they take them to the voting area diagrams of the ballot marked to show them how to vote. (Levitt 1988)

Such manipulation breeds voter cynicism and has detrimental consequences both for the integrity of the party organization and for the subsequent political involvement of the ethnocultural communities implicated.[42] At the extreme, such manipulation involves clear abuses of rules regarding membership and candidate selection, such as the duplication of names on the membership lists of two parties. For example, during the 1988 Toronto-area nomination contests, there were two documented cases of names of individuals from the Portuguese and East Indian communities appearing on both Liberal and Conservative membership lists.[43]

The dual party membership of recruits from ethnic minority communities contravened only the Liberal party constitution. Fred Clark, then director of operations for the Ontario wing of the federal Conservatives, in fact stated that "double memberships are no problem for us ... It's an open party for us because we practise the politics of inclusion" (Webb-Proctor 1988b). Interviews with party activists, however, revealed that disapproval existed among both Liberals and Conservatives with the practice of double memberships (interviews with Avi Flaherty, Albina Guarnieri, Rocco Sebastiano). In a brief to the Commission, political scientist William Christian explains why irregularities and improprieties are a common feature of both delegate selection and constituency nomination conventions:

> Most local organizations hold their nominating conventions on the basis of poorly understood rules, and in a condition of uncertainty, since they are normally not certain even how many members they will have until shortly before the convention is to be held. How chaotic this process becomes depends on the organizational skill of the riding and their organizers. It is often not a pretty sight, and *my guess is that there are few contested nomination meetings which could stand close scrutiny if their practices and procedures were examined.* (Christian 1990, 28; emphasis added)

Similarly, according to Brodie and Vickers (1981, 36), "most political observers would argue that when the party's nomination is contested by two or more political aspirants 'dirty tricks' invariably occur."

The unexceptional nature of irregularities during nomination contests must be kept in mind when reviewing the types of "dubious" behaviour engaged in by supporters of contending candidates, which received close scrutiny in 1988 and 1990, seemingly for two reasons: the magnitude of the growth in Liberal party memberships, and the minority ethnic backgrounds of the participants.

Nonetheless, the need for some reforms has concerned minority activists and politicians. Liberal MP Albina Guarnieri, who emerged the victor after two nomination battles for the same Liberal party candidacy in 1988, has compiled one of the most comprehensive lists of common abuses in party nominations. Several of these practices were also mentioned in interviews with MPs and individuals who had contested party nominations as part of the arsenal of dirty tricks played by their opponents, and in the media coverage of several hotly contested battles preceding the 1988 election and the 1990 Liberal leadership convention (see Stasiulis and Abu-Laban 1990, 585–90). These practices include: fraudulent and (deliberately) lost memberships; inaccessible cut-off registration locations (sabotaging registration during critical last hours to cut-off time); changing the registration location without proper notice; changing membership qualifications (such as the amount of membership fee) without adequate notice; selective challenges to qualifications; changing time or location of nomination meeting; selecting biased officers to oversee meetings; capriciously changing, limiting or extending voting times; arbitrary rules about location and access to polls; arbitrary and selective ID criteria; arbitrary elimination of right of challenge; issuing multiple or fraudulent ballots; appointing biased people to appeal panels; and arbitrary procedural rules of appeal (Guarnieri 1990, 10–12; see also Levitt 1988).

Guarnieri and other Liberal MPs, such as Rey Pagtakhan and Sergio Marchi, argue that the best way to eliminate some of the common abuses in candidate and delegate selection conventions is to have Elections Canada supervise the nomination process for all political parties. Guarnieri's argument in favour of state regulation is based on her perception that abuses occur most frequently because the process is controlled by small groups of interested party officials. Thus, any reform must go beyond internal party reform so that the arbitration and appeal processes are not subject to being hijacked by biased party officials.

Currently, Elections Canada has very little jurisdiction over the candidate and leader selection for the political parties because the parties are considered to have the legal status of private clubs. But the fact that political parties are provided with public funds through rebates and tax credits, as well as the importance of candidate selection, particularly for the leadership of parties and governments, are arguments used to justify greater state regulation of nomination procedures. Guarnieri accordingly recommends that "the nomination meetings themselves should either be conducted by or supervised by Elections Canada officials" (1990, 16).[44]

Other Liberal MPs and activists interviewed offered other suggestions for reform of the nomination process. One recommendation was for the issuing of ID photo cards for members to eliminate the fraudulent memberships and unfair challenges that currently turn packed nomination meetings into chaotic brawls; however, MP Derek Lee suggested that ID photo cards would be overkill (interviews with Tony Ianno, Armindo Silva, Derek Lee). The most common recommendation was for an earlier cut-off date, different time periods being suggested for the interval between membership registration and eligibility to vote, ranging from 45 days to 18 months.[45]

Most members of the NDP and the Conservative party [46] were happy with the current membership rules, arguing for the need for criteria that are not unduly restrictive and that will attract new members. NDP members were apt to point out that their earlier cut-off, relative to the other parties, prevented abuses and inhibited the creation of instant New Democrats (interviews with Abby Polonetski, Howard McCurdy, Margaret Mitchell).

Some MPs were willing to countenance more drastic reform of the leadership selection process, arguing that it is more important than individual candidate selection. Several Liberal MPs favoured a universal ballot of all party members, with stricter control (earlier cut-off) of party membership for leadership selection only. MP Derek Lee, for instance, favoured a universal ballot for all party members, arguing that the current process of leadership selection "now permits anyone to participate in choosing the leaders, whether or not they are Liberal. This is not fair for current members. The only thing that becomes important is sheer numbers" (interview).

Liberal party activist Tony Ianno regarded "direct voting for leadership as the more democratic option" (interview). But not all Liberals were in favour of the universal ballot. MPs Rey Pagtakhan and Sergio Marchi, and party member Jasbir Singh Mangat argued that the universal ballot would replace one type of abuse with another – specifically, that the leadership race would be stacked in favour of the candidates with the most money and the highest pre-election profile.[47] Party strategists have also objected to a universal ballot on the grounds that "a party would be foolish to give up the intensive publicity engendered by a convention" (Wearing 1988, 216–17). In line with this thinking, MPs Charles Caccia, Rey Pagtakhan and Sergio Marchi spoke of the benefits to the party of leadership conventions such as the excitement engendered by the leadership race and debates, and the involvement of party members at the convention (interviews).

In general, the benefits of greater external regulation of and state intervention in the internal affairs of the political parties must be weighed carefully against the costs. Wearing (1988, 216) states that the "call for legislation also raises the question of how desirable it is to follow the American model of asking government to regulate the parties' internal affairs." Liberal MP and organizer Sergio Marchi warns about the deleterious effects of too much regulation:

> When the Liberal party is an open shop, it will become more reflec
> tive of the community. If you regulate too much, it will close the party
> to some and become stifling. The system is fairly open now. It allows
> for challenges to the MPs, and at the executive level. (Interview)

The reasons underlying current pressures to regulate the system of nominations and leadership selection must also be scrutinized. As Elvio DelZotto (then president of the Ontario wing of the federal Liberal party) pointed out, the magnitude of growth of the Liberal party membership as a result of nomination-centred recruitment – from approximately 50 000 before 1 May 1988 to 124 724 by the end of July 1988 – was bound to cause problems of administration by a financially weak party organization (DelZotto 1988).

The concern of party establishment and party stalwarts was also based on the fact that they were facing challenges to their own power through "unhampered grassroots democracy" organized by ethnic minority activists and supported through the recruitment of ethnic networks (Howard 1988).[48] Here it should not be overlooked that at a time when political scientists were discussing the "decline of political parties," ethnic minorities, however unruly and mismanaged, were actively and enthusiastically participating in party democracy. Sergio Marchi attempted to place the disruptions in party process in the context of increased ethnic minority activism:

> There are problems in allegations that power plays are occurring, buy
> ing up of memberships, shunting long-time members aside. I'm happy
> to have these problems, as we no longer have to ask how these groups
> can participate. We must find ways of managing these problems.
> (Interview)

Instant Members or Temporary Members?
While ethnic minorities were clearly being recruited in record numbers during recruitment drives, one question raised by the sudden growth in party membership was the effect on the subsequent development of local party organization. One objection to mass recruitment practices is that the members who are newly recruited exercise power through

numbers, yet "do not understand the process." Recruited for the purpose of single-event votes, such members are "not philosophically committed to the party." Furthermore, they do not remain active in the riding association and indeed generally fail to renew their memberships (interviews with Elaine Collins, Jill Marzetti, Rocco Sebastiano). As articulated by the World Sikh Organization in its submission to this Commission, "The problem ... is not of 'Instant' Party Members, but rather of 'Temporary' Party Members. Political parties should involve people, not only at times of election, but in between as well" (1990, 11).

Activists within all three parties provided stories in which riding association membership declined drastically or disappeared following recruitment through ethnic mobilization. But do the reasons for such declines pertain to the characteristics of the new members, or to the nature and narrow purposes of the riding association? Currently, riding associations are dormant in between elections. The inactivity of the majority of local riding associations except during elections acts as a disincentive to the active involvement of new members, regardless of their ethnicity.[49] At the same time, the problem of retaining members may be particularly acute for some new Canadians who are unfamiliar with the Canadian political system and who may face additional linguistic and cultural obstacles to participation.

Currently, membership rules in all three major parties are meant to allow for the participation of noncitizens who are resident in Canada. The less restrictive criteria for party membership, compared with the criteria for electors (who must be Canadian citizens), means that the parties can serve as forums for citizenship training.

In discussions of reforms to membership, a few MPs and party activists have argued that the current system of permitting candidates to be selected by those who do not have the right to vote in general elections can lead to serious distortions. Their recommendation that follows is to make the qualifications of voting party members consistent with those for the general electorate.[50]

The majority of MPs, party officials and activists either did not suggest restrictions on criteria for party membership (beyond earlier cut-off dates before voting) or else they defended the current openness to noncitizens, both for reasons of party health and rejuvenation and to provide new Canadians with encouragement to participate politically and become full citizens. Typical in this regard were comments made by Liberal MP Charles Caccia, who argued for the need for an earlier cut-off: "But this should not exclude noncitizens. New Canadians must be given a chance to explore the Canadian system of democracy. And you want to bring in fresh blood" (interview).

If parties are to make the full participation of ethnic and visible minorities a priority, then whatever reforms are made to deal with abuses in candidate and leadership selection must not undercut the efforts made to provide greater accessibility at all levels of party organization. This means not closing off access to one of the few avenues that exists to the meaningful participation and empowerment of recent immigrant groups such as the Southeast Asians and Portuguese, who currently have high proportions of noncitizens.[51]

Shunting Aside the "Party Faithful"?

Another concern expressed about the packing of riding associations with new recruits is its effects on long-term party members – the "party faithful," who have shown their commitment to their party and their riding association over many years. Alfonso Gagliano, Liberal MP for Saint-Léonard, stated that it was "unfair that people who have given their time should be shoved over" (interview). Charles Caccia, Liberal MP for Davenport, who was first elected in 1968, expressed his concern for the integrity of local party organization threatened by the current system of recruitment of members:

> The membership rules need to be looked at, particularly how to treat new arrivals. There can be distortions and disruptions in delegate and candidate selection that are damaging to the party when long-time members are swept off. For example, you have been a member for nine years, then you are swamped by thousands of new members. This leaves scars. (Interview)

Prefacing her remarks by saying that "it's more prevalent in the Liberal party than within the Conservatives," Conservative party official Susan Warren commented: "Ethnic minorities have taken over established riding association executives. They've wiped them out. This is not always good. Political experience is vested with riding associations" (interview).

While political experience may be vested with long-time members of riding associations, so may established biases that may prevent the recruitment and acceptance of ethnic and visible minorities. Moreover, the concept of "take-overs" of riding associations may also implicitly suggest that only members of the dominant ethnic and racial groups are legitimate office-holders within riding associations, a suggestion that Jim Coutts, former personal secretary to Pierre Trudeau, has argued is discriminatory:

When large groups of Italian, Chinese and Portuguese supporters of various candidates turned out for the nomination in Trinity–Spadina, a riding in the heart of downtown Toronto, their presence was not a reflection of some subversive plot to take over the riding. It is theirs. They are the life-blood of Trinity–Spadina. (1988)

In sum, problems pertaining to large-scale membership recruitment were seen to influence the ethics of supporters of candidates contesting nominations, the loyalty and permanence of membership in riding associations, and relations between new and long-time members. In most cases, these problems with mass recruitment were linked to the integration of ethnic minorities into the major parties in a way that implied that ethnic minority participation itself was part of the problem, thus undermining the legitimacy of "ethnic" candidates, riding executive members and supporters.

It should be noted, however, that a few critiques of the current nomination process and its attendant membership recruitment made an effort to counter the assumption (inscribed in the notion of "instant Liberal") that the involvement of ethnic minorities in party politics was itself problematic. For instance, Jim Coutts argued for the need to separate the process from the players and to concentrate reform on the former: "We must recognize that what needs reform are the rules governing nominations, not the cast of characters who are identified as taking advantage of the rules" (1988). Albina Guarnieri, a strong advocate for reform of the nomination process, cautioned that

there has been no change in abuse from the past. The only difference is that now the numbers are greater. It's not just the ethnics. Many of the officials adjudicating the nomination process were not ethnics. (Interview)

While most responses solicited from party activists regarding the problems with nomination and delegate selection processes suggested the need to tighten rules (with the most common suggestion being the advancing of the cut-off date), some party officials and MPs addressed the need to safeguard the openness of membership rules and the recruitment process so as to encourage the revitalization of their parties. For instance, Progressive Conservative official Susan Warren defended an open system of party membership:

The [current] system is open to abuse, but the abuse of a closed system is even worse. The party cannot survive unless it attracts new people. It's very easy for the riding executive to just sit there and recruit the same few people. At key times in the party, you need to bring in new people. (Interview)

Similiarly, Doug Fisher, a Liberal party candidate in the 1988 federal election, wrote in the *Mississauga News* (22 March 1988) that "rigid rules designed to guard establishment rights and to exclude new people are sure signs of decay."

The position supportive of retaining an open system of recruitment is linked to the issue of party relevance and representation in the context of social and demographic change within Canadian society. Joseph Volpe, Liberal MP for Eglinton–Lawrence, argued for the "need to recruit new members within a democratic environment. The party should reflect the community both in numbers and 'quality' " (interview). Margaret Mitchell, federal NDP multiculturalism critic, also spoke to the need for her party to be open: "We should not be restrictive. It's a healthy sign when ethnic politics are coming into the mainstream. The reality is that many of those people are being discriminated against, so their involvement is healthy" (interview).

The next section of this study explores the initiatives taken by the three traditional parties to garner the support and active involvement of ethnic and visible minorities in party structures.

PARTY INITIATIVES AND POLICIES ON MINORITY PARTICIPATION

As revealed in the previous section, ethnic minorities are no longer content merely to support the major parties, either as voters or as campaign workers, but are themselves demanding access to power and decision making at all levels of party organization. This reflects the changing nature of ethnic communities in Canada. Many are socio-economically diverse, with large professional and entrepreneurial segments. A 1986 submission to the Ontario Liberal party President's Council by a body representing visible minority Liberals describes this changed political character of ethnic communities:

> In the increasingly turbulent world of ethnic politics, the old style brokers, men and women with whom the previous Liberal government in Ottawa could deal, trading grants and favours for votes have since been rendered obsolete. They have been replaced by a new generation of assertive, self-confident minorities who are now, collectively, the majority. Perceptions aside, this new political reality has to be configured and brought to bear in future decision making processes at both the political and governmental levels. (FOLSAT 1986, 5).

The response by the political parties to this "new political reality" was described in this same document to be "indiscriminate" and "haphazard," with the net result that there was "an us/them approach to sharing the democratic instruments of power and decision making" (FOLSAT 1986, 6).

Several ethnic minority MPs and party activists regarded the approach taken by party strategists toward ethnocultural minorities to be ill-informed, instrumental or even cynical. For instance, Bhausaheb Ubale, who had unsuccessfully contested a Liberal nomination in 1988, felt that "party strategists have no knowledge about what ethnic communities are. They look at minorities as 'vote banks' " (interview). MP Albina Guarnieri also perceived that party officials underestimated the political maturity of ethnic communities:

> I think that they are baffled about ethnics. They lack some understanding that they have to include us. They lack sensitivity. What the [Liberal] party finds is that the old lines don't work anymore. The ethnic communities won't be hoodwinked any longer. I find that there is an arrogance among the traditional members. (Interview)

Similarly, NDP MP Howard McCurdy criticized his party's tendency to exclude visible minorities:

> The NDP has taken minorities for granted and failed to reach out to them. They have felt that because we have the most all-inclusive philosophy, the participation of minorities would fall behind. They did not understand inclusiveness, how to work with, become friends, etc., with visible minorities. (Interview)

Notwithstanding the criticisms by several minority party activists about the exclusionary tendencies of the parties vis-à-vis ethnic and visible minorities, all three parties have taken initiatives to become more inclusive and representative of Canadian ethnocultural and racial diversity. The philosophical openness to ameliorative, affirmative measures, and the extent and nature of integrative structures and reforms vary across the three parties. Consistent with the regional concentration of ethnocultural and visible minorities in urban Ontario ridings is the greater degree of acceptance to minority liaison structures and/or affirmative action at the provincial (Ontario) level of party organization in comparison with the national level of party organization.

Racial minorities, white ethnocultural minorities and new Canadians lacking official language skills all face somewhat different sets of barriers to party participation and representation. These differences have meant that different policy responses are appropriate to widen access for each target group. That visible minorities are afforded greater attention within party reforms than ethnic minorities reflects the fact that racial minorities are most clearly underrepresented in the House of Commons and that they face the most severe forms of systemic discrimination.

Some of the initiatives and affirmative measures are fairly recent, making it premature to evaluate their success in increasing minority representation. This is the case for the NDP's new affirmative action measures for visible minorities at the federal level (discussed below), which were the product of minority protest and party self-criticism pertaining to the minimal participation of visible minorities at the 1989 NDP leadership convention (interviews with Howard McCurdy and Dan Heap).

How have the major parties attempted to recruit the support of ethnocultural minorities at the electoral level? What initiatives have been taken to facilitate integration of minority members at different levels of party organization and, in particular, as legislative candidates? And what are the perceptions, both of party officials and minority activists, of barriers to the full and equal participation and representation of minorities within the major parties? These are the major questions providing the framework for the following discussion.

Outreach and Courting the "Ethnic Vote"

Since the early 1970s, one routine practice during national election campaigns designed to attract ethnic support has been for governing and opposition parties to advance their own versions of multiculturalism policy (Burnet and Palmer 1988, 176). The governing party has an advantage in that it can spend money and enact state policies that may win the favour of ethnic communities. While the multiculturalism policy was first introduced by the Liberals under Prime Minister Trudeau, the Conservative government of Brian Mulroney has further advanced the policy through a number of initiatives.[52]

Rocco Sebastiano, Ontario director for the Progressive Conservatives, felt that the Conservatives' demonstrated commitment to multiculturalism would have an impact in party support by ethnocultural minorities. He conjectured that "something like the prime minister's apology to Italian-Canadians [for internment by the Canadian government during the Second World War] can change party affiliation, can cause a rethinking of allegiance to a party" (interview). The fact that the Mulroney government has increased immigration levels from those of the previous Liberal administration has also won the favour of many minority groups, particularly those with a high proportion of recent immigrants.[53]

Another means open to the governing party to win popularity among ethnic voters is through patronage appointments. In October 1986, a report prepared for the federal Progressive Conservative party by the Tory Metro Caucus Subcommittee on Special Concerns argued that the party's stated objective for political appointments – Governor-in-Council appointments to agencies, boards and commissions (ABC) of 30 percent women and 20 percent from ethnocultural backgrounds – was not being met. The fact that until March 1986, 92 percent of all Tory appointees from Ontario were Anglo males created dissatisfaction among supporters of the two targeted groups (Malarek 1986).

Steven Coupland, the current director of the Appointments Secretariat in the Prime Minister's Office, stated that while the Secretariat does not keep statistics on the percentage of ethnocultural ABC appointments, "a good number" have gone to ethnocultural minority individuals.[54] The process of making appointments to ethnic minority individuals is encouraged by meetings with heads of the Canadian Ethnocultural Council (CEC) and by maintaining stable lines of communication between the CEC and the secretariat. Many of the recent appointments to the immigration and refugee boards have been drawn from ethnocultural minority groups. The representation of ethnic minorities joins other considerations in making patronage appointments, including representation of visible minorities and women,[55] and regional and linguistic representation. The percentage of appointments that are ethnocultural is, however, difficult to calculate. Citing the recent appointment of Don Oliver, a Black Nova Scotian, to the Senate, Coupland discussed the difficulty of using surnames to categorize an appointment as ethnocultural: "Is Mazankowski an ethnic? Who is a minority? Some people find it insulting to be labelled an ethnocultural appointment" (telephone interview).

While the governing party has the advantage over other parties in its capacity to make policies and appointments beneficial to ethnic minorities, all parties can forge other types of contacts with minority groups. The attendance of party leaders and MPs at functions arranged by ethnic community organizations is one common means of establishing direct contact with ethnic minorities. The garnering of support at community functions is assumed to stem from the symbolic recognition by politicians and party leaders of different ethnic communities and their particular concerns.[56]

Many MPs from all parties attend ethnic community functions in their ridings as a part of their constituency work. Typical in this regard

were remarks made by Liberal MP Derek Lee, who represents an ethnically diverse riding:

> I treat ethnics as constituents. I don't make it a priority to link up with
> the 15 communities in my riding. I respond to any initiative with a
> cultural/national/linguistic origin. For instance, I attend events such
> as *Divali* (a Hindu holiday) and Prophet Mohammed Day. (Interview)

Constituency-level contact with ethnic minorities often also occurs
through casework. In areas with large populations of new immigrants
such as Trinity–Spadina, the riding held by NDP MP Dan Heap, where
21.4 percent of residents are noncitizens (Canada, Statistics Canada
1988), much of this casework revolves around immigration and is
conducted by office staff who have fluency in the nonofficial languages of some of the larger minority communities. As described by
Dan Heap:

> Some of the pages in my *Householder Report* [constituency newsletter
> of MPS] are in Spanish, Chinese, Italian, Portuguese. In my office, I
> staff Chinese-speaking capability (a practice which I continued from
> my years as alderman). Due to budgetary considerations, I had to cut
> back to half-time on Portuguese language casework. Occasionally, I
> put out mailings in Chinese. I deal with the Chinese on problems
> within immigration. I have had workshops on immigration with
> Chinese and Portuguese language interpreters. I maintain contacts
> with ethnic community organizations. But I don't make it as high a pri-
> ority as others to attend all their dinners. It depends on the kind of ser-
> vice they have given to the riding. (Interview)

Different MPs have different practices regarding the linguistic capa-
bility of their constituency offices and the languages printed in their
constituency literature such as the *Householder Report*. For instance,
Liberal MP Alfonso Gagliano, who represents the Quebec riding of
Saint-Léonard, which is heavily French and Italian, puts out his constituency mail in three languages: French, English and Italian. In contrast, Charles Caccia, who now represents a Toronto riding with a
declining percentage of Italians, prints his constituency literature only
in English (interviews).

Not surprisingly, during elections, candidates in ethnically diverse
ridings are more apt to translate literature into several nonofficial languages of the major language groups in their area. However, in ridings
with a variety of language and immigrant groups, party candidates

face a challenge in reaching voters in their language of preference, through literature and canvassing, while remaining within the bounds of campaign spending (Brunt 1988).[57]

During the 1988 campaign, the Conservatives distributed third-language literature produced by the national campaign office. One standard brochure distributed in six nonofficial languages (Italian, Portuguese, Chinese, Greek, Hindi and Punjabi) was a "motherhood piece, explaining what the PC party is in Canada" (interview with Elaine Collins).

Following the 1988 election, there was major consternation in the NDP among some minority ethnic activists over the national campaign's failure to spend money on advertising in ethnic media, an omission that was interpreted as showing the party's disregard of non-British, non-French supporters. The limited advertising in ethnic newspapers and the absence of advertising in electronic ethnic media was justified by the federal secretary in terms of "budgetary considerations."[58]

Generally speaking, the Canadian electoral system and the system of party financing have not been accommodating of the ethnolinguistic map of the potential electorate. Given that most of the national election campaign is conducted in English and French, immigrants lacking competence in one of the official languages[59] are shut out. Margaret Mitchell, the multiculturalism critic for the NDP, spoke about the need to address questions of accessibility for non-English-speaking, non-French-speaking immigrants. One type of reform in federal elections designed to widen access is suggested by a set of recommendations recently passed by the Toronto City Council, pertaining to ballots in municipal elections. Some of the recommendations were for simpler language on ballots. Further recommendations called for

> color-coded ballots ... , ballots in different alphabets and languages, ballots with photographs of the candidates, candidate posters in the polling booths and numerical designations for candidates corresponding to numbers on the ballots. (Valpy 1990)

Political parties often are not equipped to deal with the political integration of immigrants at the level of providing political education, such as the basics of the electoral and voting process. At least three submissions to this Commission spoke of the need for education and voter information in various languages and for greater use of the "ethnic media" (both print and electronic, as well as mainstream radio and television).[60] As discussed below, the ethnic liaison structures and committees established at more local levels of party organization are among the few arenas where political parties are claiming to do basic political education for new Canadians.

Since 1987, the federal Tories have made outreach to ethnic communities a priority during and between elections. At the PC national office the director of multicultural communications, Elaine Collins, worked to "educate ministers, caucus members, especially western and East Coast MPs who do not have the same sensitivity to ethnic issues" (interview with Elaine Collins). Collins also urged greater use of the ethnic media in communicating the Conservative government's policies to ethnic communities:

> I would hound chiefs of staff to get their minister's message into press releases of the ethnic media, even if it was done in English or French. Some of the ethnic media would be glad to receive these releases and would translate them. Other groups such as the Ukrainians and Germans would print them in English. We also asked ministers to go on multicultural cable TV shows such as Channel 47. (Interview)

In the Ontario office of the Progressive Conservatives of Canada, a Multicultural Advisory Committee was established to keep the director of operations and the party informed about ethnocultural community events. This committee of 14 people is composed of individuals who are themselves from a variety of minority backgrounds, such as Italian, Chinese, Muslim, Hindu and Pakistani. It was felt that a clearing-house on information about such ethnocultural community events as festivals and national and religious days would be useful in helping to build a relationship between MPs from dominant ethnic backgrounds and their often ethnically diverse constituencies.

The chair of the PC Multicultural Advisory Committee spoke of its liaison function between the party and the government:

> It is difficult to run the party when the party is in power. Sue [Warren, Ontario director of operations] wanted to keep the party informed and abreast about the communities. She tried to keep party officials informed of community events and policy discussions, and what party staff could do to match ministers to professional associations. Its purpose was also to inform riding associations about the demographics of ridings and what outreach could be done, e.g., giving them the names of cultural community association presidents. We have been doing this, but it's not been too successful because riding associations are dormant between elections. (Interview with Rocco Sebastiano)

The Liberals and New Democrats have also developed liaison structures with ethnocultural communities. The following discussion examines the development, organization and objectives of liaison committees and structures in the federal Progressive Conservative, Ontario Liberal and Ontario New Democratic parties.

Conservative Party: Ethnoculturally Based Affiliated Organizations

The Progressive Conservative Party of Canada has a series of affiliated associations that operate under the same constitution as the extra-riding associations (such as campus associations). For an association to be recognized, it must have a minimum of 100 members. Affiliated associations can send delegates to meetings and are allowed one delegate for every 50 members up to a maximum of three delegates.[61]

There are several affiliated associations organized on an ethnic basis. The first affiliated ethnic club was Eastern European; formed in the early 1980s, it is now defunct. An Italian club also had a brief life. The PC Chinese Business Association was formed in the early 1980s and is still operating. Other associations include a PC Korean Business Association, a recently formed PC Portuguese Business Association, and an Afro-Canadian PC Association. Most of these affiliated associations are de facto locally based in Toronto.[62]

The major purpose of these affiliated associations is to do political training within the ethnocultural communities, to sensitize the members to the policies of the party, and to help to integrate the members into the mainstream party structures. They also act as a source of funding for the PC party.

As reflected in the names of many of the PC ethnic clubs, the membership tends to be drawn from the entrepreneurial segments of minority communities. Additionally, the clubs provide a "comfort zone" for new immigrants who lack knowledge about the Canadian political system and who are able to meet with others of the same language and culture in familiar venues (such as ethnic restaurants). As well, one Conservative organizer felt that the motivation for many of the members of the ethnic clubs was their desire "to be represented in the PC party because we are in government. It's a status thing" (interview with Avi Flaherty).

Progressive Conservative officials felt, however, that the ethnic clubs "have not been terrifically good in getting members of the group on to other, e.g., riding, executives" (interview with Rosemary Dolman). Thus the affiliated organizations have not acted effectively as mechanisms for the integration of ethnic minorities into mainstream party structures. Interestingly, this also emerged as a concern among Liberals about the visible minority liaison structure established by the Ontario Liberal party.

The Federation of Ontario Liberal Satellites

The Federation of Ontario Liberal Satellites (FOLSAT)[63] emerged as a result of the organizing efforts of visible minority activists, primarily in Metro Toronto, who were demanding a more prominent role in the Ontario Liberal party. It is an umbrella organization of several visible minority Ontario Liberal associations: Korean, Chinese, East Indian, South Asian (East Indians outside India), Filipino, and Black and Caribbean.

FOLSAT was conceived in 1986 as a means of developing Liberal political leadership within visible minority communities – using a different approach from the old style of brokerage politics that had predominated in the Chinese, Black and other visible minority communities. The objective was to attract minority groups to the Liberal party so as to integrate them into local ridings. The promotion of the interests of visible minority Liberals was to occur through building institutional channels of communication with the Ontario Liberal party leader and with cabinet ministers, Liberal MLAs, the Executive Committee and other committees of the Ontario Liberal party. The resources of FOLSAT's members were also to be used to support the Liberal candidacy of visible minorities in provincial, federal and municipal elections.

The visible minority focus and membership of the structure reflected its founders' views that white ethnic communities, such as the Italian and Jewish, had been successful in obtaining representation within all levels of the Ontario Liberal party. The founders also felt that there were:

> substantial differences in issues: for us, it was discrimination, based on colour. What was lacking was people of colour on the convention floor, party executive. The integration of visible minorities is different than for other minorities. At the 1982 leadership convention, there were very limited numbers of people of colour, tokenism. Visible minorities still feel that we have been used when we are needed. In between elections, visible minorities are not involved, only during elections. (Group interview with FOLSAT leaders)

The visible minorities involved in the Liberal party felt that in their respective communities they had leadership potential and a lot of financial resources that were not being tapped by the political parties. In

return, they wanted "employment equity targets, patronage appointments and access to power" (group interview with leaders of FOLSAT).

Altogether, the various member organizations (some of which were
formed at the same time as the umbrella organization) brought
in about 6 000 new members. This was undoubtedly a factor in the
support given to the structure by David Peterson, whose special assistant, Trevor Wilson, was a key strategist in FOLSAT's formation. At the
Ontario Liberal convention in June 1986, two amendments were made
to the Liberal party constitution, recognizing FOLSAT as part of the
Ontario Liberal party and reserving space at the convention for
FOLSAT (but without delegate status). All accounts suggest that the introduction of FOLSAT was not an easy battle at the convention, finding
opposition both from Executive Committee members and from some
visible minority party members.

Among the achievements claimed by FOLSAT members was the successful candidacy of three visible minority Liberals in the 1987 Ontario
election: Bob Wong, Murad Velshi and Alvin Curling, from the Chinese,
East Indian and Black communities respectively. FOLSAT was able to
obtain regular access to higher levels of the party through quarterly
meetings with the premier and through regular meetings with the
provincial minister of citizenship, who was in charge of both multiculturalism and employment equity. The members of FOLSAT also claim
that their influence was felt in the commissioning of a study on over-
seas qualifications by the Peterson government and in pressing the government toward employment equity.

Leaders of the satellite ethnic clubs argue that their organizations
have also played a significant role in the political education of new
immigrants. The president of the Filipino-Canadian Liberal Association
stated:

> With the birth of FOLSAT, Filipinos are more aware of political struc-
> tures in Canada, the different kind of government in Canada, the fact
> that you do not elect the prime minister directly. Other than FOLSAT,
> there was no other focus for this type of political education. Twelve
> hundred Filipinos came out in the first meeting. The Filipino
> Association would meet once a month. We have had workshops con-
> cerning political issues. Some board members also attend Ontario
> Liberal party workshops. We try to find qualified Filipinos to run as
> MPs, MPPs and aldermen. (Interview)

A major objective of the satellite organizations was the integration of previously uninvolved minorities into mainstream party

organizations at the constituency level. FOLSAT was thus meant to provide a transitional step toward integration in the Liberal party structure. While most leaders agreed that the presence of FOLSAT meant that there was greater involvement of visible minorities in party politics than before its establishment, they also acknowledged that the integration of visible minorities into riding associations has not been too successful.

Theoretically, this integration was to occur by having membership in one of the FOLSAT organizations entitle people to have automatic membership in local riding associations for the first year. However, the majority did not renew their memberships, and there were conflicts between FOLSAT member organizations and riding associations about the apportionment of membership fees. In addition, some riding associations did not want to accept FOLSAT members, fearing a take-over. A president of one of the affiliate organizations also raised the issue of the internal politics of FOLSAT. He felt that alienation existed among the members of the minority clubs, who did not always accept the legitimacy of the leadership of their organizations.

For many of the first-generation immigrants participating in FOLSAT, the satellite organizations provided a culturally supportive atmosphere among people who spoke the same language and were familiar with the same traditions. As one member stated, "People who come in are shy and they are shy of parties." A member of the Korean Liberal Association said that the barriers to political participation of Koreans include:

> language, knowledge of the system. One of the cultural traits of Koreans is political apathy. They are culturally trained to respect power. Even if they are qualified, they do not jump into the arena. This also applies to the other Oriental communities. (Interview)

The notion of a satellite organizational structure to liaise between visible minority communities and the various levels of party organization was rejected at the national level of the Liberal party. Liberal MPs Charles Caccia and Sergio Marchi both spoke of their fight against the establishment of FOLSAT at the federal level. Caccia explained his opposition to FOLSAT as being based on his perception that it would "produce power brokers who receive undue importance." Marchi proclaimed his philosophical opposition to FOLSAT, which he viewed as slowing down rather than facilitating integration of minorities into mainstream political institutions:

I fought this concept at the federal level because it creates two levels of members. The satellite concept is telling. It means that it is orbiting. We have riding associations and members. FOLSAT retards people's entry and political development. Peterson created it as a way of penetrating ethnocultural communities. You should bring people into the front door, and not the back door. FOLSAT also builds tensions in the community – for example, the Italian-Canadian FOLSAT versus the Afro-Caribbean. If the Berlin wall can come down, so can FOLSAT! (Interview)

Several other ethnic minority Liberal MPs and party activists expressed their resounding opposition to FOLSAT on the grounds that the satellite organization ghettoizes and segregates the group. They argued that, far from integrating minorities into the mainstream political structures, FOLSAT segregates them and discourages mainstream involvement.[64]

Members of FOLSAT gave other reasons for the opposition at the federal level of the Liberal party to visible minority liaison structures. Some felt that "the party strategists at the federal level were not in tune with the power potential within visible minority communities." In particular, they saw former national leader John Turner as uninformed about visible minorities and interested only in their potential as voters rather than as leaders and decision makers.

In addition, there was some recognition among FOLSAT supporters that "federally, the Liberal structure is more complicated. Not all provinces have visible minorities." Also, the ethnocultural politics at the federal level are more likely to be dominated by French–English issues, as well as by Aboriginal politics.

The membership of FOLSAT has declined since the Peterson government lost the September 1990 election. This lends credence to the hypothesis that ethnic minorities gravitate toward the governing party – a hypothesis supported by the recent growth in interest shown by some minority groups in the Ontario NDP since its September 1990 electoral victory.

The Ontario NDP Ethnic Liaison Committee

The impetus for the formation of the NDP Ethnic Liaison Committee in 1985 was similar to that underlying the development of FOLSAT. New Democrat ethnic minority activists felt that their concerns were ignored or were underrepresented in the party, and this in turn left the minority communities with a disinterested or sceptical outlook toward the NDP. To redress this deficiency within the party, it was deemed essential for minorities to have a higher profile through the establishment of a formal structure of ethnic minority committees. Currently, committees exist to represent Black, Chinese, Korean, Italian, Portuguese, Greek and South Asian communities, and thus liaise both with visible minority communities and with white ethnocultural communities.

The objectives of the individual minority committees and the liaison structure were threefold. First, they aimed to raise the political priority of minority group issues within the NDP. Second, the minority committees were to encourage minority group party members to hold office and be represented at all levels of the party, and to fill leadership roles within the party at all levels; to be convention and council delegates; to hold senior party executive and committee positions; to become candidates for the party at municipal, provincial and federal levels; to work to enhance job opportunities for minorities within the party; and to increase party memberships within the minority groups (Ontario NDP 1985). Third, the minority committees were established to provide a liaison between the party and the minority group communities. This was to be done through the ethnic print and electronic media, through community functions to convey the message of the NDP to minorities and through education of the NDP membership about minority concerns.

The Ethnic Liaison Committee was created to play a more formal role than the FOLSAT structure, where FOLSAT members met directly with Liberal party leaders. In the case of the NDP liaison committee, policy resolutions would be forwarded to the party executive and then, if passed, would be presented by the executive either to a council meeting or to the biennial convention of the party. Thus, the NDP liaison committees took on the status of riding associations within the larger structure of the party, and indeed in 1986 they were entitled to name two delegates, with voting rights, to the provincial convention.[65] As in the case of FOLSAT, the intention of the structure was to integrate minority members within the mainstream party organization. Members who took out membership with the NDP were entitled to the full privileges of party membership, including being listed as members of the riding association for the area where they lived.

One priority of the Ethnic Liaison Committee was the promotion of minority participation and minority issues during elections. The minority committees were to work with the Elections Planning Committee to promote the candidacy of minorities, to provide financial and volunteer assistance in their campaigns and to develop minority group issues as a central part of electoral campaigns. The support given to minority candidates by the individual committees in the 1988 federal election appeared to have mixed results. While Paul Simon of the Black Advisory Committee (BAC) expressed disappointment in the support he received from the BAC in his campaign as a federal candidate, Raymond Cho was reported to have been provided with substantial financial and campaign support from the Korean Advisory Committee (KAC) in his candidacy in the riding of Scarborough–Rouge River. Moreover, Cho attributed his success in a contested election to the Policy Review Committee and to the work done by the KAC and the larger Korean community during his federal campaign (Ontario NDP 1989).

The concept of ethnic liaison committees within the NDP had its genesis in the early 1970s, when an Italian association was formed within the Ontario NDP. At that point, minority influence was extremely limited: the members of the committee asked Stephen Lewis (the Ontario NDP leader at the time) whether they could say a few words in Italian to the provincial convention (interview with Joe Pantalone).[66]

More recently (1983), Bob Rae, as Ontario NDP leader, convened a meeting with Black community members, out of which was formed the BAC. This committee was developed as a nonpartisan liaison with the Ontario New Democrats. In 1985 the impetus for the formation of ethnic liaison committees was driven by white ethnic groups to counteract the traditional attraction of ethnic minorities to the Liberals, because of the latter's immigration policies. The fact that one did not have to be a New Democrat to be a member of a liaison committee was something of an anomaly, particularly when the committees were granted delegate status (interview with Jill Marzetti). Joe Pantalone argued that the opportunities provided by the minority committees to work with non-NDP members of the community were beneficial to all participants, citing as one example the work done by the Italian Advisory Committee on pensions for Italian-Canadians. This one issue enlisted the participation of 600 people (interview).

Currently, recruitment to the ethnic liaison committees reverses the conventional pattern; that is, rather than being recruited directly from the communities without prior involvement in the party, now "recruitment occurs through the riding associations, and then members are rolled into the advisory committees" (interview with Jill Marzetti). Interestingly, since the NDP took power in Ontario, there has been new interest expressed, from communities like those of the Filipinos and Lithuanians, in establishing such committees for their communities. According to Marzetti, the Ontario NDP is "on the horns of a dilemma. Are the committees meant for outreach, or are they committees made up of party members who happen to be from specific communities?" (interview).

Unlike FOLSAT, the NDP Ethnic Liaison Committee is an umbrella group both for visible minority committees and for white ethnic minority committees. Given that issues of discrimination are likely to be seen somewhat differently by people of colour than by white, nondominant ethnic minorities, such differences could become an issue in political structures that bring together both constituencies. Indeed, Jill Marzetti stated that there is dissension within the committee on issues such as affirmative action:

> The Black Advisory Committee has been pushing for affirmative action for candidates. But the other communities such as the Italian and Greek feel that affirmative action for visible minorities is disadvantageous for them. Oddly, the Chinese and Korean committees have sided with the Greeks and Italians against the Blacks. They have seen an affirmative action policy only for visible minorities as a divisive policy where visible minorities will lose out ... The question is where do you draw the line in affirmative action? Should it be only for visible minorities? Or is there something more general about the immigrant experience? (Interview)

The affirmative action guidelines for nomination and candidacy in the Ontario NDP reflect a compromise position, with priority given to visible minorities, but with attention also given to the running of all minority ethnic candidates. These guidelines and other affirmative measures introduced by the provincial and federal levels of the NDP will be discussed below.

The federal structure of the NDP is not as advanced as that of Ontario on issues of visible minority and ethnic minority participation. Criticisms of the "white TV face of the 1989 leadership convention" have served as a catalyst for the federal NDP to redress the underrepresentation of ethnic and visible minorities and of Aboriginal peoples within the national party. According to Abby Polonetski, the women's director of the federal NDP, after having achieved gender parity in the representation of women, "it's only now [in 1990] that we've been mandated to address our affirmative action program to include visible minorities and Aboriginal people" (interview).

Much of the work done in developing programs to "build a party that reflects the ethnic and racial diversity of working people in Canada today" is centred in the Multiculturalism Committee of the federal party, which is composed primarily of visible minorities (NDP n.d.) The Multiculturalism Committee has proposed that:

a Participation of Visible Minorities Committee be created as a permanent committee of the Party to assist and encourage the participation of members of racial minorities in all aspects of the Party,
including as candidates, Executive and Council members, delegates
to conventions, members of federal committees, riding members and
executives, and employees of the Federal Party proportionate to their
representation in the general population. (NDP 1990)

In addition, in December 1989 an amendment to the Constitution
created a Council of Federal Ridings, which will provide a new type of
organizational representation for visible minorities by making a council of visible minorities one of six councils in a new federative structure.[67]

The next section addresses the affirmative action measures within
the NDP, both in operation at the Ontario level and "in process" at the
national level, and the stance of the Liberal and Conservative parties
toward affirmative action for visible and ethnic minorities. This discussion will pay particular attention to party differences in philoso-
phies and institutional measures to promote the participation of
minorities as candidates for elections.

Affirmative Action Measures

The brief to the Royal Commission on Electoral Reform and Party
Financing from the Canadian Ethnocultural Council (1990) made the following recommendation:

That parties (and leaders) be called on to encourage affirmative action
type policies to increase the number of candidates (in winnable ridings) from ethnic and visible minorities, and to increase such participation in the party apparatus. Each party should adopt its own policy
in this regard.

It is evident that as it stands, the three parties have important differences in their position on the integration of ethnic and visible minorities. As is evident in the following discussion, these differences have
affected the development of each party's affirmative action and community liaison policies and structures.

New Democratic Party

In December 1989 the Ontario Provincial Council of the NDP approved
affirmative action guidelines for nomination and candidacy, which
were then included in the "prospective candidate information package"
sent out to all NDP provincial riding associations for use in the 1990

Ontario election. These affirmative action guidelines are listed in appendix B.

The Ontario NDP guidelines identify as target groups women, visible minorities, persons with disabilities and Aboriginal peoples. The process is meant to address the complaint of female and other target group candidates that they are put into unwinnable ridings and made the sacrificial lambs in elections. Thus, the guidelines specify that 75 percent of the "priority" or winnable seats are to have candidates from the target groups. Among the target groups, women are marked for special attention in the specification that 60 percent of the candidates in the priority seats should be women.[68] In addition, what Joe Pantalone referred to as a "permissive policy" exists for 25 percent of the priority seats, where priority is given to "running ethnic candidates, especially in those ridings where such groupings are a major element in the riding population." This policy guideline to run ethnic candidates in heavily ethnic ridings continues a strategy of capturing the ethnic vote that has a long historical tradition in Canadian politics, as documented in the first section of this study.

Riding associations submit the names of candidates to the Elections Planning Committee. If names of candidates from target groups are not included, then the riding association is asked to present reasons for this omission. Also, the services of the Central Search Committee are provided to assist in recruiting target candidates. Thus, while the process of searching for target candidates and accounting for the results of this search are mandatory, the affirmative action policy is not mandatory in the sense of producing specified results (in the manner that fulfilling quotas would be). According to Jill Marzetti:

> There may be fights if the local (nontarget) candidate is very popular, for example, a municipal councillor. I see the blockage out in riding associations outside Metro [Toronto] and places like Windsor – in the rural ridings. (Interview)

Similarly, the women's director in the national office of the NDP saw riding autonomy to be one of the biggest barriers to implementing affirmative action:

> Because the NDP formulates policy from ridings, the ridings are very important, even if you're talking about two or three activists. *The concept of riding autonomy is a sacred cow, and a barrier to implementing affirmative action programs.* (Interview with Abby Polonetski; emphasis of the authors)

It is in part because of the strong regard within the NDP for the grassroots democracy of the riding-level associations that the Ontario director spoke of the necessity to have a more "organic" approach to affirmative action. This would entail voluntary compliance rather than mandatory rules, which Marzetti argued "fly in the face of local democracy." Instead, Marzetti favoured more education and development, and more support and encouragement given to target candidates to run. The current NDP guidelines also include a financial "carrot" to those riding associations that implement affirmative action in their candidacy selection:

> We have an "Affirmative Action Fund," $60 000 in the budget that is divided among candidates in the affirmative action program. Affirmative action expenses include child care, such things as dry-cleaning and wardrobe expenses for women. But we give the same amount of money to visible minority candidates as to women. (Interview)

During the last Ontario election (in 1990), the NDP ran five visible minority candidates – three Black and two South Asian. Of these five, one candidate, Zanana Akande, won and was appointed to the Rae Cabinet as Minister of Social Services, making her the first Black woman cabinet minister in Ontario. Marzetti attributes the fielding of all five visible minority candidates to the affirmative action program.

NDP supporters for affirmative action for visible minorities also point to the success that has been attained in their program of affirmative action for women (Bashevkin 1985, 86–89). While there are only five women out of a total of 44 NDP provincial members of Parliament, at other levels of the party gender parity has been achieved. The federal leadership of Audrey McLaughlin is symbolic of the gains made by women at top levels of decision making. NDP multiculturalism critic Margaret Mitchell felt that success for the representation of visible minorities could similarly be achieved through actions such as sending letters to riding executives informing them of party policy.

It is clear that the affirmative action program initiated by the Ontario NDP has served as an important model – both in letter and in spirit – for the formation of a similar program at the federal level. Thus, suggested guidelines brought to the 1991 federal convention borrowed heavily from the Ontario NDP, as did the understanding that there are differences in the disadvantages experienced by racial versus ethnic minorities:

The impediments to racial (visible) minority participation are significantly different and their resolution therefore requires different approaches to the problems of ethnocultural participation. In the former, the application of specific affirmative action techniques are necessary. In the latter the more effective outreach strategies (also necessary for visible minorities) should suffice. (NDP n.d.)

The goal for visible minority representation at all levels of the national party organization is approximately 7 percent, the estimated percentage of visible minorities in the larger population. One problem acknowledged in the implementation of this goal is the "heterogeneous distribution of visible minorities in various parts of Canada" (NDP n.d.).

Howard McCurdy, who has been centrally involved in drawing up the affirmative action guidelines for the federal party, also argued that such a program for candidate selection cannot be imposed on riding associations:

At the riding association level, the NDP is talking now only about [affirmative action for] membership – getting them in. Those who are capable will get selected as candidates. In a place like Toronto, it will happen naturally, without an affirmative action program. You cannot set hard-fast targets for all riding associations. (Interview)

In January 1992, the Federal Affirmative Action Program comes into effect. Thus it will be some time before the results of such a program will be known. Nonetheless, the federal guidelines, like those of the Ontario NDP, reflect sensitivity to the need to balance riding autonomy with greater representation of Aboriginals, the disabled, women and visible minorities.

Additionally, the federal NDP is also in the process of implementing employment equity for visible minorities and Aboriginal persons in NDP federal offices. A permanent Employment Equity Committee comprising caucus and staff union representatives has been established to implement and monitor this program. According to Wendy Jang, legislative assistant to MP Margaret Mitchell and a Chinese-Canadian who has worked on the employment equity program, progress has already been made. Currently, there are eight visible minorities and two Aboriginal persons out of a total of 177 NDP parliamentary staff, which means that they are more than halfway to the goal of a total 10 percent combined visible minority and Aboriginal staff.

Progressive Conservative Party

Unlike the NDP, the federal Progressive Conservative party does not have any formal outreach or affirmative measures to increase the participation of ethnocultural or visible minorities. Nonetheless, organizers within the Tory party are cognizant of the need for local party constituency associations to become more representative of the ethnic and racial composition of local populations. This awareness is linked to a desire to maintain electoral strength within areas of high ethnic and racial diversity. Rosemary Dolman, the acting federal secretary of the Conservative party, stated that during the 1986 general meeting "there was a discussion about the demography of the ridings and the country as a whole. There was a recognition that you cannot really represent a riding if you have a WASP executive and half of the riding is not" (interview).

One of the roles of the Multicultural Advisory Committee, established at the Ontario office of the federal party, was to assist ridings to recruit candidates from ethnic communities that were heavily represented within particular ridings. Conservative party officials were not in favour of mandatory affirmative action. Elaine Collins, who had been director of multicultural communications during the 1988 election, stated that the Conservatives tried to get active recruitment of minority candidates, but that this was done on a "more personal level" and "without issuing dictums from Ottawa, and without a structural policy." She added, "We prefer to get people involved in ways other than through quotas. It helps to get good [ethnic minority] candidates – for example, Alex Franco, who is Portuguese, got more people involved in the process. We prefer to see it evolve naturally."

Similarly, Rocco Sebastiano, a member of the federal executive, echoed sentiments conveyed by Ontario NDP secretary Jill Marzetti:

> As far as affirmative action is concerned, I would prefer that the national level not send directives, but rather engage in persuasion. The organization is built on the strengths of volunteers. We need to respect the autonomy of riding associations. We have an arm's-length relationship with the riding associations. If the party tried to actively recruit visible minority candidates, the riding associations would oppose this. (Interview).

Sebastiano, like Marzetti, argued for a more "organic" approach to recruitment of minority candidates. He argued that one of the best ways for minorities to become candidates for federal elections is to begin by entering at the municipal level. The cultivation of party candidates first at the municipal level was seen to have worked well in the NDP, where the party placed its resources behind promising candidates. Some of the ethnic minority MPs in the Liberal party, e.g., Sergio Marchi, John Nunziata, Rey Pagtakhan, had also cut their teeth in municipal-level politics and spoke of the exposure and legitimacy this had provided for their successful federal campaigns. At the PC Ontario provincial convention, delegates argued that the Tories ought to become similarly involved in municipal politics:

> Municipal politicians tend more to reflect the community. After eth-
> nic minorities have been cultivated locally, [the Conservative party]
> could approach them to run provincially or federally. This will avoid
> the conflicts with the riding associations and also recruit good can-
> didates. (Interview with Rocco Sebastiano)

According to Sebastiano, the best way for the Tories to overcome their image – "that they represent big business, white Anglo-Saxon interests" – is to get good, credible ethnic minority candidates to run in winnable ridings. This would prove that there is effective representation of ethnic communities. Sebastiano emphasized the importance of the minority candidates running in winnable ridings, even at the expense of alienating some of the people in those riding associations (interview).

Liberal Party

As discussed previously, the national level of the Liberal party rejected the ethnic satellite structure developed at the Ontario provincial level of the party. Consistent with this was the opposition expressed by most minority Liberal MPs to any formal affirmative action program to promote the representation of racial or ethnic minorities within the party.[69] Typical responses to the question as to whether reforms were needed to better represent ethnic minorities in the Liberal party were:

> I don't agree with quotas or levels. Within the Liberal party, the
> assumption is that we are all equal. It is up to the respective com-
> munities to take their places. I don't favour a multicultural commis-
> sion. We should have the same rules for everybody. (Interview with
> Alfonso Gagliano)

> You cannot prescribe these things. Political organizations are no dif-
> ferent than businesses. You need to meet the clients' needs. There is
> no systematic way of getting people involved within the political pro-
> cess. (Interview with Joseph Volpe)

I am not in favour of special measures. (Interview with John Nunziata)

MP Rey Pagtakhan, the only visible minority person in the Liberal caucus, suggested that the party should give visible minorities support and encouragement to run. He also recommended that sensitivity to the issue of visible minority candidacy would be facilitated by having a visible minority member on the Elections Committee. Pagtakhan laid particular emphasis on the need for commitment and activism of the party *leadership* in the search for good visible minority candidates.[70] Party activists in the NDP and the provincial Liberal party also spoke about the importance of leadership commitment to the participation of visible minorities as a key factor in the success of any affirmative action program.[71]

Barriers to Participation

Currently, the main parties are far from representative of the racial and ethnic diversity of the Canadian population. Members of all three parties were of the opinion that racism and ethnic discrimination exist within their parties in the same measure as they exist within society at large. Officials in the New Democratic and Conservative parties acknowledged that the top ranks of decision making in their parties are "all white." What, then, are the obstacles to participation and representation of ethnic and racial minorities within these three parties?

The views of ethnic minority MPs and minority candidates are instructive about prevailing perceptions of constraints and opportunities among those who are actively involved within the party system. A small number believed that no obstacles existed to the participation of nondominant ethnic groups within the parties and felt that their parties were characterized by equality of opportunity for all, regardless of racial or ethnic background. This liberal position on questions of race and ethnicity was articulated by Gus Mitges, a Tory MP of Greek-Canadian background:

> Your racial background doesn't count much. It's the work you do.
> You work from the ground up – whether you are Jewish, Greek, etc.
> It's entirely up to the individual. You'll get biases from people whether
> they're visible minorities or other minorities. People look for scape-
> goats when the economy is bad. There is nothing [discriminatory]
> within the institutions. It's no longer the case that we are a white party
> ... At one time, discrimination was so hard that people changed their
> names. This is no longer the case. If you're a good organizer, you're

welcomed with open arms. If you're a good worker, your chance is as good as anyone else. (Interview)

A few MPs of minority backgrounds argued that more is expected of ethnic minorities, that success hinges on working harder for respect within the parties (interviews with Gagliano, Volpe, Guarnieri). Several MPs, particularly among the Liberals, stated that while their party had a long way to go before ethnicity and race were irrelevant for participation, there was a far greater openness within the traditional parties than there had been in the past.

Liberal party activists were apt to emphasize that, comparatively speaking, the Liberal party was "light-years ahead of the other parties in attracting Canadians of other origins" (interview with Tony Ianno). MP Joe Volpe argued against the conventional wisdom about the attraction of ethnic minorities to the Liberal party based on its immigration policy, on the evidence that the Liberal party had in fact curtailed immigration flows in the 1970s and 1980s. Rather, Volpe suggested that

> Ethnic minorities are attracted to the Liberals because they have projected an image of a party open to newness and change without massive turmoil. This image has been reinforced by some policies that confirm that image, such as social welfare. (Interview)

It was striking how frequently Liberal party activists of minority backgrounds talked about the "comfort factor" in their decision to join and work within the Liberal party.[72] In contrast, Conservative party officials talked about their party's "image problem." For instance, Susan Warren, Ontario director of operations, stated:

> From our "focus groups" (a form of intensive polling using stratified samples), we know that ethnic and visible minorities are not comfortable with the Tories. We suffer from the image of "uptight Bay Street and WASP big business." Historically, in the forties and fifties, we were still blue-suited and excluded ethnic and visible minorities. We were also rural and predominantly English, Scottish and Irish. Now, the PCs who want to remain exclusive are moving to the Reform Party. (Interview)

Despite the growing attraction to the Tories of racial and ethnic minorities, particularly among business people, Warren felt that the majority within the Conservative party would continue to be of British and French origin. Her explanation for both the historical and contemporary ethnic composition of the party was based on ethnonational differences in political traditions of participation:

> The day-to-day participants will continue to be French and English in the majority. They've grown up in the system and understand the system. The new communities have no history of this. The British grew up in a party tradition where there was a long history of working for your party and of volunteerism. The Italians volunteer for their church. It is not part of the socialization of the Greeks and mideastern countries to be volunteers. But for WASPs, it's "Old Lady Bountiful." (Interview)

The NDP has also suffered from an image as a "white party," as witnessed both in the 1984 national election campaign literature (which lacked people of colour in the photos) and in the poor representation of visible minorities at the 1989 leadership convention. Howard McCurdy, the NDP's only visible minority member of Parliament, stated that his bid for the federal leadership in 1989 "was intentionally symbolic, to say to the Black community and visible minorities that the NDP gave them a place to participate" (interview).

Within the NDP, other obstacles were felt to exist to the recruitment of activists from minority backgrounds. For many ethnic minorities who have left repressive Communist regimes, the fear of left-wing parties has been translated in the Canadian context to reluctance to support the party perceived to be the most socialist. Given the historical bias within Canadian refugee policy, favouring refugees leaving repressive left-wing regimes, the "natural" constituency of immigrants who would be inclined to support the NDP has been limited.[73]

In addition, according to Howard McCurdy, the level of "ideological purity" demanded of NDP members acts as a deterrent to participation. In particular, it blocks access to visible minorities, who are external to the white networks of NDP party activists. Thus, McCurdy regarded the "puritanical bent" within the NDP as a serious impediment to recruitment, an argument he elaborated further: "People almost have to petition to get in because there is the assumption of some absolute adherence to belief. There are the 'fundamentalist NDPers'" (interview).

Abby Polonetski, the NDP's women's director, suggested that the NDP has fewer instant party members because the party demands of its members a higher level of commitment to party ideology and policy in comparison with either the Liberals or the Tories. Relating her own history of NDP involvement since early youth, Polonetski remarked that "you have to be a political junkie to get in" (interview).

However, there was a sense among New Democrats that this barrier to participation was weakening as a result of the combination of the pragmatic style of the new NDP leadership of Audrey McLaughlin and Ontario Premier Bob Rae, and the recent electoral success of the NDP in Ontario. According to Joe Pantalone, a chair of the Ontario NDP Ethnic Liaison Committee:

> There is no litmus test for democratic socialism. The NDP has not been in power historically, so they've held to their philosophy. Now they are in power in Ontario and they will change. They may become more like the Liberals. (Interview)

A structural hurdle for the participation of ethnic minorities within all three parties is the "incumbency factor." An unwritten, widely accepted rule within political parties is that one does not challenge the renomination of incumbent members of Parliament without due cause. The electoral success of a party is regarded as of extreme importance, and therefore there is a strong belief that it is better to field an incumbent who has a proven electoral appeal than to field an unknown and unproven candidate (see Gallagher 1988, 248–49). The successful nomination challenge in Eglinton–Lawrence of Joe Volpe to sitting member Roland de Corneille during the 1988 federal election, and the implicit endorsement of incumbent challenges by then Liberal leader John Turner, was met with considerable disapproval both within and outside the ranks of the Liberal party.

Yet the informal rule that discourages challenges to incumbents is a barrier to the placement of minority candidates within winnable or safe seats. Conservative party officials accounted for the low number of ethnic minority candidates within recent federal elections in terms of the incumbency factor:

> We don't face the same issues as Liberals. This is because in Ontario we have only 15 seats and with all incumbents we have a de facto coronation. The ridings that are left are heavily Mediterranean and therefore part of the "dead zone." (Interviews with Susan Warren and Avi Flaherty)

Similarly, the multiculturalism critic for the NDP stated that "the problem federally is that there are a limited number of seats held by incumbents. There has to be a conscious effort to have affirmative measures" (interview with Margaret Mitchell). To avoid incumbent challenges, NDP women's director Abby Polonetski suggested that NDP affirmative action for visible minority candidates would involve "a strategy of looking for incumbency seats where incumbents retire" (interview).

While the prevailing view within the parties is against contesting the candidacy of sitting MPs, this view is currently debated, precisely because it appears to be a major obstacle to the entry of minorities into representation within the party as serious rather than token candidates. MPs Sergio Marchi and, not surprisingly, Joe Volpe both regarded incumbency challenges as legitimate, as did NDP Metro councillor Joe Pantalone, Liberal Jasbir Singh Mangat, some leaders of FOLSAT and NDP Ontario provincial secretary Jill Marzetti. Marzetti stated that while the tradition of challenging incumbents does not exist within the Ontario NDP, in other provinces such as British Columbia and Manitoba they do allow for incumbent challenges; indeed, in British Columbia the NDP has helped women candidates challenge incumbents to promote gender parity (interview).

One barrier to contesting nominations and elections that was mentioned by several minority party activists was financial. Members of FOLSAT argued that "new Canadians are trying to build resources and it takes several years to save the fifty grand required for a campaign." At another meeting with FOLSAT leaders it was similarly suggested that:

> Financing is a deterrent to the candidacy of visible minorities. You require a network to generate financing, just as do the Bay Street Boys. The Bay Street mentality prevails – as when businessmen say, "We'll buy all the tables" at a party event. "Why try to generate funds from ethnic communities?" (Interview)

This is not to imply that all ethnic communities – even those comprising new immigrants – are economically disadvantaged or are without links to potential funding sources. Indeed, the majority of ethnic minority candidates in recent federal elections share similar class and occupational backgrounds and ideological positions with candidates from the dominant ethnic groups. However, it must be suggested that some minority groups (the more newly arrived, those facing considerable discrimination, and those concentrated in low-income jobs) face major financial barriers to participation at the level of contesting nominations or elections. Moreover, given the need in ethnically diverse constituencies to distribute campaign literature in nonofficial languages, the ethnic minority candidates running in such ridings may have higher campaign expenses in comparison with dominant group candidates who are running in ridings that have smaller numbers of ethnic minorities.

Another barrier to the representation of ethnic minorities within the main parties lies in the conventional patterns of recruitment of volunteers and activists, which are heavily reliant on personal networks. It is ironic that much of the criticism of recent ethnic activism in the Liberal party has centred on the purported abuse of ethnic community networks. Networks of participants within the main parties have followed traditional patterns of recruitment and therefore have tended to be within white and, depending on region, also British and French communities. As Howard McCurdy stated,

> Structural discrimination does not necessarily mean racism. The people who are already there don't know about visible minorities, who are then shut out. You need to work from the bottom up, rather than the top down. Your chances of getting a "token" are enhanced if you identify "leaders" to insinuate people into any area. (Interview)

Margaret Mitchell described the exclusionary impact of networks in arguing, "People in parties form cliques. This is a barrier to all outsiders, including Caucasians" (interview).

Another barrier that some minority party activists linked to that of exclusionary networks is the reluctance among those who have power to share it with those who are defined as outsiders by virtue of their ethnicity or race. As voiced by Tony Ianno:

> There is only one pie to be shared. People don't want to give up their part of the pie. The longer established people are part of Anglo networks. They've known "Joe Blow" for many years. There's familiarity, the trust factor. It takes time to build trust. Now I'm friends with those I fought. (Interview)

Similarly, several party officials and activists spoke of the "fear of take-overs" within riding associations.[74] FOLSAT leaders explained the rejection by the federal Liberal party of a structure to represent visible minorities in terms of the reluctance to give up power and the "fear that through the process of immigration, visible minorities are taking over" (interview).

Albina Guarnieri, one of the few female ethnic minority MPs, also spoke of the disadvantages for minority women in not being part of the "old boys' network." The ethnic liaison committees, particularly their leaders, in both the NDP and the Ontario Liberal party, are overwhelmingly male. The interviews also suggested that the vast majority of ethnic minority participants in riding association executives are male, although the gender balance was more equitable among nonimmigrant minorities (second-generation and further).

Both structural and cultural explanations have been provided for the underrepresentation of women within the party system (see Brodie 1985, 77–97; Bashevkin 1985; Maillé 1990, 2–4). Structural explanations refer to such constraints as the division of labour in most households, where women have primary responsibility for child care and housework, and the "double day" of women who are also full-time wage earners. In addition, the financial requirements for candidacy are prohibitive for most women, who on average earn two-thirds of the male wage. As Maillé argues:

> Access to socio-economic networks is a fundamental requirement for running for office; in this respect, women are at a disadvantage because very few of them belong to the financial circles of seats of power that provide an advantage for anyone entering politics. (1990, 4)

Cultural explanations include the assumptions of the supposed incongruity between the roles of homemaker and mother on the one hand and the role of politician on the other. These attitudes continue to prevail in the dominant culture, in spite of the contrary claims and gains of the vibrant Canadian feminist movement (Brodie 1985, 81). And as Maillé (1990, 3) says, the workings of the political sphere do not make any provision for the gender roles and family responsibilities that remain at the heart of many women's lives. The organizational culture of political parties and Parliament is also viewed by feminists as embodying male or patriarchal culture and "old-boy skills [such as] the ability to dominate an argument by force of oratory, by force of personality" (ibid., 4).

In addition, obstacles to the political participation of immigrant and ethnic minority women may be further compounded by linguistic and ethnocultural constraints. Racial and ethnic minority women, as well as Aboriginal women, are especially underrepresented in the political arena (Maillé 1990, 3). The appallingly low representation of women overall in the House of Commons (40 out of 295, or 13.6 percent of parliamentary seats) must, however, be kept in mind when evaluating the specifics of minority women's political participation.

The culture of political parties may also be unfamiliar or even alienating to new immigrants or to people from non-British traditions. Abby

Polonetski stated that "we are so wedded to certain skills – speaking at microphones, Robert's Rules of Order, chairing meetings. It is those who can best speak at mikes who, to date, have participated in the NDP" (interview).

A feature of the larger political culture (discussed in the first section of this study) is the bicultural framework that has historically defined the dominant approach to ethnicity and politics within the Canadian party system.[75] Some ethnic minorities feel that the pre-eminence in federal politics of linguistic duality, French–English relations, and even the "Quebec as a distinct society" clause within the failed Meech Lake Accord relegates questions of representation of "the others" to a much lower rank of importance. One Ontario Liberal party activist of East Indian origin stated that "the bicultural framework of Canada within Meech Lake is reprehensible" (interview with FOLSAT group members).[76] The PC Ontario director viewed the entry of more ethnic minorities into the Conservative party as a positive development because "it's making the party more relevant. If we stuck with that other thing – 'two founding nations' – we would have been dinosaurs."

Howard McCurdy suggested that the informal culture of political parties (e.g., the type of social activities they sponsor, the music played at parties) needs to be examined for its impact on making people from different cultures feel comfortable (interview). It is in part the felt need of minorities, particularly those lacking official language competence, for a culturally supportive atmosphere that has spawned the development of liaison, satellite or affiliated ethnic clubs within the parties.

Some of the barriers that are associated with immigrant status in a new country disappear or grow smaller for second and further generations. Some interviews (and observation at a University of Toronto campus meeting of the Young Liberals) suggested that the second generation of ethnic minorities does not experience the same degree of barriers to participation in the political parties, and that the party youth organizations tend to reflect the diversity of the institutions where they are situated.[77]

Finally, while this study has not focused directly on the media coverage of ethnopolitics within the major political parties, it is important to point out its effects on minority participation. While some exceptions of more sophisticated journalism were cited and lauded, the overwhelming view expressed by ethnic minorities within the party system was that newspaper and other mass media coverage given to events such as Liberal nomination meetings and the Liberal party leadership convention created and perpetuated negative stereotypes about the political participation of ethnic minorities.

Many minority candidates and MPs interviewed for this study related individual stories concerning the biased and/or marginal coverage of their own political involvement, in contrast with the coverage accorded candidates of British or French origin. It was particularly striking how often ethnic minorities who had contested (nomination or general) elections mentioned that the media marginalized and delegitimated them as credible candidates for voters by placing them in the straitjacket designation of "ethnic candidate." In part, this was done by reporters who asked questions in interviews that only addressed "ethnic" issues (e.g., multiculturalism, immigration, affirmative action), and who ignored the fact that the candidates had considerable expertise and well-articulated positions on other issues.

In addition, the media were widely perceived to have done damage to the complex issue of ethnic minority political representation by focusing almost solely on the sensationalist aspects of nomination and delegate selection processes. It is worth citing a couple of the passionate comments made during interviews about the perceived role of the media:

> The last group to see that changes are occurring is the *Globe and Mail*. It's an ethnic newspaper for WASPs. (Interview with Tony Ianno)

> The media have concentrated on controversial aspects. They deny the reality of integration. They have trivialized the issues, focused on machine politics and portrayed it as an armed struggle. They perpetuate the image of a legitimate ruling class, where everyone else is illegitimate, defined by their barbaric tactics. (Interview with Joseph Volpe)

In sum, the underrepresentation of ethnic and visible minorities within the major parties is accountable in terms of a variety of structural, cultural and organizational obstacles. For recent immigrants lacking official language skills, linguistic barriers intersect with lack of familiarity with Canadian political culture. Racial minorities confront discrimination practised at the highest levels of party power and within the mass media. For women of colour and ethnic minority women, the barriers are gender as well as race, ethnicity and often class. And for all excluded groups, there is a legacy of exclusion that is reinforced by the hegemonic bicultural discourse of party politics, by patterns of recruitment through networks, and by party traditions such as the incumbency factor within the electoral process. While the elimination of some of these barriers would require fundamental societal transformations, others are significantly mediated and structured by political parties and are therefore amenable to more immediate reform. It is in the direction of such realistic and necessary reforms that our conclusions turn.

CONCLUSIONS AND RECOMMENDATIONS

The response of elements of the establishment of the major parties and the mass media to the recent entry of considerable numbers of ethnic minorities into party politics has been to question the effect that this development has had on party democracy. Frequently, the social construction of ethnopolitics within the mainstream political arena has borne alarming similarity to the concerns raised 80 years ago by J.S. Woodsworth, founder of the Co-operative Commonwealth Federation – namely, that "disreputable fellows" are herding members of their communities "unfit to be trusted with the ballot" and are undermining Canadian democratic institutions (Woodsworth 1909).

The views of ethnic minorities within the party system and the analyses of the actual participation of Canadians of non-British, non-French origin presented in this study indicate how misconceived, superficial and biased this kind of interpretation is. However, there are meaningful connections to be made between ethnic minority participation in the party system on the one hand and democracy on the other.

First, the large influx of ethnic minorities – particularly notable within the Liberal party and within large, urban, ethnically heterogeneous ridings – has pointed out some problems inherent in the party system and the limitations of grassroots democracy within the Canadian system of liberal democracy.

For instance, with few exceptions, constituency organizations have remained primarily election-fighting mechanisms, with policy discussions far removed and primarily centred in the upper echelons of the party. Given that the major role of the local party (riding associations) is to select election candidates and convention delegates, the amount of participation in decision making solicited from party members is minimal and is confined to a few votes annually.[78] The limited meaningful and effective participation of the rank and file is endemic to a party system that encourages riding associations to be dormant between elections. Thus, the problems of instant or temporary membership were related far less to the ethnicity of new members than to characteristics of the party organizations themselves.

As Doug Fisher (1988) recently observed, there have always been some nominations that are "quiet little tea parties and others that were

year-long drag-'em-out civil wars." This was true when the participants were in the vast majority British- and French-Canadian. It cannot be assumed that because a large proportion of the participants in
the larger, noisier nomination meetings are of nondominant ethnicity,
improprieties are at work. Such assumptions tend to breed ethnic bias
or racism. If reforms of membership or candidate-selection processes
are required (e.g., earlier cut-offs, registration of parties with Elections
Canada), these aspects of the process need to be considered separately
from the actors who are currently exercising their right to democratic
participation within the parties.

1. To the extent that nomination processes involve improprieties or
   abuse of rules, these need to be addressed on their own terms and
   should not be conflated with the issues of increasing minority ethnic participation within the parties.

Historically, ethnic minorities have been excluded from full
participation within the major political parties – through denial of the
franchise and through discrimination. Currently, a number of features
of the culture and operation of political parties and the electoral system
render them inaccessible or alienating to immigrant and racial minorities. These include the working languages of the parties, the bureaucratic
culture and style of political discourse, and features of the networks of
activists and officials.

2. The operation of the electoral system and organizational
   practices of political parties need to be scrutinized in the light
   of questions of accessibility for immigrant and racial minorities.
3. Elections Canada should engage in greater political education of
   new Canadians in nonofficial languages. It should disseminate
   voting information in nonofficial languages and through the use
   of the "ethnic media," and it should provide more accessible ballots for voters who are not proficient in the official languages.
4. Campaign spending limits should be adjusted to reflect the linguistic diversity (i.e., the presence of large numbers of nonofficial language speakers) of particular constituencies.
5. Political parties should ensure that all visual materials in their
   campaign, as well as other literature, reflect the cultural and
   racial diversity of Canadian society.
6. More effort should be made within the political parties to engage
   in outreach with minority communities – between as well as
   during elections.

7. Party membership with full membership rights should continue to be open to noncitizens to encourage opportunities and training for full citizenship.

A multi-party system is a key defining feature of liberal democracy. But the extent of democracy *within* the political parties also needs to be addressed. Insofar as parties are recruiting grounds for elected officials, one measure of their democracy and legitimacy is how well they reflect their constituencies. It is apparent that the major political parties are not currently representative of the ethnic and racial diversity of local constituencies or of Canadian society as a whole. This unrepresentativeness has translated into a House of Commons that is predominantly white, male and overrepresented by MPs of British and French origin. Constraints on access to participation and power within the established parties have deepened the resolve of several ethnic minorities to contest their condition of political subordination. Such constraints need to be identified and eliminated.

What difference would result from a more equitable representation of ethnic and racial minorities within the major parties and within the House of Commons? This study has underscored the two dimensions of representation: statistical representation and representation of interests. Turning to the first, a more ethnically and racially representative Canadian legislature would have symbolic significance for the many ethnocultural and racial communities that currently make up Canadian society. It would provide evidence of the openness of political parties to the participation and involvement of all groups, regardless of race and ethnicity. Such evidence would be even stronger if ethnic minority MPs represented ridings that did not have large ethnic minority populations.

With respect to the second dimension of representation, it is clear that the minority ethnic MPs who were interviewed reflect levels of philosophical and ideological diversity similar to those of other MPs. That is, through both belief and party discipline, the positions on economic and social policy of minority MPs (like dominant group MPs) divide along party lines. For instance, Liberal MP Joseph Volpe referred to the conditioning effects of party discipline when he stated, "The unfortunate part of being an MP is that your personal agenda gets submerged by the party agenda" (interview).

Furthermore, the views and positions of minority MPs within political parties reflect intraparty differences in interests and policy positions. Thus, among the growing number of minority ethnic MPs in the Liberal party, some represented the more business-oriented thrust of the party, whereas others were more focused on social policy concerns. The portfolios of minority MPs were also often related to their occupational training – as lawyers, physicians, community activists and so on. Thus, in responding to the question of the impact of greater numbers of minority ethnic MPs, Charles Caccia asked, "How do you evaluate this? Is it because you come from an ethnic group, or is it because of your upbringing, education? If we were all unanimous, then you could see it" (interview).

In spite of the interparty and intraparty diversity among minority MPs – ideologically and in terms of policy interests – the overall impact of greater representation in the House of Commons was to add a new dimension of sensitivity to the concerns of minority ethnic and racial groups. This sensitivity was reflected in several of the comments of ethnic minority MPs, party activists and officials:

> It keeps the party rejuvenated and in touch with the various ethnic communities. It leads to more tolerance. The handling of the Air India crash is an example of how the Tories are out of touch with the ethnic communities.[79] It makes it easier to achieve firsthand information about ethnic communities. (Interview with Atul Sharma)

> [The impact of the greater numbers of ethnic minority MPs] is both positive and real. They are more "in sync" with the membership because they show sensitivity about non-Anglo, non-French minorities: the Italian-Canadian, Aboriginal, Filipino. There is now a better response. We don't have to wait for a community to slap Parliament on the head. There is a greater diversity of perspectives. It also gives credence to our philosophy that is supportive of diversity. (Interview with Sergio Marchi)

8. A firm commitment must be shown by the leadership of the major parties to the greater representation of visible and ethnic minorities at all levels of party organization.
9. Political parties should make special efforts to recruit and support racial and ethnic minority women as candidates for federal and provincial elections.
10. All policies of political parties should be evaluated in the light of their probable impact on representation of ethnocultural and racial minorities. Political parties should study the most effective ways to represent and reflect the ethnic and racial diversity of Canadian society at all levels of their organizations. Experience with affirmative action policies at the level of candidacy suggests that "organic approaches" (i.e., guidelines, encouragement and support rather than quotas) are more effective and respect the principle of local riding democracy.
11. The encouragement and promotion of ethnic and visible

minorities within winnable ridings should be made a priority.

12. Ethnic minority candidates should *not* be selected only from ridings with ethnic minority concentrations.

13. Issues such as incumbency challenges and financial assistance to candidates need to be evaluated with the goal of increasing the ethnic and racial representativeness of party candidates.

In conclusion, there is a very real sense that broadening the base of the major political parties by opening the parties and Canadian legislatures to the meaningful participation of all Canadians enriches the Canadian polity. A fairer legislative representation of ethnic and racial minorities would provide a framework for more accountable representation. It would lead to a form of governance that was more relevant to the Canadian public in all its diversity; in some important areas, such as the amelioration of racial and ethnic injustices, it would encourage greater policy responsiveness.

APPENDIX A

Table 1.A1
Ethnic breakdown of Canadian population, 1986
(in percentages)

Total (noninstitutionalized) population	N	Single British origin	Single French origin	Single other origin	Multiple origins
Canada	25 022 010	25.3	24.4	22.4	27.9
Newfoundland	564 000	79.7	2.0	1.6	16.6
Prince Edward Island	125 090	47.4	8.9	2.9	40.8
Nova Scotia	864 150	48.3	6.1	7.6	38.0
New Brunswick	701 855	35.8	33.1	2.9	28.1
Quebec	6 454 490	5.0	77.7	10.5	6.9
Ontario	9 001 170	32.4	5.9	27.9	33.9
Manitoba	1 049 320	21.4	5.3	38.3	35.0
Saskatchewan	996 700	22.3	3.4	35.0	39.3
Alberta	2 340 265	25.3	3.3	30.8	40.6
British Columbia	2 849 585	30.6	2.4	28.8	38.2
Yukon	23 360	23.0	3.3	28.7	45.0
Northwest Territories	52 020	13.5	2.9	60.5	23.1

Source: Canada, Statistics Canada (1988).

Note: Percentages may not add to 100% because of rounding.

Table 1.A2
Minority ethnic ridings: Non-British, non-French, non-Aboriginal single origin, 1986

Province	N	Number of ridings with 50% or more ethnic minorities	% of total
Newfoundland	7	0	0
Prince Edward Island	4	0	0
Nova Scotia	11	0	0
New Brunswick	10	0	0
Quebec	75	2	2.7
Ontario	99	27	27.3
Manitoba	14	7	50.0
Saskatchewan	14	7	50.0
Alberta	26	9	34.6
British Columbia	32	5	15.6
Yukon	1	0	0
Northwest Territories	2	0	0
Total	295	57	19.3

Source: Canada, Statistics Canada (1988).

Note: Minority ethnic ridings are defined as ridings with 50% or more non-British, non-French, non-Aboriginal single origins.

Table 1.A3
Major urban-centre ridings with 50% or more ethnic minorities

	Urban ridings 50% or more ethnic minorities (N)	Provincial total urban ethnic ridings (N)	Urban ethnic ridings as % of all provincial ethnic ridings
Quebec		2	100.0
Montreal	2		
Ontario		26	96.3
Toronto	19		
Mississauga	2		
Brampton	1		
Kitchener	1		
Markham	1		
Thunder Bay	1		
Waterloo	1		
Manitoba		4	57.1
Winnipeg	4		
Saskatchewan		5	71.4
Regina	2		
Saskatoon	3		
Alberta		7	77.8
Edmonton	6		
Calgary	1		
British Columbia		5	100.0
Vancouver	5		

Source: Canada, Statistics Canada (1988).

Note: Major urban centres are defined as cities with a population of 50 000 or more, in 1986.
The Canadian World Almanac and Book of Facts, 1990 (1989, 76–77).

Table 1.A4
Ridings with 50% or more residents of non-British, non-French, non-Aboriginal single origins

Quebec	Manitoba	Alberta
Mount Royal	Lisgar–Marquette	Calgary Northeast
Saint-Denis	Provencher	Edmonton East
	Selkirk	Edmonton North
Ontario	Winnipeg North	Edmonton Northwest
Brampton–Malton	Winnipeg North Centre	Edmonton Southeast
Broadview–Greenwood	Winnipeg South	Edmonton Southwest
Davenport	Winnipeg Transcona	Edmonton–Strathcona
Don Valley East		Medicine Hat
Don Valley North	Saskatchewan	Vegreville
Eglinton–Lawrence	Regina–Qu'Appelle	
Etobicoke Centre	Regina–Wascana	British Columbia
Etobicoke–Lakeshore	Saskatoon–Clark's Crossing	Burnaby–Kingsway
Etobicoke North	Saskatoon–Dundurn	Richmond
Kitchener	Saskatoon–Humboldt	Vancouver East
Lincoln	Swift Current–Maple Creek–	Vancouver Quadra
Markham	Assiniboia	Vancouver South
Mississauga East	Yorkton–Melville	
Mississauga West		
Parkdale–High Park		
St Paul's		
Scarborough–Agincourt		
Scarborough Centre		
Scarborough–Rouge River		
Thunder Bay–Nipigon		
Trinity–Spadina		
Waterloo		
Willowdale		
York Centre		
York North		
York South–Weston		
York West		

APPENDIX B
ONTARIO NDP AFFIRMATIVE ACTION GUIDELINES (as approved by Provincial Council, 9–10 December 1989)

Objectives

There is a strong opinion being expressed in the party that the process of building our party and the nomination of candidates should be linked. In particular there is a desire that every effort must be made to ensure that we are much closer to our goal of electing a caucus that reflects the ethnic diversity of Ontario and has gender parity. While the outcome of elections is not within the party's jurisdiction, if we ensure that through affirmative action women,

visible minorities, aboriginal, disabled, ethnic, gay, lesbian, youth and francophone candidates have a better chance of winning nominations, the party
will have done its job.

Affirmative Action Policy

The affirmative action policy will identify a target for nominating and electing members of specific target groups.

- As a general policy, 50% of all ridings should have women candidates.
- As a general policy, riding EPC's should be comprised of representatives
  that include all of the target groups.
- In addition, a specific group of "winnable" or "priority" ridings as defined
  by the EPC should be targeted for application of a further affirmative
  action formula.
- The affirmative action formula which should be applied to these target
  seats is as follows:
  – 75% of the "priority" seats should have candidates *from affirmative action
  target groups: women, visible minorities, disabled and aboriginal.* (In the
  remaining 25% of the "priority" seats, priority attention should be given
  to running ethnic candidates especially in those ridings where such
  groupings are a major element in the riding population.)
  – 60% of the candidates in the "priority" seats should be women.

Nomination Procedures

An important mechanism for implementation of the affirmative action policy
will be the nomination process. While recognizing that this is a democratic
process, the outcome of which cannot be determined, certain steps can be taken
which will encourage implementation of affirmative action principles. These
steps include:

- Prior to the nominating process, all ridings within a designated geographic
  area (as defined by the EPC) *SHALL* meet to discuss how to implement in
  their geographic area the affirmative action measures spelled out above.
- Nomination rules which provide that, before the writ is dropped, no non-
  incumbent riding shall hold a nomination meeting until they have at least
  one target group candidate for that nomination.
- Riding associations who feel they cannot or should not fulfil this provision
  must present acceptable reasons to the EPC Steering Committee.
- If no nomination meeting is held before the writ is dropped, riding associations should make every effort to find target group candidates.
- Provincial Council, in its process of approving candidates, should be responsible for ensuring that affirmative action targets are achieved overall. Lists
  of candidates provided to Council for approval will include affirmative
  action progress reports.

Support Mechanisms

The Party can further help to implement the affirmative action policy through initiatives aimed at identifying and supporting target group nomination candidates. These *SHALL* include:

- assign an organizer to implement and be responsible for this affirmative action programme.
- a series of "road shows" in the period leading up to the election, aimed at educating riding associations on the affirmative action policy and candidate search strategies, and on identifying potential target group candidates and giving them general information on "choosing to be a candidate."
- independent candidate search activities by other interested groups in the Party.
- regular review by the EPC on implementation of the affirmative action policy.
- develop an information package for potential target group nomination candidates, outlining the Party's commitment to the affirmative action policy, and the supports available for the policy and for nominated candidates.
- offer training opportunities, across Ontario, for target group members who have expressed serious interest in becoming nomination candidates, or who are already candidates for nomination, and for their campaign workers.
- a group of volunteers who will assist potential candidates with nomination races will be assembled.
- the EPC develop a subsidy program for women and affirmative action candidates in "priority" ridings.

Contested Nominations

1. Childcare costs up to $500 will, on submitting expenses, be reimbursed by the party to declared affirmative action candidates during the period of a contested nomination.
2. Where travel costs are a factor in contested nominations in large rural ridings, they will be reimbursed up to $500 to declared affirmative action candidates upon submitting expenses.
3. Consideration will be given to imposition of limits on expenditures for nomination campaigns with particulars to be brought forward by the EPC.
4. Where a disabled candidate for nomination incurs expenses related to the disability, those expenses shall be reimbursed up to $500.

NOTES

This study was completed in December 1991.

We wish to gratefully acknowledge the support and assistance of all those individuals who agreed to be interviewed for this study. Their names are listed in the "Interviews" section. This study has benefited from the careful reading and incisive comments of two anonymous reviewers.

1. This study does not address itself to the many issues involved in the rep-
    resentation of the First Nations within the political system. The majority
    of submissions to the Royal Commission on Electoral Reform and Party
    Financing that addressed questions of group representation in the electoral
    system were from individuals and groups representing Aboriginal inter-
    ests. While Aboriginal critics have drawn attention to significant structural
    problems with the electoral system, the basis for their critique is signifi-
    cantly different from that of non-Aboriginal, ethnic and visible minorities,
    particularly as it relates to broader Aboriginal grievances and aspirations
    for self-determination and the political restructuring of present-day Canada.
    See as examples of Aboriginal critiques of the electoral system and parlia-
    mentary representation of native peoples, submissions by Senator Leonard
    Marchand, 9 March 1990; and by the Native Council of Canada, 15–16
    February 1990. For a discussion of the problematic nature of the employ-
    ment equity definition of "visible minorities," see Boxhill (1990).

2. "Legitimacy" within political studies is a "soft" concept. William Irvine
    suggests one definition of the concept when he writes, "We are not quite
    sure how to measure legitimacy, but [it appears that] a government or deci-
    sion-making body is accepted as legitimate if a group is confident that its
    interests are heard within it" (Irvine 1985, 138–39). Currently, national polls
    (e.g., Globe and Mail–CBC News Poll, reported in the *Globe and Mail,*
    29 October 1989) reveal that the legitimacy of Parliament, government,
    political leaders and the Canadian political system is very low among the
    majority of Canadians. For example, 72 percent of Canadians surveyed
    agreed or strongly agreed with the statement, "I don't think governments
    care much what people like me think." But at the same time, the majority
    of those surveyed felt that the choice of party to form the government did
    make a difference. Thus, 62 percent of interviewees disagreed or strongly
    disagreed with the statement, "It doesn't matter which party is in power –
    there isn't much government can do these days about our basic problems."

3. The interviews were conducted between 16 October and 20 November
    1990. A preliminary list of interviewees was compiled from the names of
    party activists and candidates within contested nominations preceding
    the 1988 federal election reported by the mainstream media. Both suc-
    cessful candidates (now federal MPs) and those defeated during nomina-
    tion contests were sought to provide an account of their experiences in
    their parties. Additional names were added through contact with the party
    staff and suggestions made during preliminary interviews. This study
    makes no pretence of being a report of an opinion survey, as the number
    of respondents (about 50) is too small for this purpose. Rather, interviewees
    were chosen for their presumed knowledge of the practices and policies
    of their parties and the political activism of ethnocultural minorities. As
    such, they do not constitute a rigorously representative sample. The list of
    interviewees is skewed in favour of the Liberal party and ethnocultural
    minority respondents from the Metropolitan Toronto area. In part, these
    biases are intentional, reflecting the more visible activism of ethnocultural

minorities, both within the Liberal party and within Metro Toronto ridings, in comparison with the other major parties and other regions of the country. In addition, efforts to interview several Conservative MPs were unsuccessful, reducing the intended number of Conservative party respondents. According to one Conservative party insider, the inaccessibility of Conservative MPs and ministers to researchers reflected a "bunker mentality" within a governing party that was experiencing extremely low levels of public support. Within the NDP, where the proportion of ethnic minority MPs is relatively small, interviews were also conducted with MPs of British origin who had responsibility for immigration and multiculturalism. Interviews were conducted face to face with a structured interview schedule, eliciting open-ended responses – a strength of this methodology. The majority of interviews were conducted with individuals, but a few were conducted on a group basis. They normally lasted between one and one-half hours and three hours. See the section "Interviews."

4. Asian Canadians did not gain the right to vote in federal elections until the first few years after the Second World War (1947 for Chinese and East Indians, and 1948 for Japanese) (Bolaria and Li 1988, 173; Li 1988, 2, 30, 86).

5. By 1911, people of non-British and non-French origin formed 34 percent of the population of Manitoba, 40 percent of the population of Saskatchewan and 33 percent of the population of Alberta (Palmer 1976, 85).

6. As Abella and Troper assess the situation, the three Jewish MPs (the third, A.A. Heaps, was a CCF member from Winnipeg) were themselves outsiders in official Ottawa, which was permeated by anti-Jewish feeling. "Canada's Jews, largely immigrant and working class, dismissed by many as less than desirable citizens, could never successfully combat the full force of anti-refugee and anti-Jewish sentiment abroad in the land" (Abella and Troper 1982, 283).

7. Bashevkin (1985, 89–90) makes this same point for the translation from numerical to substantive representation for female party élites.

8. The preponderance of Germans among MPs in the "other" category suggests that of all non-British groups, Germans were regarded as the most culturally similar and assimilable to the British. The exception to this perception occurred during the Second World War, when German-Canadians were considered "enemy aliens" by patriotic groups and encountered a great deal of discrimination.

9. Burnet and Palmer note that "by 1957 there were still no Jewish and Ukrainian cabinet ministers. Members of the other ethnic groups were also underrepresented as judges and senators and in the highest ranks of the civil service. Individuals of Jewish, Ukrainian, and Icelandic background were appointed to the Senate during the 1950s, but groups such as the Italians and Poles were still campaigning in the late 1950s for their first Senate appointment" (Burnet and Palmer 1988, 173–74). The increase in number of "other" origin appointments to the Cabinet in 1957–62 reflects

Diefenbaker's deliberate efforts to overcome decades of ethnic group hostility toward the Conservatives (ibid., 174).

10. The CEC's method of compiling data on the ethnic origins of MPs is not spelled out. It is unclear, for instance, whether the council has relied on single or multiple origins to determine whether MPs are non-British and non-French.

11. "Single other origins" make up about 22.4 percent of the population nationally, and multiple origins account for about 27.9 percent of the national population (Canada, Statistics Canada 1988, 1).

12. The difficulties in establishing who is a visible minority are illustrated by the discrepancies between Pelletier's count (six) and that of the Canadian Ethnocultural Council (three) of the number of visible minority MPs elected in 1988 (Canadian Ethnocultural Council 1989).

13. This is also obviously the case for the territories, where the population is largely Aboriginal.

14. See the remarks by Sergio Marchi in Winsor (1990).

15. Unless cited otherwise, all quotations are from interviews conducted by D. Stasiulis. The names and affiliations of interviewees are listed in the section "Interviews."

16. The four activists were: Joseph Volpe, now Liberal MP for Eglinton–Lawrence, and Tony Ianno, both of Italian origin; Armindo Silva, of Portuguese background; and Jasbir Singh Mangat, of Sikh origin.

17. According to Tony Ianno, who served as Roberts' Ontario co-chairperson, the four organizers gave Roberts "forty to forty-five of his one hundred and eighty-five delegates" (Dewar 1988, 46).

18. In Metro Toronto the "dead zone" includes the following ridings: York, York West, York Centre, Eglinton–Lawrence, Davenport and Trinity–Spadina (interview with Susan Warren and Avi Flaherty).

19. These sentiments were expressed by several members of ethnic minorities who ran for the nominations or as candidates for all three parties in the 1984 and 1988 federal elections. These included Rocco Sebastiano, who ran as a candidate for the Progressive Conservatives in the 1988 federal election in York Centre, one of the ridings in the Tories' "dead zone," and Jasbir Singh Mangat, who ran for the Liberal nomination in 1984 in York West. Reflecting on his decision to seek the York West nomination, Mangat had this to say: "I knew I wouldn't get in, but I wanted to awaken my community. Most of my friends thought I was a fool. I recruited 400 members. They now think that I was right – that we can get nominated and even get elected. I was the first [Sikh] to try in 1984" (interview with Jasbir Singh Mangat). Similarly, Jaime Llambias-Wolfe, of Chilean background, gave as his reason for running as the NDP candidate in the riding of Saint-Denis (Quebec) his desire to "open the doors so new Canadians will par-

ticipate and to demystify the electoral process" (Parkes 1988). Keder Hypolite, of Haitian background, gave similar reasons for running as the NDP candidate in the Montreal riding of Bourassa (Bauch 1988).

20. While MP for Parkdale–High Park, Andrew Witer chaired a subcommittee of the Tory Metro caucus, which prepared a report for the federal Conservative party, urging it to "exploit its relationship with ethnic groups if it expects to prosper at the polls in Metro Toronto in the next election" (Malarek 1986). In the 1988 federal election, Flis again ran as the Liberal candidate for Parkdale–High Park and unseated his Tory opponent, Witer.

21. Jasbir Singh Mangat, who ran for the Liberal party nomination in 1988 in Etobicoke North, contends that another Sikh candidate was deliberately brought in to split the support of the Sikh community. Mangat lost the nomination to Roy McLaren, a former cabinet minister under Trudeau (interview with Jasbir Singh Mangat).

22. As mentioned above, the fifth candidate was Jasbir Singh Mangat, of Sikh origin.

23. In reflecting on his victory in the 1984 York West nomination battle, Marchi said that his "experience in the voluntary sector and aldermanic experience" were invaluable (interview with Sergio Marchi).

24. Before the 1984 election, the Canadian Ethnocultural Council (CEC) issued a news release indicating strong disappointment with the three major parties' responses to issues relating to multiculturalism, immigration, hate propaganda, compensation for the Canadian Japanese interned during the Second World War, and the participation of visible minorities in the parties. According to then CEC president Navin Parekh, responses to questionnaires sent to the three party leaders soliciting views in the above areas were seen as containing "too many vague statements that endorse principles and commit the party to further studying and investigation" (*Toronto Star*, 17 August 1984). In addition, all three leaders declined to participate in a leaders' debate on multicultural issues advocated by the CEC (ibid.).

25. In Vancouver, 15 provincial ethnocultural groups organized a forum where MPs and a senator debated issues of racism (*Globe and Mail*, 8 August 1984). In the riding of Broadview–Greenwood, issues of racism also featured in the 1984 campaign. Conservative candidate Peter Worthington linked his defeat by NDP incumbent Lynn MacDonald to the alleged distribution by MacDonald's supporters of literature portraying him as believing that the Ku Klux Klan was harmless (Contenta 1984).

26. A Toronto telephone poll taken two months before the 1984 election revealed that 45 percent of respondents of ethnic minority origins (Italian, Greek, Portuguese, Chinese and West Indian) chose the Liberals when asked "If a federal election were held today, for which party would you vote?" The Progressive Conservatives were endorsed by only 8 percent of respondents, while the New Democratic Party drew 7 percent. There

were variations between the groups in their support of the three parties. Thus, the Liberals received the most support from West Indians (56 percent) and the least support (35 percent) from the Greek community. The Conservatives received less than 10 percent support from every group except the Portuguese, among whom 14 percent chose the Tories. A similar poll taken in Vancouver also revealed the support of ethnic minorities for the Liberals at the expense of the other parties. In Vancouver, 44 percent of decided ethnic minority voters chose the Liberals, while the Conservatives received support from 17 percent (Walker 1984).

27. One reason that patterns of party support might change among recent immigrant groups is the fact that, since the mid-1980s, the governing Tories have brought in many new Canadians, who might be expected to show their gratitude in the same manner that earlier immigrant groups did under Liberal administrations. Indeed, Nam Nguygen, president of the Communauté Vietnamienne au Canada, said that "most Vietnamese in Canada, if they vote, will vote Conservative" (Parkes 1988). Vietnamese support for the Conservative party would be based both on gratitude for immigrant entry and on the perception among a group fleeing communism in its homeland that the Conservatives are the most anticommunist party (ibid.).

28. However, as for any candidate, support might also partly be based on friendship, kinship or associational and community ties.

29. For example, one report in 1988 suggested that the strategies of ethnic minority organizers employed in the 1984 campaign were being questioned by other party activists. Dewar (1988) writes that "[Tony] Ianno was first stuck with the label of the 'instant Liberal' organizer in the federal election of 1984 when he stood for the federal nomination in York–Scarborough."

30. In 1984, Alvin Curling, the Jamaican-born Liberal who expressed his disagreement with the lack of support of the party leadership for his candidacy in York–Scarborough, commented that he would remain active in the Liberal party because "the time is ripe. Minorities have a better understanding of the issues and know there are procedures to make changes" (Serge 1984). Many ethnic minority Liberal party activists interviewed for this project commented that the Liberal party is "light-years ahead of the Tories and the NDP."

31. The Liberal candidates running in 1988 in Metro Toronto were reported to include members of the Italian, Greek, East Indian (Sikh and Hindu), Polish, Hungarian, Armenian and Tanzanian-Ismaili communities. The New Democrats were fielding candidates of Italian, Caribbean, Polish, Greek, Austrian and Korean backgrounds. The Conservative minority candidates were of Dutch, Italian, Czech, Ukrainian and Portuguese origin (Smith 1988).

32. In an earlier federal election (1979), the Quebec wing of the Liberal party had used its system of reserved ridings for parachute candidates to ensure

that an Italian-Canadian candidate was chosen in the heavily Italian riding of Bourassa (Cleroux 1988).

33. Members of the native communities were also accused of being "instant Liberals." One article reported that in Calgary outside the Sarcee Reserve Sportsplex, a bus heading for a delegate-selection meeting was full of natives given free memberships by pro-Chrétien supporters (Barnett 1990).

34. This marks a change from the 1983 Tory convention and 1984 Liberal convention, where it was found that "only about a quarter of Conservative and Liberal delegates had been elected as part of a slate supporting a particular candidate and only half of those had defeated an opposing slate" (Wearing 1988, 206).

35. In the case of the Liberals, the requirement is that the member not hold membership in another *federal* political party.

36. Some members of the Kamloops party association threatened to quit after the delegate-selection committee was attended by last-minute members. Crosbie defended the attendance of the Amway backers on the grounds that "you're not barred from being a supporter of a political party because you know nothing about (the party)" (*Toronto Star* 1983).

37. Interview with Joe Pantalone.

38. This point was made by John Nunziata, Albina Guarnieri, Joseph Volpe, Bhausaheb Ubale and Tony Ianno (interviews).

39. An editorial in the *Mississauga News* (1988) also criticized the ethnic double standard on the acceptance of certain types of behaviour surrounding nominations: "As long as there have been nominations there have been participants (usually the losers) decrying the manipulation of the rules. It is interesting that when a handful of powerful male white Anglo-Saxon businessmen controlled the nomination process for most parties for many years, little concern was expressed about the potential danger to our democratic freedoms. But when a group of new Canadians of a particular ethnic origin express interest in putting forward their own candidates and manage to bus in enough bodies and sell enough memberships to oust sitting members or pillars of the party establishment, the calls for reform echo throughout the corridors of power."

40. Similarly, John Nunziata stated, "Nomination meetings and delegate-selection meetings are both based on a numbers game. They are no different than they were in the past" (interview).

41. A third concern expressed by some MPs about mass recruitment is that it does not permit sufficient time for the efficient administration of new memberships, a weakness that encourages the degeneration of nomination meetings into chaotic brawls. Earlier cut-off dates were recommended to ease administrative problems, particularly for party organizations staffed largely by volunteers.

42. See the submissions to the Commission by Peter Regenstreif and the World Sikh Organization (WSO). In the latter brief, the WSO asks, "Have individual candidates used the lack of understanding of issues or the process among voters within [the Sikh] community in an unfair or misrepresented way?"

The response in the brief reads as follows: "Yes! Exploitation of minorities is always there. The onus is on the targeted minority to see through the sham, and do something about it. This is not always easy. Electoral candidates often show a little superficial understanding which they then try to manipulate to their own advantage ... Minorities are considered too ignorant to know the difference. They are used as pawns, exploited and then forgotten. To make matters worse, this type of electioneering results in conflict within the community" (WSO 1990, 8–9).

43. In Mississauga East, 401 Liberal supporters for Liberal candidate Armindo Silva were also signed up as Conservative party members by Carlos de Faria, a contender for the Conservative race. Both Silva and de Faria were unsuccessful in their candidacy bids. According to Silva, de Faria used deception to sign up members of the Portuguese community as members of the Conservative party, having them sign raffle tickets at a banquet, tickets that offered free trips to Portugal. The tickets were allegedly photocopies of Conservative party membership forms (interview with Armindo Silva; Webb-Proctor 1988a; Dewar 1988). The director of operations for the Conservatives in Ontario characterized de Faria as "not an instant Tory, just desperately ambitious."

In Brampton–Malton, it was discovered that 124 names of people of East Indian origin appeared on both Liberal party and Conservative party lists (Thorson 1988).

44. Guarnieri further proposes two types of regulation of nomination meetings by Elections Canada – direct and indirect – and appears to favour the latter. "Uniform legally prescribed procedures for conducting a nomination vote should be implemented for all registered parties. Alternatively parties could register their constitutions with Elections Canada, which would simply supervise to ensure that the rules were applied consistently and fairly at nomination meetings. It is probably preferable to continue to allow the parties to conduct these meetings themselves, but to give Elections Canada the authority to invalidate results obtained by improper procedures and to apply severe penalties for knowingly interfering with the nomination process" (1990, 16).

Christian, too, argues that it is "desirable for the Chief Electoral Officer's office to become involved in the process. Constituency or party rules could be registered with Elections Canada, which could also use its expertise in helping to organize the selection process and ensure impartiality (1990, 29). The regulation of the process through "some kind of judicial system or external authority" was also suggested by Jasbir Singh Mangat, who argued that internal reform within the parties would not lead to justice (interview).

45. The cut-off periods suggested were 45 to 60 days (Derek Lee); three months (Sergio Marchi, Rey Pagtakhan); six months (Alfonso Gagliano; Rey Pagtakhan – for leadership conventions); six months to 12 months (John Nunziata) and six to 18 months (Charles Caccia) (interviews).

46. An exception was Conservative Rocco Sebastiano, who argued for the need for the cut-off to be from two weeks to one month in advance (interview). Conservative MP Gus Mitges, representing Bruce–Grey, said of the membership criteria, "They're fine, it works. Anyone can join, the more the better" (interview).

47. Sergio Marchi argued: "Universal suffrage may not change the problem. It's open to abuse. For leadership candidates with money and power, it will encourage them to spend more money and sign up larger numbers of members." Rey Pagtakhan expressed similar misgivings: "In principle, I agree with universal suffrage. But it can also be subject to undue pressure. For example, only rich candidates could afford to travel to small towns." Similarly, Jasbir Singh Mangat stated, "I do not believe in universal suffrage for leadership. The leader with the highest profile will be elected. Anyone who is forthcoming, intelligent, etc., even someone like Trudeau, will not come in" (interviews).

48. Such establishment figures in the Liberal party as John Roberts (who lost a nomination contest to Tony Ianno, then virtually unknown outside local party circles) and Roland de Corneille (a sitting MP when he lost the nomination to Joseph Volpe in Eglinton–Lawrence) were only two of the "patrician" party members who were successfully challenged by the new ethnic minority activists (Wood and Kaihla 1988; Dewar 1988; Winsor 1990).

49. In a discussion about the access of minorities to the party system, Yvette Souque, executive assistant to Secretary of State Gerry Weiner, argued: "It's more difficult for those who have no familiarity with the political system. But the average person is also unfamiliar with the nomination process. You don't have to be an immigrant to find the system perplexing" (interview).

50. In her submission to the Commission, Liberal MP Albina Guarnieri recommended that noncitizens should be "encouraged to become members of parties, [but should not] have the privilege of selecting candidates for election until they themselves have achieved the necessary qualifications to vote in that riding" (Guarnieri 1990, 14). Liberal party member Howard Levitt, in an article entitled, "Wading through Liberal Nomination Mire," recommends that "all members eligible to vote at nominations should be able to vote in a general election. That is, they should be at least 18, Canadian citizens, and residents of the riding" (Levitt 1988).

51. In 1986, 41.6 percent of the Vietnamese in Canada and 31.4 percent of the Portuguese were noncitizens (Canada, Statistics Canada 1989).

52. Since 1984, these have included the establishment of a permanent Standing Committee on Multiculturalism, the sponsorship of a national symposium on race relations, increased resources to combat racial discrimination and encourage cultural diversity, employment equity in the public service, contract compliance legislation, the establishment of a national advisory committee on ethnic broadcasting, the sponsorship of a "Multiculturalism Means Business" symposium, the appointment of a new assistant deputy minister of multiculturalism, the establishment of a Heritage Languages Institute to help train teachers in more than 60 nonofficial languages, compensation to Japanese-Canadians interned by the Canadian government during the Second World War, and apology to Italian-Canadians for wartime treatment by the Canadian government. Perhaps the cornerstone of the Tory commitment to multiculturalism policy was the passage of the *Multiculturalism Act* (Bill C-93) – which entrenched multiculturalism in Canadian law – just months in advance of the November 1988 election (FOLSAT 1986, 16–17; Douglas 1988).

53. The Conservative immigration policies have, however, also been criticized by immigrant groups. In particular, changes to refugee law have been viewed by refugee support groups as unduly restrictive. The absence of support for immigrant integration (e.g., official language training, support for education) commensurate with increased immigration levels has also been the subject of censure.

54. Armindo Silva, an unsuccessful candidate in the 1988 Liberal nomination race in Mississauga East, said: "The Tories have been smart in relation to the Portuguese. They have given appointments, judgeships in the citizen court and appointments to the immigration board to the Portuguese. These are not high standard by Canadian standards, but they are by [Portuguese] community standards. The Tories are catering to the community. They're being more responsive, attending more events than ever before" (interview).

55. According to Coupland, the proportion of women currently serving appointments on ABCs is about 31.7 percent, indicating improvement since 1986 in the representation of women, and also greater ease in keeping gender-based data (telephone interview).

56. The lack of policy content to such contacts was reflected in a "dizzying blitz of ethnic festivals" attended by Prime Minister Mulroney in July 1987 during a three-day visit to Metro Toronto. In meeting with crowds of Italians, Portuguese, Scots, Irish, West Indians, Greeks, Macedonians, Slovaks and Serbs, Mulroney was reported to have avoided discussion of "serious politics" and instead showered "praise on Canada's immigrants for building the country and for keeping multiculturalism alive" (Cohn 1987).

57. During the 1988 federal election, New Democrat MP Dan Heap's campaign manager called the riding of Trinity–Spadina "a campaign manager's horror," because translating literature, finding multilingual canvassers, and particularly carrying on a campaign in some four languages was difficult

to do within campaign spending limits (Brunt 1988).

58. Correspondence between Joe Pantalone (23 March 1989), chair of the Ontario NDP Liaison Committee, and Anna-Rae Fishman, acting federal secretary, NDP (29 March 1989).

59. Immigrants lacking competence in one of the official languages can be those who are newly arrived in Canada, but they can also include immigrants who came to Canada as adults and who have not had the opportunity to learn English or French, e.g., those who work in occupations where official language fluency is not required, or women who have remained at home for many years.

60. These submissions were from the Canadian Ethnocultural Council, the London Cross Cultural Learner Centre and Debra Wong.

61. Affiliated organizations include the PC Business Club, where the membership tends to be drawn from established business people, and the PC Blue Club, which attracts younger business-oriented members, generally recruited out of university.

62. According to Rosemary Dolman, there is also a French-affiliated organization based in Montreal and a nationwide, Aboriginal-affiliated organization, headquartered in Saskatchewan (interview).

63. Much of the information about FOLSAT was derived from three group interviews with people associated with FOLSAT. The names of respondents within the group interviews are listed in the section "Interviews." Unless otherwise indicated, all quotations in this section are taken from the group interviews and will not be attributed to specific individuals.

64. Almost identical sentiments opposing minority liaison structures were articulated by Charles Caccia, Sergio Marchi, John Nunziata, Joseph Volpe, Tony Ianno and Bhausaheb Ubale.

65. In 1990, a new proposal adopted by the Ontario NDP executive gave the same rights of representation to ethnic advisory committees as to the ridings, i.e., eligibility to send one delegate for each 25 members (Ontario NDP 1989).

66. It should be noted that Stephen Lewis is himself a member of a nondominant ethnic group insofar as he is Jewish.

67. The Council of Federal Ridings is composed of five regional councils (e.g., Metro Toronto would be one such regional council), plus one additional council that is for the representation of visible minorities. According to Howard McCurdy, this form of visible minority representation is "modelled on the structure created by Bob Rae" (interview).

68. In addition, the guidelines state that, "as a general policy, 50 percent of all ridings should have women candidates."

69. However, it should be noted that the Liberal party has recently established an Aboriginal Peoples' Commission, under the leadership of Senator Len Marchand, whose purpose is to increase meaningful Aboriginal

representation within the Liberal party and to encourage Aboriginal peoples' electoral participation generally (see Marchand 1990; Aboriginal Peoples' Commission 1990). In interviews, ethnic minority MPs in the Liberal party expressed differences of opinion about the necessity for, and outcomes of, the Aboriginal Peoples' Commission, with some MPs being supportive and others conveying criticisms of the same sort directed against FOLSAT.

70. Bhausaheb Ubale also emphasized the importance of leadership commitment to the promotion of credible visible minority candidates. Given that visible minorities are burdened with the disadvantage of racism, Ubale argued that public moral support from party leaders would send signals to white voters regarding the legitimacy and quality of racial minority candidates (interview).

71. Minority party activists variously lauded Bob Rae, Audrey McLaughlin and David Peterson for their commitment to affirmative action for visible minorities.

72. The choice of some middle-class ethnic minorities to work within the Liberal party often seemed like Goldilocks' approach to the possessions of the three bears: the Conservatives were deemed too capitalist, the NDP too socialist and the Liberals "just right" in their mix of business orientation and support for social policies.

73. Several members of the NDP spoke of the growing Latin American refugee population. As communities who have fled right-wing regimes, and as a group with a growing proportion of citizens and therefore of eligible voters, Latin Americans are seen as an important recruiting ground for support of the NDP (interviews with Abby Polonetski, Dan Heap, Margaret Mitchell).

74. Joe Pantalone, chair of the Ontario NDP Ethnic Liaison Committee, said, "We want to represent the 'new Ontario.' We have to overcome the fear of riding associations being taken over" (interview).

75. There is clearly a recognition within the NDP, however, that the party has not dealt well with French–English relations and with the question of Quebec's status in Confederation. Specifically, the underrepresentation of francophones in the NDP is reflected in the September 1990 employment equity proposals, which list "francophone persons" as one of the target groups.

76. Also, FOLSAT opposed Meech Lake for two reasons: first, it would have weakened the *Canadian Charter of Rights and Freedoms*; second, it would have paved the road for balkanizing the country (interview with FOLSAT group members).

77. Interestingly, PC Rocco Sebastiano said that the "PC Youth groups could be a vehicle for bringing in more ethnic communities into the party, but this is not happening" (interview).

78. There are variations among the parties with respect to the activism of local constituency associations, with the NDP having notably higher levels of activism. As Wearing (1988, 195) points out, the higher degree of participation of the NDP rank and file is encouraged by the fact that the New Democrats have policy conventions that produce resolutions that are assumed to be binding on leadership. The Liberals also hold policy conventions, but the resolutions are not binding on leadership. The Conservatives do not hold policy conventions.

79. The handling by the Mulroney government of the Air India crash on 23 June 1985, which killed all 329 passengers and crew members, was cited by a few respondents as an extreme instance of governmental insensitivity to the ethnocultural reality of Canadian society. As discussed by MP John Nunziata, "The initial response of Mulroney was to phone the prime minister of India to convey his condolences. The Indian PM said, 'Yes, we have lost some of our crew members, but most of the passengers I understand were Canadian' " (interview). In fact, 90 percent of the 307 passengers killed in the crash were Canadian citizens. For a further interpretation of the Canadian government's mishandling of the Air India crash, see Blaise and Mukherjee 1988.

INTERVIEWS

Liberal Party MPs

Caccia, Charles, MP for Davenport, 18 October 1990.
Gagliano, Alfonso, MP for Saint-Léonard, 17 October 1990.
Guarnieri, Albina, MP for Mississauga East, 16 October 1990.
Lee, Derek, MP for Scarborough–Rouge River, 20 October 1990.
Marchi, Sergio, MP for York West, 2 November 1990.
Nunziata, John, MP for York South–Weston, 25 October 1990.
Pagtakhan, Rey, MP for Winnipeg North, 20 November 1990.
Volpe, Joseph, MP for Eglinton–Lawrence, 16 October 1990.

Liberal Party Candidates in 1988 Federal Election

Ianno, Tony, candidate for Trinity–Spadina, 22 October 1990.
Mangat, Jasbir Singh, candidate for Etobicoke North, 23 October 1990.
Silva, Armindo, candidate for Mississauga East, 23 October 1990.
Ubale, Bhausaheb, candidate for Scarborough–Rouge River, 22 October 1990.

Group Interview with FOLSAT Leaders

8 November 1990, convened by Mike O'Neill, Liberal Caucus Services
    Bureau, Regional Desk:
Grant, Ozzie.
Shariff, Firoza.
Telfer, Norma, past president of Black and Caribbean Liberal Association.

Velshi, Murad, former MPP, Don Mills (1987–90).

Wilson, Trevor, former special assistant to David Peterson, Leader of the Opposition.

Group Interview with FOLSAT Leaders and Members
8 November 1990:

Chan, Michael, member of Ontario Chinese Liberal Association.

Falcon, Rick, president of Filipino-Canadian Liberal Association.

Khan, Sultan, president of Ontario South Asian Liberal Association.

Kwok, Susana, member of Ontario Chinese Liberal Association.

Kwok, Walker, member of Ontario Chinese Liberal Association.

Lee, Richard, president of Korean Liberal Association.

Malik, Imam, member of Ontario South Asian Liberal Association.

Shaikh, Annar, member of Ontario South Asian Liberal Association.

Yam, Irene, member of Ontario Chinese Liberal Association.

Yuen, Francis, treasurer of Ontario Chinese Liberal Association.

Group Interview with Minority Liberal Party Activists
9 November 1990:

Bak, Bob, treasurer of FOLSAT.

Beri, Sudersheen, vice-president, FOLSAT.

Khawja, Reema.

Kim, Brian, founder and past president of Ontario Korean Liberal Association.

Sharma, Atul, former special assistant to Labour Minister Gerry Philips.

New Democratic Party MPs
Heap, Dan, MP for Trinity–Spadina, 16 October 1990.

McCurdy, Howard, MP for Windsor–St. Clair, 1 November 1990.

Mitchell, Margaret, MP for Vancouver East, 25 October 1990.

NDP Candidate in 1988 Federal Election
Cho, Raymond, NDP candidate for Scarborough–Rouge River, 23 October 1990.

NDP Executive Officers and Staff: Federal Office
Polonetski, Abby, women's director, federal NDP, 17 October 1990.

Jang, Wendy, legislative assistant, multicultural organizer for Margaret Mitchell, 25 October 1990.

NDP Executive Officers and Staff: Provincial Office
Marzetti, Jill, Ontario provincial secretary, NDP, 9 November 1990.

Pantalone, Joe, co-chair of Ontario NDP Ethnic Liaison Committee, and Metro Toronto councillor, Trinity–Niagara, 8 November 1990.

Progressive Conservative Party MPs
Mitges, Gus, MP for Bruce–Grey, 27 October 1990.

Progressive Conservative Party: Federal Office
Collins, Elaine, former PC national director of Women's Bureau and
   multicultural communications (October 1987 – June 1990), 24 October
   1990.
Dolman, Rosemary, acting federal secretary, Progressive Conservatives.

Progressive Conservative Party: Ontario Office for Federal Party
Sebastiano, Rocco, Ontario director; chair of PC Multicultural Advisory
   Council, PC candidate for York Centre, 1988 federal election, 9 November
   1990.
Group interview, 8 November 1990:
Warren, Susan, director of operations, Progressive Conservatives, Ontario.
Flaherty, Avi, senior organizer, Metropolitan Toronto Progressive
   Conservatives.

Progressive Conservative Party: Federal, Other Staff
Group interview:
Souque, Yvette, executive assistant to Secretary of State Gerry Weiner.
Vicory, Hugh, senior policy adviser, Communications, to Secretary of State
   Gerry Weiner.

Other
Telephone interview:
Coupland, Steven, director, Appointments Secretariat, Prime Minister's
   Office, 31 October 1990.

BIBLIOGRAPHY

Abele, Frances, and Daiva Stasiulis. 1989. "Canada as a 'White Settler
   Colony': What About Natives and Immigrants?" In *The New Canadian
   Political Economy,* ed. W. Clement and G. Williams. Montreal and
   Kingston: McGill-Queen's University Press.

Abella, Irving, and Harold Troper. 1982. *None Is Too Many: Canada and the
   Jews of Europe, 1933–1948.* Toronto: Lester and Orpen Dennys.

Aboriginal Peoples' Commission. 1990. "Aboriginal Peoples' Commission
   Club Organization Manual." Ottawa: Liberal Party of Canada.

Albo, Gregory, and Jane Jenson. 1989. "A Contested Concept: The Relative
   Autonomy of the State." In *The New Canadian Political Economy,*
   ed. W. Clement and G. Williams. Montreal and Kingston: McGill-Queen's
   University Press.

Anwar, M. 1986. *Race and Politics: Ethnic Minorities and the British Political System.* London: Tavistock Publications.

Avery, Donald. 1975. "Continental European Immigrant Workers in Canada 1896–1919: From 'Stalwart Peasants' to Radical Proletariat." *Canadian Review of Sociology and Anthropology* 12 (1): 53–64.

Baldrey, Keith. 1988. "Ethnic Vote Blocs Hold Key to Working-Class Riding." Vancouver *Sun,* 13 August.

Barnett, Vicki. 1990. "Sarcees Board the Political Bus." *Calgary Herald,* 29 April.

Bashevkin, Sylvia B. 1985. *Toeing the Lines: Women and Party Politics in English Canada.* Toronto: University of Toronto Press.

Bauch, Hubert. 1988. "Parties Can't Take East End for Granted." Montreal *Gazette,* 14 November.

Blaise, Clark, and Bharati Mukherjee. 1988. *The Sorrow and the Terror: The Haunting Legacy of the Air India Tragedy.* Markham: Penguin Books.

Bolaria, B. Singh, and Peter S. Li. 1988. *Racial Oppression in Canada.* 2d ed. Toronto: Garamond Press.

Boxhill, Wally. 1990. "Approaches to the Collection of Data on Visible Minorities in Canada: A Review and Commentary." Ottawa: Statistics Canada.

Bramham, Daphne. 1990. "Minorities Join In: Party Machine Called Means to Sharing." Vancouver *Sun,* 23 June.

Breton, Raymond. 1984. "The Production and Allocation of Symbolic Resources: An Analysis of the Linguistic and Ethnocultural Fields in Canada." *Canadian Review of Sociology and Anthropology* 21 (2): 123–44.

———. 1986. "Multiculturalism and Canadian Nation-Building." In *The Politics of Gender, Ethnicity and Language in Canada.* Vol. 34 of the research studies of the Royal Commission on the Economic Union and Development Prospects for Canada. Toronto: University of Toronto Press.

Brodie, Janine. 1985. *Women and Politics in Canada.* Toronto: McGraw-Hill Ryerson.

Brodie, Janine, and Jane Jenson. 1988. *Crisis, Challenge and Change: Party and Class in Canada Revisited.* Ottawa: Carleton University Press.

Brodie, Janine, and Jill Vickers. 1981. *Canadian Women in Politics: An Overview.* Ottawa: Canadian Research Institute for the Advancement of Women.

Brunt, Stephen. 1988. "Ethnic Ridings Can Leave Parties Speechless." *Globe and Mail,* 31 October.

Burnet, Jean. 1978. "The Policy of Multiculturalism within a Bilingual Framework: A Stocktaking." *Canadian Ethnic Studies* 10 (2): 107–13.

Burnet, Jean, and Howard Palmer. 1988. *"Coming Canadians": An Introduction to a History of Canada's Peoples.* Toronto: McClelland and Stewart.

Canada. Employment and Immigration Canada. 1989. "Immigration to Canada: A Statistical Overview." Ottawa: Minister of Supply and Services Canada.

Canada. Royal Commission on Bilingualism and Biculturalism. 1970. *Report.* Vol. 4. Ottawa: Queen's Printer.

Canada. Statistics Canada. 1988. *Canada 1986: Federal Electoral Districts – 1987 Representation Order: Part Two.* Cat. no. 94-134. Ottawa: Minister of Supply and Services Canada.

———. 1989. "Profile of Ethnic Groups." *Dimensions.* Cat. no. 93-154. Ottawa: Minister of Supply and Services Canada.

Canadian Ethnocultural Council. 1989. *Ethno Canada* 9 (1): 7.

———. 1990. Brief to the Royal Commission on Electoral Reform and Party Financing. Ottawa.

Cashmore, E. Ellis. 1984. "Ethnicity." In *Dictionary of Race and Ethnic Relations.* London: Routledge and Kegan Paul.

Cauchon, Paul. 1988. "Le vote ethnique n'est plus un vote libéral automatique." *Le Devoir,* 9 November.

Christian, William. 1990. Brief to the Royal Commission on Electoral Reform and Party Financing. Ottawa.

Cleroux, Richard. 1988. "Liberal Calls Reserved Ridings Unique to Quebec." *Globe and Mail,* 22 March.

Cohn, Martin. 1987. "PM Woos Minorities in Metro." *Toronto Star,* 5 July.

Contenta, Sandro. 1984. "Ethnic Voters Help McDonald Beat Challenge by Worthington." *Toronto Star,* 5 September.

Coutts, Jim. 1988. "Rules for Nominations Need Reform." *Toronto Star,* 10 July.

Creese, Gillian. 1986. "Working Class Politics, Racism and Sexism: The Making of a Politically Divided Working Class in Vancouver, 1900–1939." Ph.D. dissertation, Carleton University.

DelZotto, Elvio. 1988. "Top Liberal Defends Party's Nomination Process." *Toronto Star,* 25 July.

Dewar, Elaine. 1988. "March of the Third Force." *Toronto Life,* December.

Douglas, John. 1988. "Multiculturalism Enters New Age: Ethnic Voters Courted." *Winnipeg Free Press,* 16 November.

Eagles, D. Munroe. 1990. "Political Ecology: Local Effects on the Political Behaviour of Canadians." In *Canadian Politics: An Introduction to the Discipline,* ed. Alain G. Gagnon and James P. Bickerton. Peterborough: Broadview Press.

Federation of Ontario Liberal Satellites (FOLSAT). 1986. "Presentation to the President's Council," presented by the FOLSAT Steering Committee.

Fisher, Doug. 1988. "Noisy Nominations Make for Good Politics." *Mississauga News,* 22 March.

Gallagher, Michael. 1988. "Conclusion." In *Candidate Selection in Comparative Perspective,* ed. M. Gallagher and M. Marsh. London: Sage Publications.

Gerus, O.W., and J.E. Rea. 1985. *The Ukrainians in Canada.* Ottawa: Canadian Historical Association.

Globe and Mail. 1984. "De Corneille Hoping to Hold His Ethnic Vote Against Tory." 30 August.

Guarnieri, Albina. 1990. "Notes for Remarks by Albina Guarnieri before the Royal Commission on Electoral Reform and Party Financing." 12 June.

Gwyn, Richard. 1984a. "Ethnic Vote Seen Changing." *Winnipeg Free Press,* 20 August.

———. 1984b. "The Liberation of Ethnic Voters." Vancouver *Sun,* 14 August.

Harrington, Denise. 1984a. "Ethnic Vote May Hold Balance in Parkdale–High Park Riding." *Toronto Star,* 30 August.

———. 1984b. "Strong Ethnic Swing to PCs Help Witer Topple Jesse Flis." *Toronto Star,* 5 September.

Harris, Lewis. 1984. "Rules Don't Allow 'Packing' of Quebec Delegate Meetings: Liberal." Montreal *Gazette,* 12 April.

Howard, Ross. 1988. "Fights, Charges of Rigging Mar Liberal Nominations." *Globe and Mail,* 25 July.

———. 1990. "Liberals Jump into Battle to Attract Ethnic Support." *Globe and Mail,* 29 January.

Irvine, William. 1985. "Reforming the Electoral System." In *Party Politics in Canada.* 5th ed., ed. H.G. Thorburn. Scarborough: Prentice-Hall.

Isajiw, Wsevolod W. 1980. "Definitions of Ethnicity." In *Ethnicity and Ethnic Relations in Canada: A Book of Readings,* ed. E. Goldstein and Rita M. Bienvenue. Toronto: Butterworths.

Johnson, W. 1988. "Ethnic Power Arrives with a Bang in Toronto." Montreal *Gazette,* 31 May.

Kallen, Evelyn. 1987. "Ethnicity and Collective Rights in Canada." In *Ethnic Canada: Identities and Inequalities,* ed. Leo Driedger. Toronto: Copp Clark Pitman.

Kinnear, Michael. 1984. "Four Ethnic Groups Could Swing Election." *Winnipeg Free Press,* 3 August.

Levitt, Howard A. 1988. "Wading Through Liberal Nomination Mire." *Globe and Mail,* 25 August.

Li, Peter S. 1988. *The Chinese in Canada.* Toronto: Oxford University Press.

London Cross Cultural Learner Centre. 1990. "Presentation to the Royal Commission on Electoral Reform and Party Financing." Ottawa.

McLaren, Angus. 1990. *Our Own Master Race: Eugenics in Canada, 1885–1945.* Toronto: McClelland and Stewart.

Maillé, Chantal. 1990. "Primed for Power: Women in Canadian Politics." Background paper. Ottawa: Canadian Advisory Council on the Status of Women.

Malarek, Victor. 1986. "Exploit Relationship with Ethnic Groups to Gain in Toronto, Tory Report Urges." *Globe and Mail,* 9 October.

Manzer, Ronald. 1974. *Canada: A Socio-Political Report.* Toronto: McGraw-Hill Ryerson.

Marchand, Len. 1990. "Presentation to the Royal Commission on Electoral Reform and Party Financing." Ottawa.

Mississauga News. 1988. "Reform Needed." Editorial, 22 March.

Montreal *Gazette.* 1984. "Portuguese Bloc Packing Riding Votes." 3 May.

Native Council of Canada. 1990. "Presentation to the Royal Commission on Electoral Reform and Party Financing." Ottawa.

New Democratic Party. n.d. "NDP Affirmative Action Discussion Paper." Ottawa.

———. 1989. "Affirmative Action Resolutions." Ottawa.

———. 1990. "Report of the Multiculturalism Committee to the Federal Executive and Council." Ottawa.

Ontario. New Democratic Party. Ethnic Liaison Committee. 1985. "Report of the Ethnic Liaison Committee." Toronto.

———. 1989. "Minutes of Meeting, 14 March." Toronto.

Palmer, Howard. 1976. "Reluctant Hosts: Anglo-Canadian Views of Multiculturalism in the Twentieth Century." In *Multiculturalism as State Policy: Conference Report,* ed. Canadian Consultative Council on Multiculturalism. Ottawa: Minister of Supply and Services Canada.

Parkes, Debbie. 1988. "Charting the Ethnic Vote." Montreal *Gazette,* 29 October.

Patrias, Carmela. 1978. *The Kanadai Magyar Usjag and the Politics of the Hungarian Canadian Elite, 1928–1938.* Toronto: The Multicultural History Society of Ontario.

Pelletier, Alain. 1991. "Politics and Ethnicity: Representation of Ethnic and Visible-Minority Groups in the House of Commons." In *Ethno-cultural Groups and Visible Minorities in Canadian Politics: The Question of Access,* ed. Kathy Megyery. Vol. 7 of the research studies of the Royal Commission on Electoral Reform and Party Financing. Ottawa and Toronto: RCERPF/Dundurn.

Pendakur, Ravi. 1990. "An Exploration of Race and State Policy." Ottawa: Carleton University, Department of Sociology and Anthropology.

Peter, Karl. 1981. "The Myth of Multiculturalism." In *Ethnicity, Power and Politics in Canada,* ed. J. Dahlie and T. Fernando. Toronto: Methuen.

Progressive Conservative Association of Canada. 1989. "Constitution." Ottawa, 26 August.

Regenstreif, Peter. 1990. "Public Participation in Nominating Candidates for Parliament and in Selecting Delegates to National Conventions." Brief to the Royal Commission on Electoral Reform and Party Financing. Ottawa.

Sarjeant, Patricia. 1984. "Ethnic Vote Is Crucial in Calgary East Race." *Calgary Herald,* 30 July.

Serge, Joe. 1984. "Awakening of Metro's Ethnic Voters Puts New Bite into Election Campaign." *Toronto Star,* 7 August.

Sher, J. 1983. *White Hoods: Canada's Ku Klux Klan.* Vancouver: New Star.

Smith, Dan. 1988. "Free Trade Has Changed the Rules on 'Ethnic Vote.' " *Toronto Star,* 20 November.

Speirs, Rosemary. 1990. "Chrétien Camp Playing It Safe with Leadership Bid in the Bag." *Toronto Star,* 1 April.

Stasiulis, Daiva. 1988a. "Capitalism, Democracy and the Canadian State." In *Social Issues: Sociological Views of Canada.* 2d ed., ed. D. Forcese and S. Richer. Scarborough: Prentice-Hall.

———. 1988b. "The Symbolic Mosaic Reaffirmed: Multiculturalism Policy." In *How Ottawa Spends, 1988–89: The Conservatives Heading into the Stretch,* ed. K. Graham. Ottawa: Carleton University Press.

———. 1991. "Symbolic Representation and the Numbers Game: Tory Policies on 'Race' and Visible Minorities." In *How Ottawa Spends, 1990-91: The Politics of Fragmentation,* ed. F. Abele. Ottawa: Carleton University Press.

Stasiulis, Daiva, and Yasmeen Abu-Laban. 1990. "Ethnic Activism and the Politics of Limited Inclusion." In *Canadian Politics: An Introduction to the Discipline,* ed. Alain G. Gagnon and James P. Bickerton. Peterborough: Broadview Press.

Sunahara, Ann. 1981. *The Politics of Racism: The Uprooting of Japanese Canadians During the Second World War.* Toronto: James Lorimer.

Thernstrom, Abigail M. 1987. *Whose Votes Count? Affirmative Action and Minority Voting Rights.* Cambridge: Harvard University Press for Twentieth Century Fund.

Thorburn, Hugh G. 1985. "The Development of Political Parties in Canada." In *Party Politics in Canada.* 5th ed., ed. H.G. Thorburn. Scarborough: Prentice-Hall.

Thorson, Stephanie. 1988. "Liberals Blame Conservatives for Duplications on Party Lists." *Toronto Star*, 27 August.

Toronto Star. 1983. "Crosbie Defends Packing Tory Meeting with Amway Backers." 7 April.

Trickey, Mike. 1988. "Ethnic Support No Sure Thing for Liberals." *Calgary Herald*, 24 October.

Valpy, Michael. 1990. "Making It Too Easy to Remain Diverse." *Globe and Mail*, 25 October.

Vancouver *Sun*. 1984. "Ethnic Minorities Seek Action in Return for Their Support." 8 August.

Volpe, Joe. 1988. "Tough Nomination Battles Equal a Healthy Democracy." *Corriere Canadese*.

Walker, Bill. 1984. "Liberals on Top with Ethnics Poll Shows." *Toronto Star*, 31 July.

Ward, Peter. 1950. *The Canadian House of Commons: Representation*. Toronto: University of Toronto Press.

Wearing, Joseph. 1988. *Strained Relations: Canadian Politics and Voters*. Toronto: McClelland and Stewart.

Webb-Proctor, G. 1988a. "Brampton Riding Parties' Lists in Dispute." *Globe and Mail*, 22 March.

———. 1988b. "Same Names Listed for PCs, Liberals." *Globe and Mail*, 18 June.

Winsor, Hugh. 1990. "Third Force Challenging Traditional Liberal Elite." *Globe and Mail*, 16 April.

Wong, Debra. 1990. "Presentation to the Royal Commission on Electoral Reform and Party Financing." Ottawa.

Wood, Chris, and Paul Kaihla. 1988. "Ontario's Minorities Reach for Power." *Maclean's*, 16 May, 13–14.

Wood, John R. 1978. "East Indians and Canada's New Immigration Policy." *Canadian Public Policy* 4:549–67.

Woodsworth, James S. 1909. *Strangers within Our Gates or Coming Canadians*. Toronto: Stephenson.

World Sikh Organization (WSO). 1990. "Presentation to the Royal Commission on Electoral Reform and Party Financing." Ottawa.

2

POLITICS AND ETHNICITY
Representation of Ethnic
and Visible-Minority Groups
in the House of Commons

Alain Pelletier

THE PRESENCE OF ethnic groups, and particularly visible-minority groups, is becoming more and more significant in Canada. In view of their growing significance, it is important to examine the effect they have on the Canadian electoral system (for example on candidacies and election results).

This study is divided into three parts. The first deals with the sociological, political and demographic factors that determine the impact these groups have on elections. The second examines the various electoral strategies the groups can adopt to assert their interests within a society. The third focuses on one of these strategies – the political representation of ethnic groups within the Canadian society. We have restricted our analysis to representation in the Canadian House of Commons. We highlight two facets: profiles of candidates elected between 1965 and 1988, and those of candidacies during the 1988 general election.

Ethnic groups are also represented politically at the provincial and municipal levels, as well as on school boards. The degree to which ethnic groups are represented at each of these levels may vary. If factors such as concentration in certain residential areas and the size of electoral units are combined, it can be assumed that the degree of representation is greater at the municipal level than at the federal. In fact, the higher the concentration of ethnic groups in one region, and the smaller the electoral unit, the greater the number of electoral units where ethnic groups make up a sizable part of the population. The groups, therefore, are able to exert a greater influence on the nomination of candidates and the election result. The nature of the issues and their importance to the electorate are two other aspects to be considered when explaining possible differences in the degree to which ethnic groups are represented at these different electoral levels.[1]

The overview of the political representation of ethnic groups is thus incomplete. Nevertheless, this analysis allows us to update some characteristics of their representation in the House of Commons. It is fair to assume that members of groups that are more integrated into Canadian society, mainly because they immigrated earlier, are better represented. This appears to be true not only for successful candidates but for all candidates. Furthermore, it can be assumed that the degree of representation in the House of Commons differs among political parties. In view of the electoral chances of the various parties and their degree of openness to ethnic pluralism, it can be assumed that there is greater representation of ethnic groups in the Liberal Party of Canada than in any other party.

FACTORS CONTRIBUTING TO THE ELECTORAL IMPACT OF ETHNIC GROUPS

We will deal with five factors relating to the electoral impact of ethnic groups. The first is the maintenance of ethnic characteristics, a sociological factor that emphasizes the distinctiveness of an ethnic group when compared with the majority and contributes to the development of ethnic interest. Next, we address political factors, such as citizenship, registration on electoral lists and voter turnout. Finally, we discuss a demographic factor: the numerical weight of the ethnic groups within the general population and within the ridings themselves.

Theoretically, we could assign to these various factors a hierarchy that follows the order listed above. However, they must also be considered as a whole, since the electoral impact of the ethnic groups is only maximized when they exist simultaneously.

Sociological Factors: Ethnic Identity and Ethnic Interest[2]

The intention here is not to carry out an exhaustive analysis of the literature on ethnic identity, but rather to highlight the various sociopolitical aspects that contribute to this identity, a basic factor in whatever electoral impact ethnic groups have (Wolfinger 1974, 49). The approach adopted here is the sociopsychological approach, which analyses the relationship between the individual and the group (Anderson and Frideres 1981, 7).[3]

Ethnic identity is that which enables ethnic groups to distinguish themselves culturally, socially, economically and politically from the majority in the society. Once this identity is achieved and maintained, members can decide whether to have representatives who will work to maintain this identity either at the "centre," within the ethnic group, or at the periphery – that is, within society as a whole.[4] It is clear that this identity plays a fundamental role. Let us highlight its component parts.

According to Juteau-Lee, "one is not born ethnic, one becomes ethnic" (1983, 45). To become and be ethnic, one must belong to (objective aspect) and identify with (subjective aspect) an ethnic group (Kasfir 1979; Isajiw 1980; Anderson and Frideres 1981; Taboada-Leonetti 1984).[5] By birth, therefore, an individual belongs to an ethnic group that differs from others either by its language, religion,[6] origin, culture or race. In addition, individuals contribute to the means of socialization (families, media, etc.) specific to their ethnic group, which, in the sum of its parts, refers to the collective "we." It should be noted that the group acquires "a reality in itself and an influence on the behaviour of the individuals which make it up" (Charlot and Charlot 1985, 431). In short, ethnic identity is seen here as a social phenomenon.

We note that belonging to an ethnic group is essentially involuntary. However, identification is both voluntary and involuntary. It is involuntary insofar as members are compelled, by birth, to contribute to the means of socialization specific to their ethnic group (Ringer and Lawless 1989, 5). It is voluntary in that members are not compelled to participate in these means of socialization to the maximum degree (Breton 1983, 25) once they have become socialized and aware. Furthermore, when confronted with another ethnic group, for example, in the case of immigrants, they must decide whether to maintain their original ties.[7] For this choice to exist, however, it must be determined whether such a possibility is open to them. This obliges us "to know when, why and how ethnicity is mobilized" (Juteau-Lee 1983, 53) and, therefore, to study ethnic relations.

Like Hechter (1986) and Stack (1986), we can distinguish two theoretical approaches pertaining to the formation of ethnic identity: primordial and situational. In the former case, ethnic identity is seen as being permanent, essential and static, since it results from the group's characteristics: culture, religion, language (Stack 1986, 2; Hechter 1986, 13). According to Hechter and Stack, this approach does not explain the historical change in the pattern of behaviour and attitude of certain ethnic groups. Hechter states that in the second case, ethnic identity becomes an epiphenomenon and malleable, since it is determined by the group's social standing: "structuralists posit that ethnic identity results instead from objective intergroup differences in the distribution of economic resources and authority" (1986, 15).

The functionalist theory relates to the primordial approach and the Marxist theory to the situational approach. The distinction between these two theories rests on the causes of the ethnic relationship as well as on its consequences (Juteau-Lee 1983, 42–43; Simon 1983; Lavigne 1980). Thus, the functionalists believe that ethnic relationships can be caused by such things as scarcity of resources, voluntary or involuntary migration, etc. For the Marxists, the material foundations of this relationship are, according to Juteau-Lee, the expansion of monopolistic capitalism and the growth in state domination.[8] Just as the causes of functionalism are varied, so are its consequences (e.g., problems of adaptation, integration, acculturation). The Marxist theory ignores this aspect of the problem.

The situational school is better able to account for ethnic relations and changing ethnic identity. We subscribe to this approach because it is not naturalistic. That is, the definition of ethnic groups does not result solely from their own attributes but from their relations with other groups (majority or minority) and from their sociopolitical standing. This constantly reopens the question of the boundaries of ethnic identity. In addition, we fully agree with Juteau-Lee (1983) that the culturalism of the functionalist theory must be maintained, since, like the economic and political aspects, this aspect also defines ethnic identity.

An awareness of differences and social hierarchies can help us distinguish between three types of communities: ethnic groups, nationality-based groups and nations.

> The concept of ethnic group is usually reserved for historically and culturally dominated communities, with the latter having a history but no historicity, since they are incapable of formulating a political plan that could radically alter their relations with the dominant group, which is the community that controls the state's functioning and its ideological apparatus ... The concept of nation is reserved more for those communities that control the state apparatus or those that are able to formulate a (nationalist) plan to take over the state themselves. Between the two extremes is the nationality-based group, which questions the existing institutional framework without, however, drawing up a political plan that would lead to independence or sovereignty. (Juteau-Lee 1983, 44)[9]

Thus, immigrants and their descendants (for example, Italians, Haitians and Latin Americans) are minority ethnic groups because, at least at this time, they do not control the state apparatus and they do not yet have any plans to exercise such control, nor do they have the possibility of doing so.[10]

Ethnic groups are not, however, homogeneous. Several distinctions exist and are politically latent in all of them. Among these are social stratification, regional and political distinctions of their country of origin, dialects, age, religion, time of immigration and ideological convictions (Martiniello 1988; Breton 1983). These distinctions prevail in every group, but with varying intensity. Different aspects can play a major role in maintaining ethnic identity (Anderson and Frideres 1981, 109) and in the degree of openness these groups have toward interethnic exchanges. Religion, for example, contributes to a closed system among the Hassidic Jews, whereas Lutherans characteristically have a more open system.

In addition, ethnic identity cannot and should not be ascribed solely to the will of ethnic groups. Once it is established that the identities of ethnic groups result from their relations with other groups – majority and minority – the notion which then comes into play is the principle of otherness: "we" and "they."

Factors outside the group (i.e., specific to the society), therefore, may or may not promote the maintenance of ethnic identity. This is the case, for example, with the Canadian government's multiculturalism policy and the bilingualism and biculturalism policy, both of which contribute to the persistence of ethnic identity (Anderson and Frideres 1981, 107). The same applies to the Quebec government's policy of cultural convergence[11] and the equality rights recognized constitutionally in Canada under the *Canadian Charter of Rights and Freedoms*. Immigration policies also play a major role either through quotas (Labelle et al. 1983, 82–84) or through a sponsorship and designation system. Sponsorship promotes residential concentration,[12] which "has always been synonymous with a will to resist integration and a desire to maximize contacts within one's own ethnic group" (Perron 1979, 324; see also Anderson and Frideres 1981). This concentration has repercussions of its own. A group's members have a greater tendency to favour endogamy,[13] intraethnic friendships,[14] the maintenance of traditional values such as marriage, and the formation of separate social and cultural organizations. The importance of these different aspects varies depending on the ethnic group.

The identity of minority ethnic groups can also be strengthened by the majority group's discrimination against them. This can foster a desire to re-establish the institutions and customs of the country of origin (Lane 1969; Bailey and Katz 1969; Anderson and Frideres 1981). Although there might be more discrimination against the visible minorities (Anderson and Frideres 1981), they are not the only ones to suffer from it. The discrimination in interethnic relations can be both individual and collective. The society can adopt restrictive laws aimed at immigrants,[15] and individuals can form a discriminatory attitude because of stereotypical beliefs, such as "immigrants steal jobs." The discrimination exists because immigrants are seen as a demographic, linguistic (Cappon 1974, 140) or even economic threat. Nonetheless, racism in the Canadian population appears to be decreasing, largely as a result of greater contact between groups (Economic Council of Canada 1991).

These external factors can strengthen the desire of ethnic groups to set themselves apart from the mainstream. The result is that the integration of minorities into society is delayed. Several authors have developed concepts about this integration process.[16] Wolfinger refers to three of them: acculturation, association and assimilation.

> *acculturation:* assumption of the behavior patterns typical of the majority society, including speaking English, increases in education and income ...

> *association:* integration of behavior patterns with those of nonethnics, including the disappearance of segregation in economic, social, residential, marital, educational, and recreational behavior ...

> *assimilation:* the disappearance of ethnicity as a source of identity. (Wolfinger 1974, 32)[17]

According to Wolfinger, these three concepts do not correspond to development stages, as the process is not linear.[18] There can be acculturation without an ensuing structural integration (Parenti 1969, 271).[19] Similarly, integration can be partial. Some aspects of ethnic identity, therefore, may persist over generations, and others may not.

A study by Humphrey and Brock Louis (1973), based on a survey of three generations of the Greek community in the city of Norfolk, Virginia, is relevant. It shows that ethnic identification ("Am I Greek?"), endogamy, intraethnic friendships and knowledge of the language of origin decrease by the third generation, whereas participation and leadership within Greek associations remain strong. Bredimas-Assimopoulos (1975, 130) theorizes that the ethnic culture and its institutions can persist into the fourth generation. The arrival of new immigrants generally makes it possible to maintain ethnic identity even longer (Anderson and Frideres 1981, 107).

Social mobility and the arrival of new immigrants, among other factors, can play a significant role in the degree of such integration. These aspects vary in scope depending on the ethnic group. As a rule, the members of ethnic groups who claim multiple origins are better integrated into Canadian society than those who claim to be of a single origin (see table 2.1). For example, they are more likely to claim English or French as their mother tongue, or to speak more English or French at home, and are more likely to identify fully as Canadian citizens. Among the groups selected here, Ukrainians, Germans and Italians demonstrated greater integration through these characteristics. However, in the areas of profession and education, Vietnamese, Chinese and Pakistanis can be seen to rate almost as highly as the three previously mentioned groups. Finally, the percentage of Vietnamese, Chinese and Pakistani immigrant populations who arrived after 1983 is higher than that of the Ukrainians, Germans and Italians who arrived during that same period.

Ethnic identity raises the question of solidarity. According to Balgopal (1984), solidarity is the result of a failure to satisfy two levels of needs, which can be classed as basic (families, associations, friends, etc.) and secondary (employment, political power, etc.). According to Wrong, "solidarity includes the degree of awareness of boundaries between group members and non-members, ... the intensity of mutual emotional identifications with one another based on a sense of similarity or 'consciousness of kind,' rituals symbolizing belonging and collective identity, and so on" (1974, 138). Solidarity, however, is not a sufficient condition for ethnic mobilization. It can, nevertheless, lay the grounds on which political organization can potentially be built (Hechter 1986, 17). Mobilization around ethnic interests (those that constitute a group's specificity)[20] can only take place if the individuals share the same interests (such as economic inequality) and if the group has ethnic ties that "define discourse (language, beliefs, and practices) which is required for any form of concerted action" (Leifer 1981, 28–29).

Ethnic identity is conditional on the level of institutionalization, which is evaluated on the basis of criteria such as longevity, depersonalization and organizational differentiation (Charlot and Charlot 1985, 435). As a corollary, the same applies to political action: "For a community to be able to govern itself and for its public affairs to be guided, the identity must be fixed in a certain sociopolitical organization" (Breton 1983, 28). There is, therefore, a need for structures and mechanisms for regulation and control. These structures can be found at two levels: that of the interpersonal network and that of organizations. The latter can be an associative, lateral structure[21] or a federative, vertical structure[22] (Vincent 1974; Higham 1978; Breton 1983). According to

Table 2.1
Sociodemographic characteristics of certain ethnic groups, 1986
(percentages)

Sociodemographic characteristic	Ukrainian		German		Vietnamese		Chinese		Pakistani		Italian	
	SO	MO	SO	MO	SO	MO	SO	MO	SO	MO	SO	MO
Mother tongue English / French[a]	51.2	94.8	58.8	96.8	11.3	26.0	19.2	72.6	40.3	65.0	29.2	93.9
Home language English / French[a]	88.7	99.3	89.1	99.4	11.8	26.3	27.8	79.2	58.4	77.6	55.1	97.8
University degree	9.0	10.8	7.4	12.2	13.4	5.1	18.3	12.8	27.3	21.2	6.6	12.0
Managerial, administrative, professional and related occupations	26.7	25.7	24.4	28.3	18.2	10.2	28.4	24.4	31.6	27.9	18.0	27.3
Canadian citizens (total) Canadian by birth	99.3 85.6	99.4 97.1	99.4 72.0	97.6 93.7	58.4 11.0	65.2 20.1	79.8 25.9	85.7 55.7	86.9 27.0	91.6 46.1	88.4 47.8	97.0 91.0
Immigrated after 1983	1.1	3.5	2.9	6.0	29.7	24.5	15.1	14.2	8.4	6.4	0.7	5.6
Single / multiple proportion in relation to population of the group	43.7	56.3	36.3	63.7	84.2	15.8	87.0	13.0	78.6	21.4	70.5	29.5

Source: Canada, Statistics Canada (1989b).

Notes: SO = single origin; MO = multiple origin.

[a]Percentages established on the basis of single responses only.

Higham, it is at the second level that a group enters into contact with the outside world (1978, 8). These two levels must be analysed in greater detail, but first it should be noted that the degree of participation by members can vary at each of them (Breton 1983, 25).

At the base of the interpersonal network's structure is the family, the main socialization nucleus contributing to the ethnic identification of the individual and, a fortiori, the group.[23] Additional dimensions include the school system and communications. Many ethnic communities have their own schools, usually offering classes on Saturday. They frequently have their own newspapers and radio or television programs. These enable them to keep in touch with the mother country, as well as with the community's life within the society. The media also enable immigrants to learn about the standards of the society (Black and Leithner 1988). It must be stressed that these various networks generally enjoy continued support by the members. For example, 80 percent of Jews regularly read Jewish Canadian dailies (Weinfeld 1984, 70).

Additional organizations are superimposed on this interpersonal network. For a large number of ethnic groups, such as Italians, Greeks and Jews, the Church was a very important organization whose role was "to vigilantly safeguard and develop the traditional values brought from the country of origin ... [which constitute a] decisive factor in social and cultural cohesion and, in some serious cases, national cohesion" (Lefebvre and Oryschuk 1985, 148; see also Anderson and Frideres 1981). Since the secularization of Canadian society and particularly since the secularization of the ethnic groups which followed, federations of ethnic groups have supplanted the Church and the various associations. These federations exercise a certain de facto monopoly and are becoming the only liaison between the different levels of government.[24]

These federations are run by an élite (Painchaud and Poulin 1983), which according to Breton (1983) on the one hand seeks to control the community's resources, and on the other seeks to impose a definition of the collective identity with a view to collective action. This definition can also come from the grass roots. It must be noted that resources can be acquired from the members "either by trying to meet their requests or expectations or by forcing them or by persuading them of the intrinsic value of the objectives anticipated" (ibid., 35). The issue of control over material as well as symbolic resources can lead to economic or ideological conflicts between the different social and ideological components of the community. Those who take control "will try to organize the community on the basis of their ideological preferences and (or) their economic, social or cultural interests" (ibid., 33). The question of choice between integration and nonintegration enters here. What direction will these leaders take? It should be noted that the leaders "assure the role status of pressure-interest groups and engage in interaction with the political structure" (Anderson and Frideres 1981, 239).

According to Breton (1983), conflicts are regulated or resolved when collective projects are to be carried out. This phenomenon, which makes social cohesion possible, results in the community forgetting its internal squabbles in order to form a bloc against the threats society poses to its distinctive character. Ethnic identity, and its institutional corollary, is the major factor in determining the electoral impact of ethnic groups. Although this is the decisive factor, others, such as political factors, are also important.

Political Factors: Citizenship, Registration on Electoral Lists and Voter Turnout

There are three political factors listed by Portes and Mozo (1985) whose importance cannot be isolated: the acquisition of citizenship, the obligation to be registered on electoral lists and the degree of electoral participation. These various factors are indicators of the degree of integration of ethnic groups into the electoral process.[25]

In industrialized countries, the general rule is that only citizens are entitled to vote (Bouthillier 1987). Thus, according to Portes and Mozo, "the rate at which an immigrant group acquires citizenship is important, first, as an indicator of its collective desire to become integrated in the host society and, second, as a measure of its potential political power through electoral participation" (1985, 39).

The industrialized countries grant this recognition to immigrants only after they have met the residency requirements determined by the legislature. In Canada, this period is three years (Canada, *Citizenship Act*). Some countries grant immigrants the right to vote only at the municipal level. Since 1986, for example, the Netherlands has granted this right to immigrants after five years of residence (Gérard-Libois 1990). Immigrants are also entitled to vote at the municipal level in Norway, Ireland, Denmark and Sweden. In the latter case, the period of residence is set at three years (Bouthillier 1987). It can be said, therefore, that the Canadian position is generous. Considering that citizenship is granted after only three years' residence, it should continue to be one of the criteria for being able to vote in Canada.

Acquisition of citizenship, however, is not necessarily proof of any degree of political competence or interest in the electoral process. Thus, some members of ethnic groups may be more interested in becoming citizens for economic reasons, for example, than for electoral reasons.

On the other hand, registration on electoral lists is more likely to suggest an interest in exercising the right to vote.

As a rule, all electors must be registered on an electoral list to be eligible to vote. Although this requirement is not specific to ethnic groups, it may take on a particular significance in certain cases. Since members of certain ethnic groups come from countries whose electoral process is antidemocratic, those unfamiliar with the system may be reluctant to open their doors to enumerators.[26] In addition, it is difficult to enumerate some members of ethnic groups, especially the elderly, who understand little or none of either of Canada's official languages, making it difficult for enumerators who know only these languages. A permanent electoral list, with registration based on residence and not the individual, could partially solve this problem by enabling electors to register on their own by mail or telephone. However, members of ethnic groups may be reluctant to have their names revealed before polling day.

In the United States, where the elector must travel to be registered on the lists, there are significant variations in registration rates from one ethnic group to another. Portes and Mozo (1985) report the following registration rates for the 1980 presidential election: 71 percent for whites, 62 percent for Blacks and 54 percent for those of Hispanic origin. Hamilton considers that "black politics can only be helped by any system that facilitates the registration and voting process" (1978, 26). To this end, the author believes that registration on polling day could maximize electoral participation. This measure is already in effect in Canada in rural polling divisions (Canada, *Canada Elections Act*, s. 147). As will be shown later, ethnic groups are overwhelmingly concentrated in urban areas. Extending this measure to urban constituencies could promote the registration of electors from ethnic groups. At the same time, appointing enumerators who speak the language of the target population could also further this objective. Translating the various documents needed for enumeration might also be a solution. However, this measure would only place a further burden on the electoral bureaucracy because all documents would have to be translated into all the nonofficial languages and sent to the electorate concerned. The solution to the language problem depends not only on electoral legislation but also on immigration policies (e.g., selection criteria and language courses such as the COFI – immigrant guidance and training centre – program in Quebec), which are designed to promote language skills for immigrants.

However, these two factors are not significant unless electoral participation or the exercise of the right to vote is maximized. The study by Portes and Mozo (1985) showed that the participation rates of whites

(89 percent), Blacks (84 percent) and those of Hispanic origin (82 percent) did not vary a great deal during the 1980 presidential election in the United States. In Canada, the study by Wood (1981) relating to ethnic groups of East Indian origin in Vancouver South during the 1979 federal election concludes in the same vein: the rates of participation were 91.3 percent for the ethnic groups and 98.3 percent for all others in the riding. Under certain conditions, participation by ethnic groups can prove to be even higher than that of the general population. Hamilton (1978) reached the same conclusions in his analysis of the municipal elections in certain American cities. According to Hamilton, participation by members of the Black minority is higher in some cases than that of whites. The author explains this as "candidate attraction coupled with the excitement generated by the possibility of victory. (Studies have shown that turnout is increased where the voters perceive a good likelihood of their candidate winning in a hotly contested race)" (1978, 24).

The problem of participation by ethnic groups in the electoral process, then, does not seem to depend on the rate of participation in elections as much as on registration on electoral lists: the discrepancies between the registration rates of the ethnic groups and those of the majority group are much more significant in the latter case. This last factor is the determining one because it indicates the ethnic groups' interest in the electoral process or their political ability. To increase this interest or ability, efforts are needed to "demystify" the electoral process through training courses on the political process, which could be provided by the various ethnic organizations under the supervision of Elections Canada. These courses should target not only the ethnic electorate, but also the ethnic population not yet old enough to vote.

These various factors, however, can only have a significant effect when the ethnic groups carry sufficient demographic weight.

Demographic Factor: The Numerical Weight of Ethnic Groups

The numerical weight of ethnic groups is considered in relation to two aspects: the weight of the population in general and the division of electoral constituencies. Due to the time allotted for this research, the demographic picture presented had to be limited to data from the 1986 census. It is thus not intended to establish a historical perspective on demographic weighting of ethnic groups. Further, since the analysis of the representation of ethnic groups, which is the subject of the third part of this study, is confined to the House of Commons, the portrait of electoral constituencies painted here is purely federal. Finally, a distinction is made between visible minorities and ethnic groups as a whole, in order to bring out certain comparisons.[27] The term "ethnic group" is used in its usual sense; that is, it includes both visible-minority and other minority groups. This is the meaning to be given to the concept throughout this study.

Numeric Weight of Ethnic Groups within the Canadian Population[28]

Based on the criterion of mother tongue, anglophones – who account for 60.6 percent of Canadians – form the majority language group. Francophones rank second with 24.3 percent, and those who grew up speaking a language other than English or French account for 11.3 percent.[29] However, the criterion of mother tongue provides an incomplete picture of Canada's ethnic diversity. Some ethnic groups identify their mother tongue as French (e.g., Haitians); others, English (e.g., West Indians). Furthermore, we shall consider that the loss of the mother tongue does not necessarily mean loss of ethnic identity.

Other criteria, therefore, must be used to draw the most accurate picture possible of this reality. If ethnic origin[30] is used, those of British extraction are the majority – 44.8 percent[31] of the Canadian population. Those of French origin follow with 27.8 percent[32] and Aboriginal people with 3.0 percent. Ethnic groups other than British, French and Aboriginal make up 23.7 percent of the population.[33] There are three dominant categories of ethnic groups: those from Western Europe (5.3 percent); those from Southern Europe (5 percent); and those from Asia and Africa (3.9 percent).[34] Among these, the majority are thus from Europe.

We can use country of origin as another criterion for assessing the numerical weight of ethnic groups coming from Europe. In the 1986 census, Europeans represented 62.3 percent of the immigrant population. We note that this immigration took place mostly before 1967 (65 percent), while visible-minority groups for the most part immigrated after that date (see table 2.2). Based on these data, it could be assumed that the Europeans are more fully integrated into Canadian society than the other groups.

In Canada, this ethnic diversity is not uniform throughout the country. Some provinces have had fewer immigrants than others, with diverse ethnic groups concentrated in specific provinces, notably in Ontario where more than 60 percent, for example, of Portuguese, Italian, Black and Caribbean ethnic groups are concentrated. There are, however, some sizable concentrations in Quebec, Alberta and British Columbia (table 2.3). This trend at the provincial level extends to cities; thus most of the ethnic groups are concentrated in large metropolitan areas, such as Toronto, Montreal and Vancouver.

Visible-minority groups make up 6.3 percent of the Canadian population. Asians (55 percent) and Blacks (23 percent) form the largest

Table 2.2
Immigrant population distribution according to area of birth and period of immigration, 1986
(percentages)

Area of birth	Distribution[a]	Period of immigration
Europe	62.3	65 before 1967
Asia	17.7	44 after 1978
USA	7.2	—
Caribbean and Bermuda	5.0	59 between 1967 and 1977
South and Central America	3.8	62 after 1978
Africa	2.9	56 between 1967 and 1977
Oceania	0.9	58 between 1967 and 1977
Others	0.2	—

Source: Canada, Statistics Canada (1989b).
[a]Total immigrant population was 3 908 150.

contingents of these minorities. Close to half of the visible minorities (49.1 percent) are concentrated in Ontario; of these, 37.7 percent are in the Metropolitan Toronto area. There are, however, significant concentrations in two other metropolitan areas: Vancouver (14.8 percent) and Montreal (13.1 percent). Blacks seem to come to Montreal and Halifax, whereas Filipinos come to Winnipeg and Asians to Vancouver, Toronto, Calgary and Edmonton (table 2.4).

With the exception of Chinese and Afro-Americans in the 19th century, immigration from Asia, Africa and Latin America dates mainly from the beginning of the 1970s. Nearly one-third of the members of visible-minority groups were born in Canada, and as a result there is a second or even a third generation born in Canada. This can be expected to have a positive influence on their participation in, and knowledge of, the political process because they have been raised in the Canadian system from birth. Knowledge and participation are strengthened, at least potentially, by the fact that three-quarters of the members of visible-minority groups are Canadian citizens. This favours the maintenance of citizenship as a basic requirement for exercising the right to vote. It must also be kept in mind that some immigrants might not want to become Canadian citizens.

Numerical Weight of Ethnic Groups within Federal Ridings
The more concentrated the various ethnic groups are in an electoral district, the greater their potential to influence both the nomination of

Table 2.3

Concentration rate of ethnic groups (SO) by province, 1986
(percentages)

Ethnic origin	Nfld.	P.E.I.	N.S.	N.B.	Que.	Ont.	Man.	Sask.	Alta.	B.C.	Y.T.	N.W.T.
Western Europe	0.1	0.1	2.4	0.5	3.4	36.8	9.9	11.0	18.6	16.9	0.1	0.1
German	0.1	0.1	2.4	0.4	3.0	31.8	10.7	14.4	20.4	16.5	0.1	0.1
Dutch	0.1	0.4	2.7	0.8	1.8	48.6	8.0	3.7	16.0	17.9	0.1	0.1
Northern Europe	0.1	0.1	0.6	0.6	1.6	25.1	7.3	12.2	23.2	28.8	0.2	0.2
Scandinavian	0.2	0.1	0.7	0.7	1.5	15.6	8.6	14.5	27.1	30.6	0.2	0.2
Eastern Europe	0.1	0.1	0.5	0.1	6.0	39.5	12.5	10.3	18.6	12.3	0.1	0.1
Ukrainian	0.0	0.0	0.3	0.1	2.9	26.1	19.0	14.4	25.4	11.5	0.0	0.0
Polish	0.1	0.0	0.8	0.2	8.5	53.0	9.9	6.0	12.8	8.7	0.0	0.0
Hungarian	0.0	0.4	0.5	0.2	8.7	52.4	3.3	8.3	13.1	3.3	0.1	0.0
Southern Europe	0.1	0.0	0.4	0.1	21.2	65.1	1.7	0.4	3.8	7.2	0.0	0.0
Italian	0.0	0.0	0.3	0.1	23.1	65.0	1.2	0.3	3.3	6.6	0.0	0.0
Jewish	0.1	0.0	0.7	0.2	33.0	51.7	5.6	0.4	3.2	5.0	0.0	0.0
Portuguese	0.1	0.0	0.3	0.1	14.4	70.0	3.7	0.2	3.1	7.8	0.0	0.0
Asia, Africa, Pacific Islands	0.0	0.0	0.0	0.0	11.5	45.3	3.8	1.6	12.3	24.1	0.0	0.1
Chinese	0.0	0.0	0.4	0.2	6.4	43.3	2.4	2.0	13.7	31.3	0.0	0.1
Indian	0.1	0.1	0.7	0.2	5.5	50.7	2.7	1.3	11.1	27.2	0.0	0.0
Arabic	0.1	0.4	3.4	1.1	3.5	42.1	1.8	1.0	12.5	3.2	0.0	0.0

Table 2.3 (cont'd)
Concentration rate of ethnic groups (SO) by province, 1986
(percentages)

Ethnic origin	Nfld.	P.E.I.	N.S.	N.B.	Que.	Ont.	Man.	Sask.	Alta.	B.C.	Y.T.	N.W.T.
Latin America	0.0	0.0	0.4	0.2	37.5	37.0	3.7	2.4	11.7	6.9	0.0	0.0
Black	0.0	0.0	4.5	0.5	21.4	63.3	2.2	0.7	4.6	2.7	0.0	0.0
Caribbean	0.1	0.0	0.3	0.1	26.8	62.0	2.8	0.6	5.1	2.5	0.0	0.0

Source: Canada, Statistics Canada (1989a).

SO = single origin.

Table 2.4
Distribution of visible minorities by census metropolitan area (CMA), 1986

CMA	N	% of total CMA population	Concentration/ Canada (%)
Halifax	15 025	5.1	1.0
Montreal	204 740	7.0	13.1
Toronto	586 495	17.1	37.7
Winnipeg	49 530	7.9	3.1
Calgary	72 600	10.8	4.7
Edmonton	72 560	9.2	4.7
Vancouver	230 840	16.7	14.8
Total CMA	1 231 790	5.0	79.1
Total Canada	1 557 710		

Source: Canada, Statistics Canada (1990).

candidates and the election results (Massicotte and Bernard 1985, 41). And the more important the ethnic groups' populations are within a riding, the more decisive this influence is in local associations. At the same time, the more electoral constituencies they affect, the more decisive is this electoral weight nationally.

Ethnic groups as a whole have a significant electoral weight in many ridings in Canada. There are 11 ridings where the population of ethnic origin exceeds 50 percent (table 2.5) and in 125 ridings it varies from 21 to 50 percent. Forty-six percent of electoral constituencies have a population of ethnic origin greater than 21 percent. It is important to note that 40 percent (54 of 136) of these ridings are in Ontario, which has 33 percent (99 of 295) of the country's ridings.

Even though the ridings have a strong concentration of ethnic groups, none is dominated (that is, 51 percent or more) by any particular ethnic group (table 2.6).[35] Few ridings (4.7 percent, or 14 of 295) have one ethnic group forming from 20 to 50 percent of the ridings' population. Very few have one group forming from 10 to 19 percent of their population (15.6 percent, or 46 of 296). Ethnic pluralism, therefore, characterizes the composition of federal electoral constituencies.

In spite of this tendency to pluralism, visible minorities often have the potential to influence more decisively than other minorities. If we look only at those electoral constituencies where all ethnic groups account for

Table 2.5
Breakdown of ridings by ethnic groups (SO) by province, 1987

Province	0–10%	11–20%	21–40%	41–50%	≥51%	N
Nfld.	7	—	—	—	—	7
P.E.I.	4	—	—	—	—	4
N.S.	10	1	—	—	—	11
N.B.	10	—	—	—	—	10
Que.	56	5	10	3	1	75
Ont.	16	29	36	11	7	99
Man.	—	2	9	2	1	14
Sask.	—	1	11	1	1	14
Alta.	—	3	23	—		26
B.C.	—	12	16	3	1	32
Y.T.	—	1	—	—	—	1
N.W.T.	1	1	—	—	—	2
Canada N	104	55	105	20	11	295
%	35	19	35	7	4	100

Source: Canada, Statistics Canada (1988).

Note: Ethnic groups other than British, French and Aboriginal people.

SO = single origin.

more than 10 percent of the population (table 2.7), visible minorities are the largest or second-largest group in 29 percent of these cases (56 of 191).

Do electoral-map boundaries play a negative or a positive role in the representation of ethnic groups? The *Electoral Boundaries Readjustment Act* sets out certain guidelines that the commission must follow when setting the boundaries. It divides the provinces according to a quota based on a province's population or the number of members it should have (s. 15(1)); the difference between a constituency's population and its quota must not exceed 25 percent (s. 15(2) *in fine*). The population's sociodemographic characteristics have not yet been formally taken into account.[36] The legislation, however, departs from the general principle set out above:

> 15(2) The commission may depart from the application of the rule set out in paragraph 1(*a*) in any case where the commission considers it necessary or desirable to depart therefrom

Table 2.6

Ridings where ethnic groups (SO) make up more than 50% of the population, 1987

(percentages)

Riding	Total ethnic population	First predominant ethnic group		Second predominant ethnic group	
Quebec					
Mount-Royal	62.2	Jews	37.7	Blacks	2.6
Ontario					
York South	52.8	Italians	17.7	Blacks	6.8
Don Valley North	53.0	Jews	10.9	Chinese	9.8
Trinity–Spadina	62.7	Chinese	13.1	Italians	7.9
Eglinton–Lawrence	63.3	Italians	23.7	Jews	11.3
York West	63.6	Italians	28.3	Blacks	7.9
York Centre	66.1	Italians	31.0	Jews	13.6
Davenport	73.1	Italians	21.4	Chinese	3.0
Manitoba					
Winnipeg North	71.9	Ukrainians	13.3	Jews	7.1
Saskatchewan					
Regina–Qu'Appelle	64.5	Germans	16.8	Ukrainians	5.2
B.C.					
Vancouver East	56.1	Chinese	25.4	Italians	7.6

Source: Canada, Statistics Canada (1988).

Note: Ethnic groups other than British, French and Aboriginal people.

SO = single origin.

Table 2.7

Importance of visible minorities by riding, 1987

Province	N^a
Quebec	12
Ontario	23
Alberta	4
British Columbia	16
Total	55
N	*(191)*

Source: Canada, Statistics Canada (1988).

[a]Number of ridings in which ethnic groups make up more than 10% of the population where visible minorities are the largest and/or the second-largest group, i.e. in 191 cases out of 295.

(*a*) in order to respect the community of interest or community of
identity in or the historical pattern of an electoral district in the
province, or

(*b*) in order to maintain a manageable geographic size for
constituencies in sparsely populated, rural or northern regions
of the province.

In brief, the ethnic distribution could be taken into account when electoral
boundaries are drawn. The case of the Chinese in the Vancouver area can
demonstrate this and is mentioned here for two reasons. Among the visible
minorities, the Chinese have the greatest demographic weight within the
electoral constituencies; furthermore, these ridings are in the Vancouver
area, where the distribution of the Chinese population[37] is most concentrated in the eastern part of the city and along a north–south axis.

The 1984 electoral boundaries respect this residential concentration, except in Vancouver Quadra (11.2 percent Chinese) and Vancouver
South (17.8 percent Chinese), where the boundary follows an east–west
axis. If the boundary between these two ridings had respected the
concentrations of the Chinese population, that population could have
been 21.9 percent in Vancouver South (rather than 17.8 percent) and 6
percent in Vancouver Quadra (rather than 11.2 percent). The 1988
boundary uses the same line to separate these two ridings. The ridings
are, however, extended toward the east of the city, thus encroaching
on the riding of Vancouver Kingsway as drawn in 1984.[38] The Chinese
population is increased in both cases: in Vancouver Quadra, to 16.2
percent; and in Vancouver South, to 19.7 percent.

On a broader scale, the electoral boundaries drawn in 1988
decreased the representation of the Chinese. In 1988, only the riding
of Vancouver East had a Chinese population exceeding 20 percent (25.4
percent); Vancouver South had 19.7 percent. In 1984 there were two
ridings exceeding 20 percent: Vancouver Kingsway (24.6 percent) and
Vancouver East (23.9 percent). If the 1984 boundaries for Vancouver
South and Vancouver Quadra were rearranged, as set out above, there
could have been a third riding with more than 20 percent Chinese –
Vancouver South (21.9 percent). It should be noted that, in this area
of Vancouver, the Chinese cannot exceed a third of the total of a given
electoral district. In fact, only Census Tract 57 exceeds this threshold,
with 62.3 percent Chinese residents.

Electoral boundaries serve to effect change to certain integration policies. Legislators have two choices: to maximize the weight of certain groups
or to promote ethnic pluralism within the various electoral constituencies. The results here show that it is the second option legislators have

chosen. Because residential segregation maintains ethnic identity, departure from this course would not facilitate integration of the various ethnic groups into Canadian society. Although such electoral boundaries must respect communities of interest, examples such as Vancouver Quadra and Vancouver South show that this is not always the case.

Ethnic identity, citizenship, registration on the electoral lists, voter turnout and the numerical weight of the ethnic groups, along with other factors, affect the political impact that various ethnic groups can have within a society. This impact can, moreover, be expressed in various ways.

ELECTORAL STRATEGIES OF ETHNIC GROUPS

Ethnic groups can adopt various strategies to assert their ethnic interests. Crewe (1983), who analysed the representation of Asian and Indian minorities in the British Parliament, mentioned four electoral strategies that ethnic groups can adopt. They can form their own party, nominate independent candidates, vote as a bloc, and elect candidates of ethnic origin within the established political parties. In addition, we should note that they can also abstain, reflecting either their lack of interest or "silent" opposition to the standards and policies of the society.[39] The following sections summarize the four main strategies.

Forming an Ethnic Party

Since they are in the minority, ethnic groups cannot form a party based solely on ethnic concerns and expect to gain office (Leslie 1969, 420–21). It is much the same in a single-member or proportional system, although in this system electing candidates from such parties is easier (Hahn and Holland 1976). The difficulty of taking office, however, does not prevent them from founding their own parties, especially at the municipal level: "To be sure, an ethnic party might win sufficient support to affect the prospects of the main parties – for example, by siphoning off Labour votes in marginal seats. But under Britain's electoral system it could elect only a handful of councillors and probably no MPs" (Crewe 1983, 261).

In Canada, there are no ethnic parties, at least federally. It has been tried in other countries at the municipal level, but without much success. The municipal Pakistan People's Party, for example, was formed in the town of Bradford, England, in 1970. That party's only candidate, Mr. Nawaz, won 11.2 percent of the votes in the 1970 election. He later ran as an independent in the next election, after quitting the party in 1971 over some disagreements (Le Lohé 1979).

Independent Ethnic Candidacies

According to Crewe (1983, 265), forming an ethnic party requires a collective initiative, whereas an independent ethnic candidacy depends on individual initiative. Associations, however, can choose collectively to support such a candidacy by allocating material or symbolic resources.

If forming an ethnic political party cannot lead to office, neither can running an independent candidate. That explains why in England "the number of such candidates has been surprisingly small, given the cheapness of the deposit (£150)" (Crewe 1983, 265). This strategy is not highly regarded in Canada either, even within the majority group. Only 54 independent candidates (3.4 percent of the total) ran in the 1988 federal election. Fourteen of these candidacies were held by members of ethnic groups; thus they represented only one-quarter of the independent candidates.[40]

The Ethnic Vote

To have their specific interests recognized within a society, it is better for ethnic minorities to accept the political parties of that society and vote for them. According to Crewe,

> For the exercise of ethnic electoral power the following conditions must all be met:
> a) the *full electoral mobilization* of the ethnic minority, i.e. high registration and high turnout;
> b) an *ethnic bloc vote*, i.e. uniform support for one party, or at least against one party … ;
> c) a *strategic location* of this ethnic vote in marginal constituencies such that it has the potential to deliver seats to one party at the expense of another;
> d) a net effect in terms of seats over the country as a whole that *outweighs that of the white anti-ethnic vote*. (1983, 268)

The strength of support for a particular party is much higher if the ethnic communities are concerned about government policies or affected by the policies forming the platforms of the parties involved (Lipset et al. 1954, 1129). This is particularly true when major social, economic or political changes are looming. Voter turnout is higher if the group is subjected to strong and consistent pressure (ibid., 1132–33). The role of the ethnic media reflects the partisan orientation that the group wants to impress upon the members. A study by Donefer (1984, 343–45) shows that during the pre-referendum campaign in Quebec, the

Canadian Jewish News devoted only 6 articles to the yes side and 24 to the no side.

The ethnic vote, according to Wolfinger, must be defined "as situations in which ethnic group membership is an important independent variable in voting behavior. I do not claim that ethnicity is the only independent variable ... One corollary of this point is that ethnic voting cannot be detected by examining the voting behavior of a given group in isolation from the rest of the electorate" (1974, 41).

Such electoral behaviour by ethnic groups influences what the political parties have to say. Thus a party that enjoys the overwhelming support of the minorities must respond to their concerns, while at the same time adopting policies that will be supported by the rest of the population so that the party avoids being identified as one that represents only the interests of those minorities. By contrast, a party that does have the support of minorities must avoid stressing the ethnic aspects of any controversial policy (Leslie 1969, 427). Political parties, therefore, must adopt a middle-of-the-road position (Crewe 1983, 262). These strategies allow them to garner the most votes not only from the ethnic communities but also from the rest of the population, so they have some hope of taking and keeping power.[41] However, keeping this balance involves certain risks for both the ethnic groups and the political parties.

Support given to a party is not necessarily unshakable. Changes in allegiance can result "from logical objections where the interests and social standing of a group seem threatened by the platform of its traditional party" (Lipset 1967, 304). In such a case, voting support might remain but be thrown behind another party that seems to meet the collective aspirations of the ethnic communities better or that seems to be the least likely to harm them. The case of the Black minority in the United States is one example: it abandoned the Republican Party in favour of the Democratic Party because the New Deal policy seemed more advantageous (Lipset 1967). The Cubans in Miami are another example. They have supported the Republican Party since the 1968 presidential election because of the policy pursued by President Kennedy and the Democrats during the Bay of Pigs crisis (Mohl 1986).

It must be noted that both time of immigration and desire for social mobility can play decisive roles in the choice of parties by various ethnic groups: "Ethnic minorities, especially those of recent arrival, have traditionally supported more progressive candidates and parties with more egalitarian platforms. These political preferences follow quite logically from the collective self-interest of these groups in abandoning the bottom of the social pyramid and finding avenues of economic and social mobility" (Portes and Mozo 1985, 53).[42] Bloc behaviour can only occur if there is cohesion and homogeneity within a group. Squabbles about the course of action a community should follow can split the community's vote (Jedwab 1986).

Other studies also show that mass support for one policy is not systematic in Canada. The ecological analysis by Boily et al. (1988) of the 1988 federal election in the greater Montreal area concluded that the ethnic vote seems to have split in that election. Wood's study (1981) of East Indian ethnic groups in Vancouver South, which relied on a questionnaire-based survey, showed that in 1974 61.8 percent of these groups supported the Liberals, whereas only 44 percent of non-East Indians did so. In 1979, however, the East Indian vote for the three major parties was divided almost equally (Liberals, 31 percent; Conservatives, 31 percent; New Democratic Party (NDP), 36 percent), whereas non-East Indians showed very high support for the Conservatives (Liberals, 28.6 percent; Conservatives, 64.3 percent; NDP, 7.1 percent).

Ethnic Candidacies within the Major Parties

First, we will address nominations for ethnic candidacies within the major parties as a two-pronged strategy; that is, one that benefits the political parties themselves as much as the ethnic groups. Then we will consider certain factors that facilitate or do not facilitate the candidacy of members of ethnic groups.

A Two-Pronged Strategy

Contrary to the impression Crewe (1983) gives us, the major political parties themselves may support ethnic candidacies. A party which has ethnic-group support can retain it in this way. Parties without such support may hope to shift the party loyalty of the ethnic electorate (Wolfinger 1965, 896). Such a shift, however, will take place only if there are no deep divisions between the major parties running counter to the interests of the ethnic communities. When there are no clear and major divisions between the parties that might affect the collective interests of the ethnic communities, there is unlikely to be a tendency to give mass support to one party. On the other hand, these communities may give more votes to one party than another without necessarily providing mass support.

Ethnic candidacies, therefore, play an important role not only for the political parties but also for the various ethnic groups. This strategy, like those discussed before, involves asserting ethnic interests within the political system of the society. However, it is not certain that ethnic interests will be preserved by this strategy. Even though these various candidates generally participate actively in the sociopolitical structures of their respective communities before their nomination (Pelletier 1988), their links with their communities of origin may, once they are elected, weaken with time. When these candidates are elected, they do not necessarily become spokespersons for their communities:

> The physical presence of Asians and West Indians on the floor of the Commons or Council Chamber, it is argued, would ensure the representation of the ethnic minorities' specific interests. Whether in fact a small number of coloured councillors or MPs could act – or would wish to act – as ethnic spokesmen is far from certain. Elected members of other minorities – Jews and "Irish" Catholics, for example – do not generally act in this way. Most Jews in the Commons regard themselves as "MPs who are Jewish", not as "Jewish MPs." (Crewe 1983, 276)

The mandate of candidates of ethnic origin cannot tie their hands. Especially in the context of single-member representation, it must be emphasized that these candidates represent a part of the electorate that is not ethnic. Like the political parties, they adopt a middle-of-the-road stance on ethnic issues and attempt to reconcile ethnic and nonethnic interests. Furthermore, the presence of candidates of ethnic origin may be a reflection of the greater integration either of certain ethnic groups or of the members themselves into the political system. Consequently, this ethnic élite may no longer have anything but a symbolic role to play, conforming to Higham's definition of "projective leadership," which "[wins them] their initial recognition outside the limits of the group that nurtured them. In some cases, they may feel little identification with that group, but it canonizes them as symbols of its character and submits them as evidence of the group's 'contributions' to American civilization" (1980, 646).

Factors Facilitating Ethnic Candidacies

The promotion of ethnic candidacies requires a series of factors. First, there are those of an economic order. According to the theory of mobilization, there must be a certain degree of social mobility within the group: "Middle-class status is a virtual prerequisite for candidacy for major office; an ethnic group's development of sufficient political skill and influence to secure such a nomination also requires the development of a middle class" (Wolfinger 1974, 49).

Crewe cites two key factors which impede ethnic candidacy: the perception that a Black candidate will lose votes for the party, and candidate-selection criteria within the parties that are "complex and difficult to pin down" (Crewe 1983, 277–78). As an example, parties can fix the voting hours at a time inconvenient for certain ethnic or religious groups (Guarnieri 1990).

Second, certain factors are related to the chances of a candidate of ethnic origin being elected. Le Lohé, using an inductive analysis based on observing three Black candidacies, concluded that candidates of ethnic origin can win only if they run in safe ridings; that is, where their party is sure to win or where they enjoy the support "of a relatively undivided coloured electorate" (1979, 196). However, this observation must be qualified. First, the second condition set by Le Lohé guarantees that candidates of ethnic origin will be elected only if there is a substantial ethnic presence[43] and, unless such candidacies lead to a shift in party loyalty, only if this ethnic electorate is solidly behind the party for which the candidates are running. Victory aside, Fitzgerald shows that "Black candidates, for example, did not fare particularly well or particularly badly where there was a high concentration of Black voters; nor did they have particular difficulty in areas that were mostly white" (1983, 394). Next, the candidate's image can also be important:

> The "image" of the candidate, to whites especially, is important. The candidate will have a more difficult time if he or she is perceived by whites as the "candidate of the blacks" ... Maintaining a "deracialized" image does not mean that a black mayor or candidate cannot adopt strong positions on racial justice, such as affirmative action in hiring city employees. (Hamilton 1978, 26)

Fitzgerald believes that identification with the party is what matters: "Voters – black and white – vote primarily on party lines. Specifically, they vote on party lines, rather than on racial lines. It is only when they think they are being asked to vote for a candidate on the basis of colour, rather than party, that they set up a backlash. To put it another way: white voters will sacrifice racial prejudice to party preference, but they will not vote for a candidate *because* they are black" (1983, 395).

Of the four strategies set out here, the ethnic vote and the presence of candidacies within parties of the society seem to be the most effective means, theoretically at least, for ethnic groups to gain recognition for their specific interests. These strategies, however, do involve certain risks with regard to this recognition and the electoral support shown for majority parties. Historically, of these theoretical avenues, representation is the one which has been preferred. Accordingly, the first stage will sketch the picture of political representation of ethnic groups in Canada. The second stage will make it possible to explain, at least in part, the nature of the situation of members of the House of Commons belonging to various ethnic groups by approaching it from the point of view of their candidacies.

POLITICAL REPRESENTATION OF ETHNIC GROUPS IN CANADA

Studies of ethnic representation in the House of Commons are rare. Of those that are available, most do not single out the ethnic dimension as a dependent variable. The study by Kornberg and Mishler (1976), constitutes one exception; in their profile of the 28th Parliament, the authors selected religion (Jewish) and certain categories of ethnic groups: Anglo-British and northern Europeans, French Canadians, central and Eastern Europeans, and other Canadians. These categories, however, do not take into account the presence of Asians, Latin Americans and Blacks. Also, this study was based on a survey whose response rate was 72 percent, providing an incomplete picture of the House of Commons.

The only data that indicate the number of members from the various ethnic groups are those established by March (Canada, Royal Commission 1970, 272) for the period 1867–1964. These show that during the period there were 97 members from ethnic groups, 40 of whom were German. March also counts one Chinese and one Lebanese MP. In addition, 35 of the 97 members (36 percent) were elected in Ontario constituencies. These data are not broken down by political party.

Because little work was available on this question, we updated March's data (Canada, Royal Commission 1970, 272) and then examined the question of these groups' representation in more detail with regard to both regions and political parties. We therefore selected two levels of representation: MPs and candidates. For the former, we dealt with the period 1965–88.[44] For the latter, we restricted our analysis to the 1988 election. Given the characteristics of the Canadian electoral system, we dealt only with candidacies in the three major parties (Conservatives, Liberals and NDP), since our main intention was to analyse the chances of success of candidates from the various ethnic groups. We are aware, however, that members of these groups, for the most part, belong to small parties.

Methodology

We rejected a questionnaire-based survey as a way to establish the representation of ethnic groups in the House of Commons during the 1988 election because it would not allow us to count everyone.[45] Furthermore, our intention was not to learn the views or attitudes of the candidates or members on certain questions but to establish their ethnic profile. Having rejected the survey, we had to rely on biographical notes

– the parliamentary guidebooks and the candidate biographies published by the political parties at the time of the election.[46]

Our survey of members of ethnic groups was done first by name. We selected all names without an Anglo-Saxon or French connotation. With this list in hand, we checked the information from biographical sources, going through more than 3 000 biographies. We based the verification on criteria such as country of birth,[47] religion, participation in ethnic organizations, language spoken and parents' ethnic origin. Insofar as possible, all these criteria were concomitant. Very few biographical notes contained all the information. In certain cases there was no indication beyond the name to help determine an individual's exact ethnic origin.[48] When photographs were available, we used skin colour as another criterion.

We distinguished between visible minorities and ethnic groups as a whole for this study. We used the definition established by Statistics Canada (see note 27) to classify MPs and candidates belonging to visible minorities. This gave us a basis for comparison with visible minorities in the Canadian population as a whole.[49]

Because the biographical sources are incomplete, the quantitative representation exposed here is not exhaustive. There may be omissions or improper entries. Some individuals may, in fact, be identified as belonging to an ethnic group when they no longer identify with this group. In this analysis, we assumed that all people enumerated not only belonged to a given ethnic group but also identified with that group. We recognize the random character of such a study and emphasize that politicians of ethnic origin might be more fully characterized by "projective leadership" (Higham 1980). Only a questionnaire-based survey or semi-directive interviews would allow us to establish the extent to which candidates identify with their group of origin. That could be the subject of subsequent work.

Despite some limitations, we believe this portrait gives a fairly accurate picture of the Canadian political reality: that is, "Canadians of other origins are under-represented although incidence of this discrepancy has been diminishing" (Franks 1987, 66).[50]

Representation of Ethnic Groups in the House of Commons
We next deal with the proportional representation of ethnic groups in the House of Commons and then with the characteristics of the ethnic MPs in relation to their origins and regional and party distinctions.

Increasing Proportional Representation
The majority of the members of the House of Commons are Anglo-British or French Canadians. In 1988, 48 members out of 295, or 16.3

percent, belonged to the various ethnic groups (table 2.8), while these groups accounted for 23.6 percent of the general population. The proportion of visible minorities was 2 percent of MPs and 6.3 percent of the total population. It should be noted that women constituted 13.5 percent of MPs and 52 percent of the population. Ethnic groups, therefore, achieved 70 percent of the objective of proportional representation; visible minorities, 32 percent; and women, 25 percent. The underrepresentation was greater in the case of visible minorities and women than in that of ethnic groups as a whole.

Furthermore, the proportion of members of ethnic origin among members of the House of Commons was slightly higher than the proportion of immigrant members – 16.3 and 15.4 percent, respectively (Canada, Statistics Canada 1988), since not all members of ethnic origin were immigrants. Between 1965 and 1988, only 24.2 percent (34 of 120) of members of ethnic origin had been born outside Canada. In 1988, proportions reached 42 percent (20 of 48).

The representation of ethnic and visible-minority groups has, nevertheless, improved since 1965. Representation of ethnic groups has increased significantly and continuously from 9.4 percent in 1965 to 16.3 percent in 1988. The increase was smaller for visible minorities, however, varying from 0.8 percent in 1968 to 2.0 percent in 1988 (table 2.9). Another indication of their underrepresentation was the relationship between members belonging to visible minorities and the total number of members belonging to ethnic groups. For 1988, the ratio of visible-minority MPs to ethnic MPs was 12.5 percent (6 of 48), whereas visible minorities constituted more than a quarter of the total ethnic population. This underrepresentation will probably decrease in the years to come as visible-minority groups increase their share of

Table 2.8
Parliamentary representation of ethnic and visible-minority groups, Canada, 1988

	Population 1986 (%)	Number of members required for equitable representation	Representation in the House of Commons 1988	
			N	%
Ethnic groups[a] (single and multiple)	23.6	70	48	16.3
Visible minorities	6.3	19	6	2.0

[a]Includes groups belonging to the visible minorities. This comment also applies to the tables that follow.

Table 2.9
Representation of visible and ethnic minorities in the House of Commons,
Canada, 1965–88

Election	Ethnic minorities		Visible minorities		Visible minorities as % of ethnic minorities
	N	%	N	%	
1988	48	16.3	6	2.0	12.5
1984	44	15.6	3	1.1	6.8
1980	40	14.2	4	1.4	10.0
1979	40	14.2	3	1.1	7.5
1974	33	12.5	3	1.1	9.1
1972	30	11.4	2	0.8	6.7
1968	31	11.7	2	0.8	6.5
1965	25	9.4	0	0.0	0.0
1965–88	120*	—	10	—	8.3

*An ethnic member of the House of Commons could have been elected for more than one term.

immigration (Samuel 1988), resulting in an increase in visible-minority
candidates and consequently in their representation in the House of
Commons. In addition, a corresponding decrease in racial prejudice is
likely as more contacts are made within the Canadian population,
which will result in more support for these candidates (Economic
Council of Canada 1991, 8).

Finally, it should be emphasized that the members of minority
ethnic origin include very few women. Between 1965 and 1988, only
5 percent of the members of ethnic origin (6 of 120) were women. In
1988, they numbered only 2 of the total of 48. Men are still very overrepresented in this category. Furthermore, those elected appear to
answer one of the conditions favouring their candidacy, that of social
mobility. An analysis of the professions of candidates of ethnic origin
elected in 1988 shows that more than half were business people, lawyers
or administrators. The others had such professional occupations as
professors, social workers, engineers and doctors.

Ethnic Origin, and Regional and Party Distinctions
Analysis of the ethnic origins of members of the House of Commons
in the period 1965 to 1988 revealed that membership did not reflect the
diversity found in the general population during that period. In fact,
most of the members from ethnic groups were of European origin

(88.4 percent),[51] a much greater proportion than was found in the total ethnic population (67.8 percent).[52] Two main groups of MPs stood out: first, northern and Eastern Europeans, mainly Ukrainians (18), Jews (13), Germans (9) and Poles (6); second, southern Europeans, mostly Italian (16). These two groups have different regional strongholds. In the first case, the members represented constituencies mainly in the western provinces, where immigrant populations from these countries settled most frequently. MPs from the second group almost exclusively represented electoral constituencies in Ontario and Quebec, where immigrants from southern Europe were concentrated. Having established these characteristics, we observed that the members of northern and Eastern European origin and those of southern European origin were usually Conservative and Liberal, respectively. This was largely due to the regional strongholds and the strength of the major parties in Canada. The Conservatives and Liberals were the only two parties that had been successful in forming governments, the Liberals relying mainly on the electorate in the eastern provinces and the Conservatives on that in the western provinces.

Between 1965 and 1988, the majority of the members from ethnic groups (40 percent) were elected from Ontario. Alberta was next (13.3 percent), followed by Quebec and British Columbia (each at 11.7 percent) and Saskatchewan and Manitoba (10.8 percent each). The Atlantic provinces and the territories were last, though not entirely absent. In these regions, only two members of ethnic origin were elected: Erik Nielsen, of Danish origin, was elected in the Yukon between 1958 and 1979; and Jack Marshall, of Jewish origin, was elected in Newfoundland between 1968 and 1974. Ontario elected a large proportion of members of ethnic origin because the majority of the ethnic groups were concentrated in that province. It should be noted, however, that this number of elected representatives represents a lower percentage than the ethnic population of Canada concentrated in this province which is 46.8 percent.[53] The relationship between these proportions was almost exactly the same in Quebec and Alberta. The discrepancies were the greatest in Manitoba and Saskatchewan, where the concentration rates were 6.6 percent and 5.6 percent, respectively.

The large number of members of European descent meant that the number belonging to visible minorities was minimal (8.3 percent of the parliamentary representation of the various ethnic groups). In the period from 1965 to 1988, moreover, members from visible minorities, unlike those from Europe, were more diverse: Lebanese, Chinese, Indonesian, Filipino, Guyanese and Black. In addition, a greater proportion were born outside Canada than was the case for MPs from all ethnic groups; that is, 40 percent (4 of 10) and 24 percent (34 of 120), respectively.

Most of the members from visible minorities were elected in Ontario (4 of 10) and Quebec (3 of 10). Nevertheless, there was a member of Chinese origin from British Columbia (Arthur Lee, Liberal, 1974), one of Indonesian origin from Saskatchewan (Simon de Jong, NDP, elected 1979, 1980, 1984, 1988) and one of Filipino origin from Manitoba (Rey Pagtakhan, Liberal, 1988). The three parties did not have equal numbers of visible-minority members. The Liberal Party had the most (6 of 10), the NDP were next (3 of 10), then the Conservatives, electing Alexander MacCauley, a Black (Hamilton West, Ontario, 1968).

Although the Liberals and NDP appear more open to ethnic pluralism, the Conservative party had the most members of ethnic origin elected: between 1965 and 1988, 46.3 percent of those elected ran under the Conservative banner. The Liberals followed with 38 percent and the NDP with 13.2 percent (tables 2.10 and 2.11). The Conservatives maintained this lead throughout the study period, except in 1968, when the Liberals were ahead. The fact that most of the Conservative party's members of ethnic origin come from northern

Table 2.10
Breakdown of members of ethnic origin by party, 1965–88

Ethnic origin	Liberal	PC	NDP	Others[a]	Total
Southern European	17	5	—	—	22
Northern and Eastern European	14	47	8	3	72
African and Arabic[b]	4	1		—	5
Asian, Indian, Filipino	2	—	1	—	3
Latin American[b]	1	—	1	—	2
Black	—	1	1	—	2
Jewish	7	1	5	—	13
Australian	1	—	—	—	1
New Zealander	—	1	—	—	1
Total	46[c]	56	16	3[c]	121[c]

[a]Includes Independent and Social Credit.
[b]The number of members in each of these categories does not correspond to the number of members belonging to the visible minorities (see notes 28 and 50).
[c]Horace Olson, of Norwegian origin, is counted twice here since he ran for the Social Credit in 1965 and the Liberals in 1968.

and Eastern Europe explains the phenomenon, since immigration from these countries took place much earlier and these members have more completely integrated into Canadian society. Also, as noted previously, this settlement was in western Canada, a Conservative party regional stronghold. Significantly, this distribution of ethnic groups among the three major parties reflects the distribution of seats in the House of Commons among the three parties. Between 1965 and 1988, the Conservatives held an average of 44.7 percent of the seats, the Liberals held 42.2 percent and the NDP held 10 percent.

We note that members belonging to ethnic groups are not found just in the three major parties. During the period the Social Credit party

Table 2.11
Breakdown of the members belonging to ethnic and visible minorities by party, 1965–88

Election	Minorities	Liberal	PC	NDP	Others	Total
1988	Ethnic	19	22	7	—	48
	Visible	3	—	3	—	6
1984	Ethnic	9	28	6	1[a]	44
	Visible	—	—	3	—	3
1980	Ethnic	14	19	7	—	40
	Visible	2	—	2	—	4
1979	Ethnic	12	25	3	—	40
	Visible	1	—	2	—	3
1974	Ethnic	12	17	4	—	33
	Visible	2	—	1	—	3
1972	Ethnic	8	15	7	—	30
	Visible	1	—	1	—	2
1968	Ethnic	18	8	5	—	31
	Visible	1	1	—	—	2
1965	Ethnic	8	12	3	2[b]	25
	Visible	—	—	—	—	0
1965–88	Ethnic	46	56	16	3[c]	121[d]
	Visible	6	1	3	—	10
%	Ethnic	38.0	46.3	13.2	2.5	100
	Visible	60.0	10.0	30.0	0.0	100

[a]Independent.
[b]Social Credit.
[c]One Independent and two Social Credit.
[d]Horace Olson, of Norwegian origin, is counted twice here since he ran for the Social Credit in 1965 and the Liberals in 1968.

elected two candidates of Norwegian origin: Bert Leboe (Cariboo, British Columbia, who won five elections between 1953 and 1965) and Horace Olson (Medicine Hat, Alberta, who ran successfully four times between 1957 and 1965). Olson was re-elected in the 1968 election, but as a Liberal. In addition, Antony Roman, of Czechoslovakian descent, was elected as an independent in York North (Ontario) in 1984.

Thus members from the various ethnic groups are most frequently found in the three major political organizations, usually the Conservative and Liberal parties; and visible minorities are most represented in the Liberal party.

It would be interesting to determine whether the profile of members which establishes their number, origin, and regional and party distribution corresponds to that of candidates. If these two profiles are not the same, it can be supposed that a selection process intervenes to create the differences. The main factors of this process depend on the party and community support which candidates of ethnic origin receive from their constituencies.

Ethnic Candidacies in 1988
This analysis is divided into two sections. The first concerns regional and party characteristics peculiar to ethnic candidacies. The second is directed to determining the success rate of candidates of ethnic origin and the factors that facilitate or hamper their election.

Ethnic, Regional and Party Characteristics
We found that the proportional representation of candidates belonging to ethnic groups and visible minorities was slightly better than that of members of the House of Commons. Ethnic candidates made up 18.2 percent of the candidates for the three major parties (16.3 percent in the House). For visible minorities, this proportion was 3.3 percent (2 percent in the House). Despite this similarity, there were differences.

The ethnic diversity of the population as a whole was better reflected in the origins of candidates. For example, the share of ethnic groups of European origin was 88.4 percent in the House and 78.3 percent for candidates. There are still many candidates of Italian, German, Ukrainian, Eastern European Jewish or Polish origin. Once again, Ontario provided most of the ethnic candidacies (41.5 percent, or 67 of 161). Quebec was next (21.1 percent), then British Columbia (13.7 percent), Alberta (10.6 percent), Saskatchewan and Manitoba (5.6 percent each). Nova Scotia had 1.9 percent. Unlike the situation in the House of Commons, ethnic groups were overrepresented in

Quebec, where they make up a total of 11.9 percent of the province's population. In the other provinces, the proportion of ethnic candidacies was very close to the concentration rates of the ethnic groups in each province.

Ethnic pluralism is becoming more pronounced, even within visible minorities. Certain ethnic groups, which are represented in candidacies, are not represented in the House. Thus, there were candidates of Egyptian, Kenyan, Korean, Tanzanian, Haitian, Chilean, Pakistani and Indian origin. Once again, Ontario had the most candidates belonging to visible minorities. However, most of those of Arabic origin were from Quebec (6 of 7), and there were almost as many candidates of Asian and Indian origin in British Columbia (4) as in Ontario (6).

The majority of candidates of ethnic origin, 62 percent, were born outside Canada, compared with 35 percent for the total ethnic population. According to the data obtained for members of the House of Commons, their place of birth does not seem to work against members who belong to visible minorities; in 1988 four of the six, or 67 percent, were born outside Canada. Place of birth does not seem to be a deterrent either to the candidacy or the election of members of these visible minorities. There are other negative factors, which will be discussed later, affecting the election of visible-minority candidates. From another perspective, women continue to be underrepresented at this level. Only 21 women of ethnic origin, or 13 percent of the total, have stood as candidates. This is, however, slightly more than the proportion of women members of the House of Commons of ethnic origin. We note that almost all of these candidacies are for the New Democratic Party, which ran 15 of the total 21, of whom nine were in Ontario.

In table 2.12, it can be seen that the Liberal party had the highest percentage of ethnic candidacies (36.6 percent, or 59 of 161). The NDP was close behind (34.2 percent, or 55 of 161), while the Conservatives were last (29.2 percent, or 47 of 161). Nevertheless, the Conservatives managed to elect the most candidates of ethnic origin in the last general election, three more than the Liberals (19) and 15 more than the NDP (7).

Candidacies by members of visible minorities were mainly in the parties that formed the opposition in the House of Commons in 1988, or since 1984. The Liberals and NDP each nominated 13 candidates, while the Conservatives nominated only three. The Liberals managed to get three candidates elected: Mark Assad (of Lebanese origin, in Quebec), Mac Harb (Lebanese, in Ontario) and Rey Pagtakhan (Filipino, in Manitoba). The NDP MPs elected were John Rodriguez (Guyanese, representing an Ontario riding), Howard McCurdy (Afro-Canadian, in Ontario) and Simon de Jong (born in Indonesia, representing a

Table 2.12
Breakdown of the candidates by ethnic origin by party, 1988

Ethnic origin	Liberal	PC	NDP	Total
Southern European	18	11	11	40
Northern and Eastern European	22	31	26	79
African and Arabic[a]	4	1	5	10
Asian, Indian, Filipino	9	2	5	16
Latin American, Haitian[a]	2	—	4	6
Black	—	—	2	2
Jewish	4	2	1	7
Australian	—	—	1	1
Total	59	47	55	161

[a]The number of candidates in each of these categories does not correspond to the number of candidates from the visible minorities (see notes 28 and 50).

Saskatchewan riding). The Conservatives were unsuccessful in electing any visible-minority candidates.

Success Rates and Winnable Ridings

We note, then, that not all candidacies from the different ethnic groups were successful in 1988. The success rate was 30 percent; 48 candidates of ethnic origin were elected of the 161 from all ethnic groups (table 2.13). However, candidates from visible minorities were at a greater disadvantage. Their success rate was only 21 percent; 6 of the 29 visible-minority candidates were elected. This does not differ greatly from the success rate of candidacies as a whole. In view of the single-member voting system and the number of seats in the House of Commons, the success rate for candidates of the three major parties was 33 percent (295 of 884). The rate was 19 percent for candidates of all parties (295 of 1 574).

These data can be misleading, but they do point to major problems. How can we improve the representation of ethnic groups and visible minorities when their success rates are almost comparable to those of the candidates of the three major parties or candidates as a whole? The success rate cannot be seen as a guarantee of proportional representation. It may also vary depending on the number of candidates from ethnic groups or visible minorities. Given the number of those who were elected, had the total number of ethnic candidates been higher,

Table 2.13
Representation of ethnic and visible-minority groups, 1988

Minorities	Ethnic and visible-minority candidates in relation to candidates as a whole		Ridings with ethnic and visible-minority candidates		Representation of ethnic and visible minorities in the House	
	N	%	*N*	%	*N*	%
Ethnic	161/884[a]	18.2	123/295	41.7	48/295	16.3
Visible	29/884[a]	3.3	27/295	9.2	6/295	2.0

[a]The Liberal party did not nominate a candidate in Etobicoke–Lakeshore.

the rate would have been lower. Conversely, it would have been higher had the number of candidates been lower. Absolutely proportional representation, however, is still possible. To achieve this, there must be 70 candidates of ethnic origin (see table 2.8) in different ridings, and these ridings must be safe for both the candidates and the parties they represent. In the 1988 election, this was not the case. In that election, 161 candidates of ethnic origin ran in 123 different electoral constituencies, but only 48 were elected (see table 2.13).

The assumption here is that these candidates were not nominated in the ridings where they could have been elected. Given the number of candidates elected, this assumption is supported by the fact that the three major political parties seemed reluctant to nominate a candidate of ethnic origin where another party had already done so. In 75 percent of the ridings (92 of 123),[54] there was only one ethnic candidacy among the three parties (table 2.14). The figure is even higher for visible minorities (93 percent, or 25 of 27). This was true in all the provinces where there were ethnic candidates. If the strategy of the parties was to maximize the chances of election for candidates of ethnic origin and, a fortiori, visible-minority candidates, there should have been a hope of at least 99 ethnic members in the House of Commons (seven ridings with three ethnic candidates and 92 where there was only one) and 25 visible-minority members (25 ridings where there was only one). However, only 48 candidates of ethnic origin were elected, of whom six were from visible minorities.

There are several explanations for this. Among them is shifting party loyalty within the electorate: favouring a party other than the one that had won the previous election. Thus, in Quebec, the Conservative party won a series of victories in the 1984 federal election, winning 58 of the 75 seats, when in the previous election of 1980, it had elected only one candidate, Roch Lasalle. Political parties' strategies alone cannot account

Table 2.14
Breakdown of ridings in relation to the number of ethnic and elected candidates, 1988

Province/ minorities	No. of Ridings	Candidates of ethnic origin[a]			Ridings with at least one ethnic candidate		Elected
		1	2	3	N	%	
Quebec	75						
Ethnic		18	5	2[b]	25	33.3	8
Visible		7	1	—	8	9.3	1
Ontario	99						
Ethnic		37	9	4	50	50.5	23
Visible		8	1	—	9	10.1	3
British Columbia	32						
Ethnic		11	4	1	16	50.0	5
Visible		4	—	—	4	12.5	—
Alberta	26						
Ethnic		11	3	—	14	53.8	5
Visible		3	—	—	3	11.5	—
Saskatchewan	14						
Ethnic		7	1	—	8	57.1	4
Visible		1		—	1	7.1	1
Manitoba	14						
Ethnic		5	2	—	7	50.0	3
Visible		2	—	—	2	14.3	1
Nova Scotia	7						
Ethnic		3	—	—	3	42.9	0
Visible		0	—	—	—	—	—
Canada	295						
Ethnic elected		92	24	7	123	41.7	48 (39%)
Visible elected		25	2	—	27	8.8	6 (23%)

[a]Including those who belong to visible-minority groups.
[b]Read table as follows: there are 2 ridings with 3 ethnic candidates, 5 with 2 and 18 with 1 from the 3 major parties. In total there are 25 ridings with at least 1 ethnic candidate. Among these, there are 8 ridings represented by an ethnic member in the House.

for this, at least as far as ethnic groups or visible minorities are concerned. Other factors can affect strategies, however, and it is these that should be analysed more thoroughly. Among them, two can be singled out: the community support candidates of ethnic origin have within their ridings; and their partisan support, that is, whether they are a sure win for the party. We will consider these two factors in the following examples (table 2.15).

Table 2.15
Breakdown of the number of ethnic candidates by ridings where ethnic groups make up 41% or more of the population, 1988

Total ethnic population in the riding (%)	No ethnic candidate	One ethnic candidate	Two or three ethnic candidates	Total
41–50	8	9	3	20
≥51	0	3	8	11

For the first factor, it could be assumed that where there were two or three candidates of ethnic origin, the parties would adopt a strategy that encouraged a shift in party loyalty within the ethnic electorate, especially in constituencies where there was a large ethnic population and ethnic questions were a decisive factor. This appears to be confirmed, because the number of ridings where there was a two- or three-way race and the number where the ethnic group population exceeded 41 percent were the same (31). But we observed that there were no similarities between these two types of ridings. In fact, in 20 cases out of 31, our assumption proved false. There were, therefore, other factors that led the parties to nominate two or three ethnic candidates in the same riding. Nevertheless, where the ethnic population reached 51 percent of the total population of a riding, the race was usually (8 times out of 11) between two or three ethnic candidates from the major parties.

If an ethnic population of 41 percent is taken as a threshold, the major political parties appear to have nominated most of their candidates in electoral constituencies where community support was not optimal. Had they done so, there would have been 93 ethnic candidacies in these 31 ridings, and given the characteristics of the single-member system, two out of three candidates would not have had partisan support. At first glance, it appears that the majority of the candidates of ethnic origin and those belonging to visible minorities were in ridings where the ethnic population was less than 41 percent. In fact, the different political parties tended to nominate these candidates in ridings where ethnic groups made up more than 10 percent of the population (table 2.16). This level is considered by some to be an appropriate threshold from which ethnic groups can seek electoral power (Boily et al. 1989).

However, few candidates can count solely on the support coming from their own group of origin. There were only 60 ridings out of 295 where one group made up more than 10 percent of the population. This fact is not unimportant, because it is not certain that the community's electors would have voted for a candidate from another ethnic group, especially if that candidate was running for the opposing party (Pelletier 1988). The hypothetical shift in party loyalty proposed by Wolfinger (1965) does not occur automatically in real life. The nature of the parties involved, the ideological diversity within different ethnic groups and the internal cohesive process all affect the situation.

In most cases, candidates from ethnic groups or visible minorities enjoyed the support of an ethnic electorate, since most of them ran in constituencies in which the ethnic electorate made up at least 10 percent of the population. Since this is the case, it seems at first glance that the three major parties nominated their ethnic candidates in electoral constituencies where they had an advantage. The number of ridings (104) with more than 10 percent of ethnic groups tends to confirm this. However, in view of the number of candidates elected, this supposition loses some of its force. It loses even more when the partisan bases of the candidates of ethnic origin and those belonging to visible minorities are analysed.

Table 2.16
Breakdown of the ethnic candidates in relation to the proportional size of the ethnic groups in the riding, 1988
(numbers)

Party minorities	Total ethnic groups			Same ethnic group as candidate (≥10%)
	0–10%	11–30%	≥31%	
NDP				
Ethnic	9	23	23	6
Visible	3	5	5	1
Liberal				
Ethnic	6	28	25	11
Visible	2	2	9	1
PC				
Ethnic	4	25	18	8
Visible	—	2	1	0
Canada				
Ethnic	19	76	66	25
Visible	5	9	15	2
%				
Ethnic	12	47	41	16
Visible	17	31	52	7

As for the second factor, because of the results of the 1984 election, most of the candidates of ethnic origin who ran in 1988 (71 percent) ran in ridings where their parties had not won in 1984. This trend was even more pronounced with visible minorities, where the proportion was 90 percent (table 2.17). This phenomenon was particularly evident in the case of the NDP in Quebec, where it nominated one-third of its candidates of ethnic origin (17 of 55), and where nearly half its candidates belonged to visible minorities (6 of 13).

These observations must be qualified by the consideration that the proportion of safe seats in Canada is smaller than, for example, that in either the United States or the United Kingdom (Lovink 1973, 358).[55] Thus, if the constituencies where the winning party changed between 1980 and 1984 are taken into account, as was the case for 40 percent of the ridings with candidates of ethnic origin, the unfavourable ridings rate falls from 71 percent to 60 percent. Only the Liberal party was affected, however, having won 20 favourable ridings for a total of 30.

In considering the possibility of a shift in party loyalty, another element must be used to determine the importance or lack of importance

Table 2.17
Partisan support: breakdown of ethnic candidates in relation to the ridings won by the party in the 1984 election, 1988

Party / minorities	Riding	
	Favourable	Unfavourable
NDP		
Ethnic	5	50
Visible	3	10
Liberal		
Ethnic	10	49
Visible	0	13
PC		
Ethnic	31	16
Visible	0	3
Canada		
Ethnic	46	115
Visible	3	26
%		
Ethnic	29	71
Visible	10	90

Note: A riding is called favourable when in 1988 a candidate ran in a riding the party won in 1984.

of electoral strongholds. This involves establishing the number of votes by which candidates of ethnic origin lost or won their elections in 1988. When they lost an election, most of the candidates of ethnic origin lost by a considerable margin: 79 percent of the candidates from ethnic groups and 87 percent of the candidates belonging to visible minorities lost their elections by more than 5 000 votes. These data correspond to those previously established for unfavourable ridings. On the other hand, when ethnic candidates won their elections, the situation was different. They won an absolute majority by more than 1 000 votes. Candidates of ethnic origin won their elections by more than 5 000 votes, while those belonging to visible minorities generally won by 1 000 to 5 000 votes (table 2.18).

The situation is somewhat less favourable for the visible minorities. It could be said that many were called, but few were chosen. To encourage the representation of ethnic groups, the major political parties must nominate ethnic candidates – especially those belonging to visible minorities – in winning ridings or those that are believed to be so. The

Table 2.18
Partisan support: breakdown of ethnic candidates in relation to the number of votes won in the election, 1988

Party / minorities	Elected by number of votes ($N = 48$) [6][a]			Beaten by number of votes ($N = 114$) [23][a]		
	0–999	1 000–4 999	≥5 000	0–999	1 000–4 999	≥5 000
NDP						
Ethnic	0	4	3	1	1	46
Visible	—	1	2	—	—	10
Liberal						
Ethnic	6	5	8	6	7	27
Visible	1	2	—	1	2	7
PC						
Ethnic	4	6	12	3	6	17
Visible	—	—	—	—	—	3
Canada						
Ethnic	10	15	23	10	14	90
Visible	1	3	2	1	2	20
%						
Ethnic	21	32	48	9	12	79
Visible	17	50	33	4	9	87

[a]The number in square brackets is the number of candidates or members from visible minorities; *N* is the total number of candidates from ethnic groups.

party strategy adopted in regard to these groups could be facilitated, however, with affirmative action legislation.

As noted earlier, it is partisan support that must be improved rather than community support. This can be verified by the example of electoral constituencies where only one of the three major political parties had a visible-minority candidate. Nazir Ahmad, for example, is a Pakistani who ran under the Liberal banner in the riding of Churchill (Manitoba), where ethnic groups made up 11.3 percent of the population. Ahmad lost to the NDP candidate by more than 9 000 votes. But in 1980 and 1984, the electors in this riding had already shown their preference for the NDP. In another example, the Liberals nominated a candidate of Chinese origin, Raymond Leung, in Vancouver East, where the Chinese population is 25.4 percent of the total (56.1 percent of the ethnic groups as a whole). However, he was not elected, placing second with 11 692 votes. The electors in this riding preferred to vote for the NDP, as they had done in both 1984 and 1980.

At the same time, it is not impossible for a candidate of ethnic origin to get elected without partisan support. Even if a riding's electors have voted for another party in the last two elections, such candidates can get elected if they have the solid backing of the community. That is what happened in Winnipeg North (Manitoba) in the last election. In 1988, that riding's electors, 71.9 percent of whom were from ethnic groups (13.3 percent Ukrainian), voted for the Liberal candidate, Rey Pagtakhan, a Filipino. This was despite the fact that the NDP had won the riding in 1980 (with a 9 044 vote majority) and 1984 (with a 5 504 vote majority). Furthermore, Pagtakhan won by 1 763 votes.

It is always possible for a candidate to get elected without either partisan or community support. For example, Howard McCurdy, an Afro-Canadian, successfully ran for the NDP in the riding of Windsor–Lake St. Clair (Ontario), where only 0.4 percent of the population is Black (24.2 percent for ethnic groups). In 1988, McCurdy was re-elected with a 2 723 vote majority. In 1984,[56] he had been elected by a 1 058 vote majority, even though the Liberals had won in 1980 with a 6 409 vote majority.

Ideally, a candidate of ethnic origin wants to have both community and partisan support. The candidacy of Alfonso Gagliano for the Liberal party in Saint-Léonard (Quebec) is an example. He had considerable community backing, with an Italian population making up 32.5 percent of the riding (44.2 percent for ethnic groups as a whole). In 1988, he was elected by a 5 959 majority (getting 23 014 votes). He had also won the 1984 election, by a 1 245 vote majority (getting 24 520 votes). In that election, he had the advantage of being in a riding that was already favourable to the Liberals since Monique Bégin had won the 1980 election there by a 38 487 vote majority (getting 42 228 votes). This solid backing helped Gagliano get elected. He did not, however, succeed in holding all the votes that had been won by the Liberals in 1980; therefore, one might assume based on the earlier discussion that the ethnic electorate, particularly the Italian electorate, made a big contribution to his victory.

The profile of candidates of ethnic origin is thus different from that of MPs of ethnic origin. The former have a much greater ethnic diversity than the latter. Moreover, while the Conservative party had the lowest number of ethnic candidacies, it had more elected than either the Liberals or the NDP. This was due mainly to the fact that all the parties, especially the Liberals, tended to nominate candidates of ethnic origin in electoral constituencies where, at least in 1988, the party was not sure of a victory.

In spite of this, candidates can get elected even if they do not have community or partisan support. The specific election issues, especially in local associations; what is said by a candidate of ethnic origin, and more generally by the various political parties; and the candidate's own personality, for example the degree of his or her socioprofessional involvement in the riding, can play a determining role.

CONCLUSION

We have dealt with five sociological, political and demographic factors that affect the political impact of ethnic groups. Among them, the maintenance of ethnic identity is the most decisive. Also, becoming a citizen (a condition for the right to vote), registration on electoral lists (a condition for exercising the right to vote) and electoral participation (exercise of the right to vote) are all important. Ethnic groups, however, must still represent a sizable part of the population and, more importantly, be concentrated in the electoral constituencies. As we have observed, this last condition does exist in Canada. We note that legislators, as they draw the electoral boundaries, seem to favour ethnic pluralism over the concentration of one ethnic group. If they intend to promote the political integration of different ethnic groups, this appears to be the most desirable approach.

The political activities of different ethnic groups can also take various forms. Crewe (1983) identifies four types of strategies that they can adopt: form their own party; nominate independent candidates; give overwhelming voting support to a candidate; and nominate candidates of ethnic origin to run for the major political parties. Abstention is another possible strategy. The first two of these strategies are not really practised in Canada: there is no ethnic party on the federal scene, and there were only 14 independent candidates of ethnic origin (out of 54) during the last federal election. Only one independent candidate of ethnic origin was elected to the House of Commons between 1965 and 1988. Moreover, we have seen that the ethnic vote is not always guaranteed because of ideological diversity within the group. Finally, we note that having candidates of ethnic origin within the major political parties is a strategy designed by the parties to win over that part of the electorate, and by the ethnic groups, wanting to assert their specific interests. In Canada, particularly in the House of Commons, this last strategy has been given practical empirical verification.

This study was conducted in two phases: on candidates elected between 1965 and 1988; and on ethnic candidacies during the 1988 election. It shows that representation of ethnic groups in the House of Commons is not proportional to the total ethnic population, although it closely approaches the level of the immigrant population. Visible minorities are in an even less favourable situation. However, whether we are talking of ethnic groups as a whole or more specifically of visible minorities, their representation has improved greatly since 1965. For the whole period studied, it was the Conservative party that was the most successful in electing members of ethnic origin. This is explained by the fact that almost all of these had northern and Eastern European ancestry, and that most of the ethnic groups they sought to represent also had these origins. In addition, these Europeans settled in great numbers in western Canada, traditionally an electoral stronghold for the Conservatives. NDP members of ethnic origin also have mostly northern and Eastern European origins.

The Liberal party, however, has the most MPs belonging to visible minorities. This is because the ethnic groups that have immigrated recently (as have most visible minorities in Canada) tend to support more progressive parties (Portes and Mozo 1985). It was a Liberal government, for example, that adopted the policy of multiculturalism and the *Canadian Charter of Rights and Freedoms.*

Analysis of these candidacies shows that the diversity of their origins reflects the ethnic pluralism of the Canadian population; however, this is not found in the Conservative party. Although the proportion of ethnic candidacies does not correspond perfectly to that of ethnic groups in the population, the number of candidates of ethnic origin is significant. In 1988 there were 161 candidates of ethnic origin running in 123 ridings. As our electoral system could permit election of only one member per riding, there was a potential for 123 ethnic candidates to be elected. However, only 48 candidates won election in 1988. Two factors could explain this: community support and partisan support.

We note that candidates of ethnic origin generally run in ridings where the ethnic community makes up more than 10 percent of the population. This seems to have a more favourable impact on candidates belonging to visible minorities than on candidates of ethnic origin as a whole. However, very few can count on such support from their ethnic group of origin. This is because few ridings have such populations (60 of 295). Here the situation is less favourable for those belonging to visible minorities. The weakness of support from the group of origin is largely because of the electoral boundaries, which favour ethnic pluralism.

The majority of the candidates, however, do not have partisan support. The (absolute) majority run in ridings where their party lost during the previous election. In addition, the defeated candidates generally lose by more than 5 000 votes. In both cases, candidates from visible minorities have less of a chance than candidates of ethnic origin as a whole.

The results show that the most decisive factor is partisan support; however, it is not indispensable. In fact, some candidates of ethnic origin are elected with the solid backing of the whole community. This community support neutralizes the lack of partisan support. A candidate of ethnic origin, however, may succeed in getting elected without either community or partisan support. In this case, other factors play a decisive role; for example, candidates' assets (speaking ability, degree of socioprofessional involvement within the riding) and the way they are perceived by the electorate. The candidates' degree of ethnic identification probably plays a significant role here; however, we need a more thorough analysis of these factors to verify their scope. After all, it is clear that candidates of ethnic origin are at an advantage when running in electoral constituencies where they can benefit from both community and partisan support.

In view of the increase in ethnic groups within the population, their representation is also likely to increase in the years to come. It could be accelerated, however, through affirmative legislation aimed at encouraging political parties to nominate more candidates from the ethnic communities, particularly those belonging to visible minorities, and to nominate them in constituencies that are favourable. Political parties, especially those that are most likely to form the government, must be able to reflect the ethnic pluralism in Canadian society adequately, thereby avoiding situations that could lead to ethnic or racial tension.

RECOMMENDATIONS

As a result, we recommend the following:

1. Citizenship should be retained as a condition for the right to vote.
2. A permanent electoral list should be drawn up and polling-day registration extended to the electorate in the urban areas.
3. Enumerators should be appointed who are able to speak the language of the target ethnic electorate.
4. Political training programs should be run jointly by ethnic organizations and Elections Canada.
5. Respect for ethnic pluralism and the localization of communities of interest should be considered as a basis for drawing up electoral boundaries.
6. Affirmative measures should be implemented to encourage political parties to respect the pluralist nature of Canadian society. These measures should favour the nomination and election of candidates from ethnic groups.

ABBREVIATIONS

am.	amended
c.	chapter
R.S.C.	Revised Statutes of Canada
s(s).	section(s)
S.C.	Statutes of Canada

NOTES

The author would like to thank Kathy Megyery and Robert Boily for their valuable comments on some elements of this research as well as an anonymous reviewer for comments on an early draft of this text. Thanks also to Cécile Boucher, who helped to compile some of the data, and to Élise Juneau, for secretarial support.

In this study, quoted material that originated in French has been translated into English.

1. As far as we know, there is no study comparing ethnic groups' representation at the different governmental or administrative levels in Canada. Such an analysis was done in the United States on the situation of Black Americans for the period 1970–77 (Hamilton 1978). However, that study has the drawback of presenting the absolute number of Afro-Americans at the various governmental levels without indicating what proportion they made up of all those elected.

2. This section is a modified and augmented version of Pelletier (1988, 2–46).

3. Anderson and Frideres (1981) list four other approaches: Marxist, evolutionist, structuro-functionalist and sociodemographic.

4. The distinction between centre and periphery was established by Lewin (1965). To some extent, these divisions are called into question by Higham, who asks in particular whether the centre is located in the traditional or innovative strata. Moreover, unlike Lewin, Higham considers that the periphery can be "an expanding frontier or a zone of reciprocal influence and mutual accommodation" (1978, 2). Despite reopening the question, Higham (1980) identifies three types of ethnic leadership, of which the first two refer to the centre and the third to the periphery: "received leadership," authority structure deriving from the country of origin; "internal leadership," putting down roots within the group; and "projective leadership," putting down roots within the society. For his part, Martiniello (1988, 20) distinguishes between leaders who almost entirely limit their actions to the centre or the periphery and those whose action takes place in between the two. This is the classification with which we agree.

5. It must be stressed here that certain authors refer solely to objective criteria; see, for example, Banton (1971).

6. On religion as a factor contributing to ethnic identification see, in particular, McLellan (1987), who analyses the case of those of Tibetan origin in Ontario.

7. According to Bredimas-Assimopoulos, "desocialization and resocialization often occur at the same time" (1975, 139). In this regard, see Newman (1978, 45).

8. On the role and management of the immigrant workforce in advanced capitalist societies, see Labelle et al. (1983, 81–82).

9. For his part, Lieberson (1985, 31–43) basically recognizes only two social groups, namely "migrants–indigenous" based on "superordinate-subordinate distinctions."

10. It should be pointed out that this study will be confined to immigrants and their descendants. Thus, Aboriginals, who are recognized as a people (*Canadian Charter of Rights and Freedoms*, s. 5(2)), are not included here. Owing to historical and social factors, British and French are not included either.

11. For an analysis of these policies see, in particular, Guay (1986). It should not be thought that all government policies to this end are received favourably. Such was the case, for example, with the PELO (heritage language training) program, which threatened the power of the Greek élite (Bredimas-Assimopoulos 1983, 114).

12. According to Ringer and Lawless (1989, 10), "Dispersion of the ghetto of the first-generation immigrant did not generally mean the dissolution of the ethnic enclave; instead there arose what Kramer and Leventman have called the 'gilded ghetto' of the second and third generation."

13. As an example, the study by Abu-Laban (1981, 173) reveals that 54 percent of Arabs favour endogamy. It should be stressed that according to Alpalhâo and Da Rosa (1980, 141), "endogamy should increase in proportion to the density of ethnic concentration."

14. In this connection see, in particular, Bredimas-Assimopoulos (1983, 109), whose study reveals that 44 percent of Greeks limit their friendships exclusively to the members of the group, and Anctil (1984, 444), who shows that Jews make up to 90 percent of their friends within the Jewish community.

15. In this regard, reference can be made to the adoption in Canada in 1923 of the federal Act relating to Chinese immigration, "which affected all people of Chinese origin or descent, except for diplomats, tradespeople, students and children born in Canada" (Bouthillier 1982, 113). For the United States, see the *Chinese Exclusion Act* of 1882.

16. For a review, albeit incomplete, of the literature on integration concepts (accommodation, acculturation, cultural pluralism, social integration and assimilation), see Gavaki (1977, 4–10).

17. According to Bredimas-Assimopoulos, the term *assimilation* has an ethnocentric character insofar as the "objective to be attained [thus] consists in bringing about the ideological and cultural standardization of the ethnic components" (1983, 115–16), whereas the term *integration* "does not necessarily imply that the individual loses his identity but rather signifies 'trouble-free entry' into the host society" (ibid.).

18. Milton Gordon (cited by Newman 1978, 43) saw assimilation as being cumulative and linear, with cultural assimilation inevitably leading to structural integration. This concept of linearity, linked to the theory of assimilation and that of integration, has proven to be a failure (Bredimas-Assimopoulos 1975, 130; 1983, 115). However, Driedger (1985) sees the assimilation–pluralism axis as a continuum. On the basis of this continuum and the voluntary–involuntary axis, Driedger arrives at a conceptual model involving three outcomes: assimilation, amalgamation and pluralism: "In the case of assimilation, minorities lose their separate identities and become like the majority group. In the case of amalgamation, all melt into one pot, with no one remaining distinct. In the case of pluralism, each group has a right to maintain a distinct identity if it has the will and can maintain a distinctive structure" (ibid., 172).

19. It should be stressed that Parenti (1969) does not use the term *integration* but (cultural) *assimilation*.

20. It should be pointed out that the situational school treats the formation of ethnic groups in the same way as that of any other group: "this is a necessary consequence of the premise of individually self-interested action" (Hechter 1986, 19).

21. That is to say, "problem-specific, temporary, voluntary, and lateral (rather than vertical) ... no one of which is sufficiently powerful to determine the actions of the rest" (Turk 1973; cited by Breton 1983, 31).

22. Here, "the member organizations keep part of their autonomy, but agree to delegate certain powers or functions to the central body. The latter has its own field of initiative. It also has a co-ordinating role and is responsible for managing services which are common to all the organizations in the field" (Breton 1983, 31).

23. For an analysis of the relationships between the family and the humanization and ethnicization of the newborn, see Juteau-Lee (1983, 44–53).

24. This was the case, for example, with the Greek community in Montreal, which was founded in 1980 and is restructuring and overseeing four Greek churches and several associations. For a retrospective view of the evolution of this community and the feuds within it, see Gavaki (1983, 133–36).

25. Note that Bredimas-Assimopoulos (1975) develops the concept of civic integration. The indices of such integration are length of stay, acquisition of the nationality, the decision to stay and the degree of language skill.

26. As far as we know, no study in Canada has delved into this question. These comments result from reflections on televised reports during the 1989 election campaign in Quebec and the depositions of ethnic organizations before the Royal Commission on Electoral Reform and Party Financing.

27. Statistics Canada establishes 10 categories in its definition of visible minorities: Blacks (Haitians, West Indians, etc.); Indo-Pakistanis; Chinese; Koreans; Japanese; Southeast Asians and Filipinos; west Asians and Arabs; Pacific Islanders; and Latin Americans (except Argentinians and Chileans). These groups must not be confused with ethnic origin. To make up these groups, Statistics Canada combines a series of criteria such as ethnic origin, place of birth and mother tongue. See Canada, Statistics Canada (1990).

28. The demographic profile was established on the basis of Statistics Canada data (1986 census). It should be stressed that these data involve a certain margin of error related, in particular, to the hypothesis of underenumeration, which is usually estimated at 3 percent (Serré 1989).

29. These percentages are established on the basis of single responses only. In the 1986 census, 3.8 percent were multiple responses.

30. Although this criterion has some advantages, it also has limitations: "Unlike country of birth, ethnic origin makes it possible better to define a particular ethnic group; it does not involve the problem of ethnic coexistence at the territorial level or that of national boundaries. However, this criterion

also has its limits since it does not correspond to a person's cultural affiliation but rather to that of his ancestors at the moment they arrived on the continent unless he immigrated on his own" (Baillargeon and Ste-Marie 1984, 116).

31. Includes 19.5 percent British multiple responses.

32. The first group includes 3.4 percent French multiple responses; the second, 1.5 percent Aboriginal people's multiple responses.

33. Includes 4.7 percent multiple responses other than British, French or Aboriginal people.

34. Based on single ethnic origin.

35. Based on the categories available: Black, German, Italian, Ukrainian, Chinese, Dutch, South Asian, Jewish and Polish (Canada, Statistics Canada 1988).

36. Even though the commissions perform this operation on the basis of the demographic map of the province, which is broken down, in particular, by census tract and represents a relatively homogeneous sociodemographic unit.

37. Considered here are the electoral constituencies of Vancouver Kingsway (Burnaby Kingsway in 1988), Vancouver South, Vancouver Quadra, Vancouver East and Vancouver Centre.

38. So that in 1988 the boundaries of Vancouver Kingsway (Burnaby Kingsway) were essentially in Burnaby.

39. On the importance of abstention from elections see Goguel (1954) and Dupeux (1954).

40. Note that, in some electoral constituencies, there is more than one independent ethnic candidature. That was the case, for example, in the riding of Lincoln (Ontario), where we find A. Papazian, D. Olchowecki and A. Stasiuk.

41. For an analysis of actual instances of the strategies political parties adopt with regard to ethnic groups, see Layton-Henry (1978), Le Lohé (1979), and Stasiulis and Abu-Laban (1991).

42. See also Parenti (1969). As an example, we note that Abu-Laban's study (1981, 79) reveals that 45 percent of Arabs have immigrated to obtain social and professional advancement.

43. The size is difficult to assess. If an overwhelming vote in favour of one party on the part of the ethnic electorate is assumed, it is possible for an ethnic group to hold the balance of power even if it does not constitute an absolute majority (51 percent) of the electorate, depending on the size of any partisan split that exists within the majority ethnic group.

44. It should be noted that the portrait presented here is that of the composition of the House of Commons after a general election. This portrait does not, therefore, include members elected during by-elections.

45. In this regard, it should be noted that the study by Kornberg and Mishler (1976, 52) on the 28th Canadian Parliament met with a 72 percent response rate even after "the good offices of friendly MPs, cabinet ministers, colleagues in Canadian universities, and even members of the media, were used to try to persuade recalcitrant MPs to change their minds and participate in the study."

46. See New Democratic Party (1988); Liberal Party of Canada (1988); Progressive Conservative Party of Canada (1988); Bejermi (1982, 1985, 1989); *Canada's 28th Parliament* (1971); Canada, Library of Parliament (1987); Canada, House of Commons (1989); *Canadian Parliamentary Guide*. There are already studies based on such documents, for example, Kornberg et al. (1982), which paints a portrait of the members of the provincial legislatures in 1977, and Barrie and Gibbins (1989), which deals with the careers of Canadian members of Parliament from 1867 to 1984. For Quebec, there are studies by Boily (1969) and Pelletier (1984).

47. Despite the fact that ethnic identity is a concept generally reserved for immigrants and their descendants, some were excluded because they belonged to or had a sociological link with the groups of British or French origin. That is the case for those who were born in Great Britain and France. It is also the case for Americans of Anglo-Saxon origin. There is some merit in specifying that the country of birth did not in itself constitute a selection criterion. Some people born abroad were excluded from this enumeration owing to their British or French origin; that is the case for Pat Carney (born in China) and John Fraser (born in Japan).

48. Let us mention a few examples where there was no biographical information to enable us to determine the exact ethnic origin. Among MPs: Mark Assad (Liberal, Quebec, 1988), Stan Hovdebo (NDP, Saskatchewan, 1980–84–88) and Pat Sobeski (Conservative, Ontario, 1988). Among the candidates: Tariq Anwar Alvi (NDP, Quebec), Tony Csinos (Liberal, Ontario) and Ken Boschcoff (Conservative, Ontario).

49. Sergio Marchi (Argentinian, MP, Liberal, Ontario, 1984–88) and Jaime Llambias-Wolff (Chilean, candidate, NDP, Quebec, 1988) were thus not included in the visible minorities (see note 27). The same goes for Latin Americans whose exact ethnic origin could not be determined, which was the case for Tony Csinos (Liberal, candidate, Ontario, 1988) and Alice Lambrinos (NDP, candidate, Ontario, 1988). MP George Chatterton (born in South Africa, Conservative, British Columbia, 1962–65) and the candidate Anne Adelson (born in South Africa, NDP, Ontario, 1988) were also not included among the visible minorities.

50. However, Franks (1987) does not refer to any source to support this assertion.

51. This percentage includes MPs of Jewish origin, many of whom personally immigrated from Europe, rather than their ancestors.

52. Single ethnic origin only.

53. Based on ethnic origin only.

54. This situation is not peculiar to the national parties; the same goes for the major provincial parties in Quebec (Pelletier 1988, 156).

55. Note that Lovink (1973) used the periods 1952–60 (five elections) in the case of the United States, 1950–60 (six elections) in the case of the United Kingdom and 1953–65 (six elections) in the case of Canada. The proportions of seats that remained with the same parties in these elections were 78.2 percent, 77.0 percent and 23.6 percent, respectively.

56. This was the riding of Windsor–Walkerville, now Windsor–Lake St. Clair.

REFERENCES

Abu-Laban, B. 1981. *La Présence arabe au Canada*. Ottawa: Cercle du Livre de France.

Alpalhâo, A., and V. Da Rosa. 1980. *A Minority in a Changing Society: The Portuguese Communities of Quebec*. Ottawa: University of Ottawa Press.

Anctil, P. 1984. "Double majorité et multiplicité ethnoculturelle à Montréal." *Recherches sociographiques* 25 (3): 441–56.

Anderson, A.B., and J.S. Frideres. 1981. *Ethnicity in Canada: Theoretical Perspectives*. Toronto: Butterworths.

Bailey, H., and E. Katz, eds. 1969. "Ethnic Groups and Political Behavior." In *Ethnic Group Politics*. Columbus, OH: Merrill.

Baillargeon, M., and G. Ste-Marie. 1984. *Quelques caractéristiques ethnoculturelles de la population du Québec*. Cahier no. 2. Montreal: Ministère des Communautés culturelles et de l'Immigration du Québec.

Balgopal, P.R. 1984. "Ethnic Minority Leadership: A Theoretical Perspective." *Journal of Sociology and Social Welfare* 11 (2): 381–408.

Banton, M. 1971. *Sociologie des relations raciales*. Paris: Payot.

Barrie, D., and R. Gibbins. 1989. "Parliamentary Careers in the Canadian Federal State." *Canadian Journal of Political Science* 22:137–46.

Bejermi, J. 1982, 1985, 1989. *Canadian Parliamentary Handbook*. Ottawa: Borealis Press.

Black, J.H., and C. Leithner. 1988. "Immigrants and Political Involvement in Canada: The Role of the Ethnic Media." *Canadian Ethnic Studies* 20 (1): 1–20.

Boily, R. 1969. "Les candidats élus et les candidats battus." In *Quatre élections provinciales au Québec 1956–1966,* ed. Vincent Lemieux. Quebec: Presses de l'Université Laval.

Boily, R., A. Pelletier and P. Serré. 1988. "Le Pluralisme ethnique et les élections fédérales." *Le Devoir.* Series of two articles, 8–9 December.

———. 1989. "Pluralisme et élections." *Le Devoir.* Series of two articles, 15–16 September.

———. 1990. "Bilan des connaissances : le comportement électoral des groupes ethniques dans la région de Montréal." Paper presented at *25 ans de science politique,* a colloquium held by the Quebec Society of Political Science, ACFAS Congress, May, Université Laval.

Bouthillier, G. 1982. *Immigration et politique dans les pays industriels depuis 1945.* Studies and Documents no. 10. Quebec: Ministère des Communautés culturelles et de l'Immigration du Québec.

———. 1987. *Les Politiques menées par certains États de democratie libérale à l'endroit des communautés issues de l'immigration internationale.* Studies and Documents no. 11. Quebec: Ministère des Communautés culturelles et de l'Immigration du Québec.

Bredimas-Assimopoulos, N. 1975. "Intégration civique sans acculturation. Les Grecs à Montréal." *Sociologie et sociétés* 2 (2): 129–42.

———. 1983. "Dynamique et évolution socio-politique du Québec : le cas de la population grecque de Montréal." *Sociologie et sociétés* 15 (2): 105–16.

Breton, R. 1983. "La Communauté ethnique, communauté politique." *Sociologie et sociétés* 15 (2): 23–38.

Canada. *Canada Elections Act,* R.S.C. 1985, c. E-2, s. 147.

———. *Canadian Charter of Rights and Freedoms,* s. 5, Part I of the *Constitution Act, 1982,* being Schedule B of the *Canada Act 1982* (U.K.), 1982, c. 11.

———. *Chinese Immigration Act, 1923,* S.C. 1923, c. 38.

———. *Citizenship Act,* R.S.C. 1985, c. C-29.

———. *Electoral Boundaries Readjustment Act,* R.S.C. 1985, c. E-3, s. 15, am. S.C. 1986, c. 8, s. 6.

Canada. House of Commons. 1989. *Photo Album of the Members of the House of Commons, 34th Parliament.* Ottawa: House of Commons, Public Information Office.

Canada. Library of Parliament. 1987. *Parliamentarians of Ukrainian Origin.* Ottawa: LOP, Information and Technical Services Branch.

Canada. Royal Commission on Bilingualism and Biculturalism. 1970. *Report,* Book 4. Ottawa: Queen's Printer.

Canada. Statistics Canada. 1988. *Federal Electoral Districts – 1987 Representation Order: Part 2.* Cat. no. 94-134. Ottawa: Canadian Government Publishing Centre.

————. 1989a. *Ethnicity, Immigration and Citizenship.* Cat. no. 93-109. Ottawa: Minister of Supply and Services Canada.

————. 1989b. *Profile of Ethnic Groups.* Cat. no. 93-154. Ottawa: Minister of Supply and Services Canada.

————. 1990. *Profile of Visible Minorities and Aboriginal Peoples. Employment and Equity Program.* Ottawa: Statistics Canada.

Canada's 28th Parliament: A Guide to the Members, Their Constituencies and Their Government. 1971. Toronto: Methuen.

Canadian Parliamentary Guide. 1966, 1969, 1973, 1975, 1979, 1980, Spring 1989. Ottawa.

Cappon, P. 1974. *Conflits entre les néo-canadiens et les francophones de Montréal.* Quebec: Presses de l'Université Laval.

Charlot, J., and M. Charlot. 1985. "Les groupes politiques dans leur environnement." In *Traité de science politique,* ed. Madeleine Grawitz and Jean Leca. Paris: Presses universitaires de France.

Crewe, I. 1983. "Representation and the Ethnic Minorities in Britain." In *Ethnic Pluralism and Public Policy,* ed. Nathan Glazer and Ken Young. London: Heinemann Educational Books.

Donefer, R. 1984. "Les Juifs québécois et le changement politique au Québec : une analyse du *Canadian Jewish News* : 1967–1981." In *Juifs et réalités juives au Québec,* ed. Pierre Anctil and Gary Caldwell. Montreal: Institut québécois de recherche sur la culture.

Driedger, L. 1985. "Conformity vs. Pluralism: Minority Identities and Inequalities." In *Minorities and the Canadian State,* ed. Neil Nevitte and Allan Kornberg. Oakville: Mosaic Press.

Dupeux, G. 1954. "La Sociologie électorale. 2. Pays anglo-saxons." In *Sociologie politique. Esquisse d'un bilan : guide de recherche,* ed. F. Goguel and G. Dupeux. Paris: Colin.

Economic Council of Canada. 1991. *Au courant* 11 (3).

Fitzgerald, M. 1983. "Are Blacks an Electoral Liability?" *New Society,* 8 December, 394–95.

Franks, C.E.S. 1987. *The Parliament of Canada.* Toronto: University of Toronto Press.

Gavaki, E. 1977. *The Integration of Greeks in Canada.* San Francisco: R & E Research Associates.

————. 1983. "Urban Villagers: The Greek Community in Montreal." In *Two Nations, Many Cultures. Ethnic Groups in Canada*. 2d ed., ed. Jean Leonard Elliot. Scarborough: Prentice-Hall Canada.

Gérard-Libois, J. 1990. Élections et électeurs en Belgique. Brussels: CRISP.

Goguel, F. 1954. "La Sociologie électorale. 1. France." In *Sociologie politique. Esquisse d'un bilan : guide de recherche*, ed. F. Goguel and G. Dupeux. Paris: Colin.

Guarnieri, Albina. 1990. Testimony before the Royal Commission on Electoral Reform and Party Financing, 12 June. Ottawa.

Guay, D. 1986. *Réflexions critiques sur les politiques ethniques du gouvernement fédéral et du gouvernement du Québec*. Montreal: Centre international de documentation et d'information haïtienne-caraibéenne et afro-canadienne.

Hahn, H., and R.W. Holland. 1976. *American Government: Minority Rights versus Majority Rule*. New York: John Wiley and Sons.

Hamilton, C.V. 1978. "Blacks and Electoral Politics." *Social Policy* 9 (1): 21–27.

Hechter, M. 1986. "Theories of Ethnic Relations." In *The Primordial Challenge: Ethnicity in the Contemporary World*, ed. J.F. Stack. New York: Greenwood Press.

Higham, J. 1978. "Introduction: The Forms of Ethnic Leadership." In *Ethnic Leadership in America*, ed. John Higham. Baltimore, MD: Johns Hopkins University Press.

————. 1980. "Leadership." In *Harvard Encyclopedia of American Ethnic Groups*, ed. Stephen Thernstrom. Cambridge, MA: Harvard University Press.

Humphrey, C.R., and H. Brock Louis. 1973. "Assimilation and Voting Behavior: A Study of Greek-Americans." *International Migration Review* 7 (1): 34–45.

Isajiw, W. 1980. "Definitions of Ethnicity." In *Ethnicity and Ethnic Relations in Canada*, ed. Rita M. Bienvenue and Jay E. Goldstein. Toronto: Butterworths.

Jedwab, J. 1986. "Uniting Uptowners and Downtowners: The Jewish Electorate and Quebec Provincial Politics 1927–1939." *Canadian Ethnic Studies* 18 (2): 7–19.

Juteau-Lee, D. 1983. "La Production de l'ethnicité ou la part réelle de l'idéel." *Sociologie et sociétés* 15 (2): 39–54.

Kasfir, N. 1979. "Explaining Ethnic Political Participation." *World Politics* 31 (3): 365–88.

Kornberg, A., and W.T.E. Mishler. 1976. *Influence in Parliament: Canada*. Durham, NC: Duke University Press.

Kornberg, A., W.T.E. Mishler and H.D. Clarke. 1982. *Representative Democracy in the Canadian Provinces*. Scarborough: Prentice-Hall Canada.

Labelle, M., S. Larose and V. Piché. 1983. "Émigration et immigration : les Haïtiens au Québec." *Sociologie et sociétés* 15 (2): 73–88.

Lane, R. 1969. "The Way of Ethnics in Politics." In *Ethnic Group Politics*, ed. H. Bailey and E. Katz. Columbus, OH: Merrill.

Lavigne, G. 1980. "Le Pouvoir ethnique : ses assises et ses objets." In *La Transformation du pouvoir au Québec*. Montreal: Albert St. Martin.

Layton-Henry, Z. 1978. "Race, Electoral Strategy and the Major Parties." *Parliamentary Affairs* 31 (3): 268–81.

Lefebvre, M., and Y. Oryschuk. 1985. *Les Communautés culturelles du Québec*. Montreal: Fides.

Leifer, E.M. 1981. "Competing Models of Political Mobilization: The Role of Ethnic Ties." *American Journal of Sociology* 87 (1): 23–47.

Le Lohé, M. 1979. "The Effects of the Presence of Immigrants upon the Local Political System in Bradford, 1945–77." In *Racism and Political Action in Britain*, ed. Robert Miles and Annie Phizacklea. London: Routledge and Kegan Paul.

Leslie, P. 1969. "The Role of Political Parties in Promoting the Interest of Ethnic Minorities." *Canadian Journal of Political Science* 2:419–33.

Lewin, K. 1965. "The Problem of Minority Leadership." In *Studies in Leadership*, ed. Alvin Gouldner. New York: Russell and Russell.

Liberal Party of Canada. 1988. *Notes biographiques des candidats*. Ottawa.

Lieberson, S. 1985. "A Societal Theory of Race and Ethnic Relations." In *Ethnicity and Ethnic Relations in Canada*. 2d ed., ed. Rita M. Bienvenue and Jay E. Goldstein. Toronto: Butterworths.

Lipset, S.M. 1967. *L'Homme et la politique*. Paris: Seuil.

Lipset, S.M., P. Lazarsfeld, A. Barton and J. Linz. 1954. "The Psychology of Voting: An Analysis of Political Behavior." In *Handbook of Social Psychology*, vol. II, ed. G. Lindszey. Reading, MA: Addison-Wesley.

Lovink, J.A.A. 1973. "Is Canadian Politics Too Competitive?" *Canadian Journal of Political Science* 6 (3): 341–79.

Martiniello, M. 1988. *Élites, leadership et pouvoir dans les communautés ethniques d'origine immigrée : vers une approche théorique*. Brussels: Sybidi-Academia.

Massicotte, L., and A. Bernard. 1985. *Le Scrutin au Québec : un miroir déformant*. Cahiers du Québec. Montreal: Hurtubise HMH.

McLellan, J. 1987. "Religion and Ethnicity: The Role of Buddhism in Maintaining Ethnic Identity among Tibetans in Lindsay, Ontario." *Canadian Ethnic Studies* 19 (1): 63–75.

Mohl, R.A. 1986. "The Politics of Ethnics in Contemporary Miami." *Migration World* 14 (3): 7–11.

New Democratic Party. 1988. *Notes biographiques des candidats*. Ottawa.

Newman, W. 1978. "Theoretical Perspective for Analysis of Social Pluralism." In *The Canadian Ethnic Mosaic: A Quest for Identity*, ed. Leo Driedger. Toronto: McClelland and Stewart.

Olsen, D. 1985. "The Political Elite." In *Party Politics in Canada*. 5th ed., ed. Hugh G. Thorburn. Scarborough: Prentice-Hall Canada.

Painchaud, C., and R. Poulin. 1983. "Italianité, conflit linguistique et structure de pouvoir dans la communauté italo-québécoise." *Sociologie et sociétés* 15 (2): 89–104.

Parenti, M. 1969. "Ethnic Politics and the Persistence of Ethnic Identification." In *Ethnic Group Politics*, ed. H. Bailey and E. Katz. Columbus, OH: Merrill.

Pelletier, A. 1988. "Minorisation politique des francophones au Québec : les élections provinciales dans la région métropolitaine de Montréal (1966–1985)." MA thesis, Department of Political Science, Université de Montréal.

Pelletier, R. 1984. "Le Personnel politique." *Recherches sociographiques* 25 (1): 83–102.

Perron, J. 1979. "Les Minorités au Québec." In *Dossier Québec*, ed. Jean Sarrazin and Claude Glayman. Montreal: Stock.

Portes, A., and R. Mozo. 1985. "The Political Adaptation Process of Cubans and Other Ethnic Minorities in the United States: A Preliminary Analysis." *International Migration Review* 19 (1): 35–63.

Progressive Conservative Party of Canada. 1988. *Notes biographiques des candidats*. Ottawa.

Ringer, B.B., and E.R. Lawless. 1989. *Race – Ethnicity and Society*. New York: Routledge.

Samuel, T.J. 1988. "Immigration and Visible Minorities in the Year 2001: A Projection." *Canadian Ethnic Studies* 20 (2): 92–100.

Serré, P. 1989. "De quelques paramètres d'une victoire anti-dépendantiste au Québec : impact électoral du pluralisme ethnique dans la région métropolitaine. Tendances actuelles et prospectives (1970–1986)." MA thesis, Department of Political Science, Université de Montréal.

Simard, C. 1991. "Visible Minorities and the Canadian Political System." In *Ethno-cultural Groups and Visible Minorities in Canadian Politics: The Question of Access*, ed. Kathy Megyery. Vol. 7 of the research studies of the

Royal Commission on Electoral Reform and Party Financing. Ottawa and Toronto: RCERPF/Dundurn.

Simon, P. -J. 1983. "Le Sociologie et les minorités : connaissance et idéologie." *Sociologie et sociétés* 15 (2): 9–21.

Stack, J.F. 1986. "Ethnic Mobilization in World Politics: The Primordial Perspective." *The Primordial Challenge: Ethnicity in the Contemporary World*, ed. J.F. Stack. New York: Greenwood Press.

Stasiulis, D.K., and Y. Abu-Laban. 1991. "The House the Parties Built: (Re)Constructing Ethnic Representation in Canadian Politics." In *Ethno-cultural Groups and Visible Minorities in Canadian Politics: The Question of Access*, ed. Kathy Megyery. Vol. 7 of the research studies of the Royal Commission on Electoral Reform and Party Financing. Ottawa and Toronto: RCERPF/Dundurn.

Taboada-Leonetti, I. 1984. "Les élites d'origine étrangère." *Les Temps moderne*, Nos. 452–453–454: 2067–90.

Turk, H. 1973. *Interorganizational Activation in Urban Communities*. Washington, DC: American Sociological Association.

United States. *Chinese Exclusion Act*. Sess. I, ch. 126, 1882.

Vincent, J. 1974. "Brief Communications." *Human Organization* 33 (4): 375–79.

Weinfeld, M. 1984. "Le Milieu juif contemporain du Québec." In *Juifs et réalités juives au Québec*, ed. Pierre Anctil and Gary Caldwell. Montreal: Institut québécois de recherche sur la culture.

Wolfinger, R.E. 1965. "The Development and Persistence of Ethnic Voting." *American Political Science Review* 59:896–908.

———. 1974. "Ethnic Politics." In *The Politics of Progress*. Englewood Cliffs, NJ: Prentice-Hall.

Wood, J.R. 1981. "A Visible Minority Votes: East Indian Electoral Behaviour in the Vancouver South Provincial and Federal Elections of 1979." In *Ethnicity, Power and Politics in Canada*, ed. Jorgen Dahlie and Tissa Fernando. Toronto: Methuen.

Wrong, D. 1974. *Power. Its Forms, Bases, and Uses*. London: B. Blackwell.

3

VISIBLE MINORITIES AND THE CANADIAN POLITICAL SYSTEM

Carolle Simard
with the assistance of Sylvie Bélanger,
Nathalie Lavoie, Anne-Lise Polo and Serge Turmel

INTRODUCTION TO THE RESEARCH AND SCOPE OF THE STUDY

The Research

IN CANADA, THE GENERAL QUESTION of ethnic groups, and the more specific question of visible minorities, is important enough to be treated as a social problem that also expresses itself in political terms. As a democracy that guarantees every citizen, regardless of origin, the right to vote and eligibility for elected office, Canada must develop rules for its democratic process that give all people and groups the opportunity to organize and act to promote their interests, while respecting institutional rules that establish methods of political participation.

It is nevertheless important to acknowledge that there is no such thing as a perfect democracy. Relying on an egalitarian philosophy and enshrined in political and administrative institutions, democracy is constantly tested in the struggle among various groups as they compete for control of its institutions. In a society like Canada's, there are divergent, even conflicting, options. This is why removing some of the structures that are supposed to be embodied in a democratic society raises problems of measurement where many groups are excluded.

In the recent past the emphasis on this issue has been on the difficulties encountered by women and Aboriginal peoples. We now know that there are social, cultural, economic and institutional obstacles that limit access by these people to representative institutions, when they are allowed to participate at all. Measures supposed to promote the integration of women at all levels and in all places are already in place, but results are still inconclusive and women's groups demand a much firmer commitment from government. As for Aboriginal peoples, the Oka crisis brought into the open the exclusions that they have suffered and still face. For these people, moreover, the problem is unchanged and solutions remain to be found.

It is no different for visible minorities, the many nonwhite peoples who arrived in Canada in the late 1970s and settled in large cities. These new immigrants have changed the racial and cultural characteristics of the immigrant population of Canada. The result has been great cultural diversity, as the Canadian population now increasingly includes groups whose origin is neither British nor French (in 1989, the proportion was around 33 percent). Another result is racial diversity; people of non-European descent are estimated to make up more than 10 percent of the Canadian population. A final result is social diversity, as most of the non-European immigrants who arrived since 1980 live in Montreal, Toronto and Vancouver.

Such diversity has political consequences because these different groups, belonging to various political cultures, do not necessarily participate in the same methods of political representation and participation. Too often, we are ignorant of these methods; their systems of political representation travel avenues that are strange to us. To learn more about the relationships between the Canadian political system and visible minorities, we have sought answers to many questions. Chief among these are: Do visible minorities participate, and do they want to participate, in political life? If they do not participate as they should, why don't they? What constraints do they face? Are there constraints of time and money? Are there constraints connected with the electoral process itself and the role of party politics? What do they think of the way elections are financed? How do they view the role of the media?

These important questions were the main theme of our research and echoed the concerns of the Royal Commission on Electoral Reform and Party Financing. We had two reasons for choosing an inductive rather than a deductive approach. First, we needed answers to our general questions on the various modes of political expression of visible minorities and explanations for them, and we needed answers to our more specific questions on their participation in elections. To obtain these answers, we had to work at the grassroots level by seeking the opinions and viewpoints of members of visible minorities themselves. Second, we had to be able to reconstruct the political universe of visible minorities through both their practices and their perceptions, since one is as structured as the other. This choice makes it clear that our research results will not lead to theoretical breakthroughs on visible minority participation in the political system. Also, our choice shows a preference for a more empirical approach that results in the formulation of recommendations.

Authors from other countries have already dealt in various ways with a number of the questions in our research. Their contributions have been theoretical, methodological or political. Given the needs of the Commission, we have concentrated on works that deal with the theory of political participation and those that evaluate participation experiences.

This theoretical review enabled us to complete a general portrait of the communities surveyed and helped us to formulate our questionnaire. It also provided a general look at different approaches to the ways ethnic groups participate and are represented in the political system, as well as at the solutions brought forward to increase political integration of ethnic minorities in countries with large immigrant populations.

The Survey: Procedures and Strategies

As we have said, we wished to reconstruct the political world of visible minorities, as much from their practices as from their representation. Our goal was to see how political cultures and attitudes are connected with political practices, political representation and visions of the future.

We used intense direct observation of the leaders of six visible minority communities for our in-depth analysis because we wished to learn about the opinions, behaviour and perceptions of the élites, rather than the masses, of these communities. This choice was based on our belief that only economic, political and community leaders know certain things about politics, and that their political behaviour is not necessarily shared by the general population. Also, leaders' perceptions of political relationships and the political system must be considered when evaluating proposed changes. Their perceptions speak volumes on the way political life in Canada is seen and understood. Awareness of these perceptions is also essential for anyone who wishes to identify problems and propose solutions.

All the communities in the survey belong to so-called visible minorities, that is, non-European communities of Arab, South-, East- and Southeast-Asian, and Caribbean origin. Using data from the 1986 census, we identified six sizable communities with significant community organizations. We also wanted these communities to be sufficiently represented in Montreal, as we planned to hold most of our interviews there. Finally, we wanted these communities to be integrated enough in Canadian society for us to find people with various types of economic, community and political experience. We therefore used the following communities for the survey: the Arabic-speaking, Indian, Chinese, Vietnamese, Haitian and Jamaican communities (see appendices B and C for the composition of the major ethnic groups in Canada based on data from the 1986 census).

We used the list of ethnic and community associations provided by the Multiculturalism Branch of the Department of the Secretary of State to help us select respondents. This list enabled us to contact various associations with infrastructures in the cities involved in our survey: Montreal, Toronto and Vancouver. These cities have the highest concentrations of the communities we were studying (see appendices B and C). The selection was made following informal interviews with those in charge of various community associations (from four to six interviews in each community). The informal interviews followed a general outline rather than a rigid questionnaire. In addition to helping us identify possible participants in the survey, these informal interviews enabled us to complete documentary research on the communities, particularly on community organization and membership, types of activities and working budget, relationship with Canadian society, and attitudes to the Canadian political system. This exploratory phase was carried out in the three cities in the survey; we also used this period to formulate the interview guide that we pre-tested during this first phase.

Most of the people interviewed are political, economic or community leaders within their communities. They are highly educated men and women, many of whom have an annual income higher than the Canadian average. Tables 3.1, 3.2 and 3.3 outline some of their characteristics.

With one exception, the interviewees were or are activists in community or political associations. They are not representative of their communities at the socioprofessional level, given their income and level of education (see detailed survey analyses). However, to varying degrees, all the respondents can certainly speak not only for themselves, but also on behalf of their communities. Given their community and political experience, these people are well aware of the problems that are peculiar to members of their communities, and their remarks are definitely reliable.

The interview questionnaire was mostly made up of open-ended questions. It was formulated around the four priority areas identified by the Commission: political parties and participation; candidacy and representation; electoral financing; and images and the media. The questionnaire contained 40 questions and was administered to 57 respondents (we had expected 60 respondents but two from Vancouver and

Table 3.1
Distribution of interviewees by community and city

Ethnic community	Montreal	Toronto	Vancouver	Total
Arabic-speaking	6	3	—	9
Chinese	4	—	4	8
Haitian	10	—	—	10
East Indian	3	3	4	10
Jamaican	3	7	—	10
Vietnamese	6	4	—	10
Total	32	17	8	57

Table 3.2
Distribution of interviewees by ethnic community and by sex

Ethnic community	Male	Female	Total
Arabic-speaking	5	4	9
Chinese	6	2	8
Haitian	6	4	10
East Indian	8	2	10
Jamaican	6	4	10
Vietnamese	7	3	10
Total	38	19	57

Table 3.3
Distribution of interviewees by ethnic community and by profession

Ethnic community	Public servants and similar	Professionals	Blue collar workers	Business people
Arabic-speaking	6	—	—	3
Chinese	4	—	1	3
Haitian	6	—	1	31
East Indian	6	—	—	4
Jamaican	5	—	4	1
Vietnamese	7	3	—	—
Total	34	3	6	42

another from Toronto had to withdraw at the last minute). The interviews, all individual, took place in Montreal (32), Toronto (17) and Vancouver (8). Five interviewers shared the task, sometimes in English and sometimes in French, depending on the interviewee's preference. In most cases they stayed in the workplace (sometimes a restaurant, a hotel room or even the office of an association). Interviews lasted between 45 minutes and three hours. On the whole, the inquiry was well received and only a few individuals were at all reticent or refused to answer certain questions.

Each interview was recorded on tape and then transcribed in French, to make it easier to compile and compare the material gathered. This transcription yielded more than 550 double-spaced pages.

In analysing our survey results, we were faced with a number of problems related to the diversity, volume and unevenness of the data. We first divided the survey questions for each community (see the questionnaire in Appendix A) into five main topics – the Commission's four topics were divided into five headings to make analysis easier. Then, again for each community, we compared the answers with each group of questions using information we had synthesized from the transcripts.

The resulting analyses are based on these main topics and contain facts, opinions and behaviours. All six analyses – one per community – were completed according to the same plan and organized as follows:

- electoral behaviour, political pressures and actions (questions 1 to 10, 20 to 23, 32 to 36);
- representativeness of the political system and politicians (questions 11, 12, 15);
- interest in Canadian politics (questions 13, 14, 28 and 29);
- Canadian politics and visible minorities (questions 16 to 19, 24 to 27, 30 and 31); and
- communities and the media (questions 37 to 40).

Because the length of time spent during the interviews varied so widely, the analyses vary in depth and accuracy. This also explains why some community analyses are shorter than others and why some topics are less developed than others.

THEORETICAL APPROACHES AND COURSES OF ACTION

Renowned as a land of welcome par excellence, during the past 20 years Canada has experienced major changes in the flow of immigration. Immigration from the Third World, particularly southern Asia and the Caribbean, has increased continuously since 1980. Consequently, immigration and the integration of immigrants have become burning issues in Canada, particularly in large cities such as Montreal, Toronto, Vancouver and Halifax.

It is not only in Canada that these questions are hitting a nerve; in many regions of the world, immigration, ethnic minorities and their integration into the society have been and continue to be subject to question and reflection by the governments concerned and by researchers preoccupied with the issue. The same is true of Australia, which adopted a Canadian-style policy of multiculturalism; of several European countries that are experimenting with various arrangements to improve integration of immigrants into the decision-making process; and even of our neighbour to the south, where some states are known to be more Mexican than American.

We complemented our research on visible minorities and their participation in the Canadian political system with a literature review that illustrates this diversity and the diversity of experience throughout the world. And, again, we chose four dimensions: political parties and participation; candidacy and representation; electoral financing; and images and the media. In reviewing monographs and articles, we also explored all these topics except electoral financing, which seems to have been skirted by both Canadian and foreign researchers.

Although this documentary research could not be exhaustive because of time limits, we believe it gives an adequate picture of the problems ethnic minorities face with respect to political participation all over the world, and that it will help corroborate or refute certain findings of the interviews. Although easy generalizations must be avoided, there is no doubt that the books and articles reviewed shed light on a number of common problems.

Our review of articles and monographs has three main sections. The first deals with the methodology and selection criteria for books and articles. The second, more detailed section contains, first, a summary of the constants and differences identified by the authors in the various countries concerned, then an overview of the main variables used. The second section also brings out the salient points on problems the authors raise and highlights the action they recommend on integration, relations between the state and minorities, and the role of the media. Finally, in the third section we return to the problems raised in the documentary research by emphasizing the different solutions the authors have advanced.

Approach Taken in the Review

As mentioned above, we wanted to survey the problems that concern us on an international scale to draw lessons from others' experiences.

Although we set no geographical limits on ourselves at the outset, we thought it useful to focus on societies that compare to our own in one way or another, namely Australia, India, North America (Canada and the United States) and Europe (mainly the Netherlands, France, Germany and Great Britain).

We also thought it advisable not to exclude any discipline. Nevertheless, the sociological approach predominates, in that several books and articles are the work of researchers who specialize in social anthropology, political science, social psychology and statistics.

Given the abundant literature on ethnic minorities, two criteria became immediately apparent. On the one hand, monographs and articles had to deal mainly with the four main research topics. On the other hand, we concentrated on the period from 1980 to 1990, because, as in Australia (Hawkins 1982), the influx of refugees from Southeast Asia was established in large Canadian cities at the end of the 1970s. It should be noted, however, that some material published before this period was reviewed because authors cited its importance, or because it is particularly relevant to an aspect of this research. Also, we reviewed some material that does not deal specifically with one of the four topics chosen because the work dealt with a related subject or with a subject closely connected to the Canadian situation.[1] Because of time constraints, we decided not to review doctoral and masters' theses.

The documentary research was completed in Montreal. Although the results would have been different if it had been done elsewhere – Vancouver, for example – we believe the overview is complete enough to be useful and to make it possible to identify the main directions of the research. Furthermore, we consulted several international databanks (Francis, Sociological Abstracts, PAIS and Bibliographie nationale française), the various Montreal universities, as well as the usual directories and card indexes. We used several classification categories, namely minorities and ethnic groups, candidacy and representation, political parties and representation, financing, and assimilation and discrimination, connected with the four dimensions of the research.

In this national and international overview we noted one weakness in the literature on ethnic minorities in Canada: while there are many general articles on the issue, we found few articles on our chosen topics and topics related to political participation. This was surprising, given the importance of immigration to this country. Perhaps this situation can be explained by the fact that immigration from developing countries is relatively recent.

It goes without saying that the monographs and articles reviewed, especially the articles, are of uneven value. Some were not consulted for their scientific rigour but for their opinions or discussions aimed at promoting debate on such a complex issue (Isajiw 1983; Jazouli 1986, 24).

Theoretical Approaches: Similarities and Differences

In this section, we present the various theoretical approaches we used to analyse minority ethnic groups' methods of participation and representation in the political system. To widen the range of works in the study, we considered all ethnic groups, not simply those that belong to visible minorities.

We also examine what the authors have to say about integration, representation and participation, the last two factors depending on the first, as they are the means of integration. The review deals with minority ethnic groups and points out the typologies the various authors have advanced. The limitations of these models are highlighted where necessary.

Another section deals with the salient points of problems raised by the authors. First, we examine integration in its various forms. Our study also covers the perception and representation of ethnic groups by the groups themselves and the majority group in power.

We then go on to government, and how it manages relations with minorities according to the authors reviewed. This can take the form of an official multiculturalism policy aimed at developing ethnic minorities within national society, or a series of measures focused on individual integration. Canadian- and Australian-style multiculturalism receives particular attention.

Finally, we deal with the media and the image they convey of ethnic groups, as well as the extent to which they can, according to some authors, link the political system to its participants.

The expression "ethnic minority" has been defined by several authors. Lemieux (1986) maintains that ethnic identity is defined first by how so-called ethnic groups perceive themselves: "[the group] would be *least* in numerical terms, a *minority* in societal terms, and *less* at the cultural level." De Marchi and Boileau (1982) define a minority "as a social group that finds itself in an inferior position, in relation not only to geographical boundaries but also to political, national, ethnic and social boundaries."

According to Isajiw (1983), there are two types of ethnic groups: minority groups and majority groups, classified not by numbers but by whether they dominate the main institutions of their society.

Finally, Enloe (1986) distinguishes between ethnic groups by their capacity for political influence. For the purposes of this study, and in recognition of the important contribution of Anderson and

Frideres (1981), we take an ethnic minority to mean a group that is smaller than another group in a society, and whose ethnic characteristics and spoken language are different from those of other larger groups.

Such a definition is not necessarily accepted unanimously by authors interested in the political participation mechanisms of minority ethnic groups or in how they are represented politically. However, it is certainly broad enough to allow us to describe the political participation and representation models of ethnic groups having one or more of these characteristics.

It is not easy to set out systematically the many existing theoretical trends which we had to clarify in our coverage of the main works studied. We also had to take account of analysis that has evolved simultaneously in the United States, Canada and Europe during the period studied, in which it has not always been possible to see a dominant trend emerging.

Given these limitations and the needs expressed by the Commission, we decided to concentrate on two groups of works. The first includes research into how members of various ethnic groups participate in political life – why some have a given type of behaviour, attitude or perception, while others do not. The second group deals mainly with studies that measure the effectiveness of certain integration policies, or at least of policies that encourage greater participation at the electoral level.

Participation in Political Life, Attitudes and Behaviour
Verba et al. (1971, 1978) and Olsen (1982) produced a series of works on these questions. In 1961 Verba, with Robert Dahl, was one of the first American social science researchers to propose modelling of the interaction of socio-economic status with electoral behaviour and mobilization for political participation. Verba et al. (1971) compared American Blacks and Harijans (Untouchables) in India in a study that revealed two minority groups' methods of political participation within their societies.

To explain the motivation of these groups, the authors formulated four hypotheses for the road to political participation. The first relates to socio-economic resources; the second to group consciousness; the third to the timely, productive use of political institutions (Miles and Phizacklea (1979) and Ehrlich and Wootton (1980) also approximate this point of view); and the fourth to partisan mobilization. This last type of mobilization was later taken up by Olsen (1982) in his study of participatory democracy and participatory pluralism as modes of participation.

Verba et al. (1978) in their work on political participation (which covered several years and seven countries (United States, Japan, Yugoslavia, Nigeria, India, the Netherlands and Austria) and continued the early work of Verba et al. (1971)) tried to explain the under- or over-representation of certain groups or segments of society. In principle, they said, political systems are egalitarian, although there are considerable differences in the influence exercised by different groups of citizens. Verba et al. (1978) advance the premise that political stratification tends to mirror socio-economic stratification. To support their hypothesis, the authors use the variable socio-economic status multiple.

The authors point out first that in all the countries examined, high socio-economic status gives an advantage to citizens in their political participation and representation. On the other hand, Verba, Nie and Kim find considerable variation among countries in the extent to which wealthy people directly or indirectly discourage the participation of less privileged citizens. They also point out that the rate at which people tend to convert their socio-economic resources into a motivation to participate seems to be the same in most countries, provided that there is no interference from groups or institutions.

Olsen (1982) examines models of political participation operating in the United States and Sweden and advances a theory of participatory pluralism, which he juxtaposes with participatory democracy. Participatory democracy involves the citizen's direct participation, although sociological pluralism places greater emphasis on collective action through voluntary associations. Olsen reviews six indicators of political participation: cognitive, expressive, electoral (the exercise of the right to vote), organizational, partisan and governmental. Like Verba et al. (1978) and Fugita and O'Brien (1985), Olsen establishes that, after socio-economic status (including the independent variables of income, education and profession), education is the single variable most likely to promote political mobilization.

For the rest, the variable socio-economic status multiple can be criticized for its overly monolithic character and its tendency to over-generalize. This tendency to generalization seems to be inherent in the American theoretical models, which draw largely on behaviourism.

These models do not always permit an appreciation of all the nuances and contradictions inherent in the phenomenon of political participation. Thus Wolfinger and Rosenstone (1980) and Olsen (1982) point out the methodological weaknesses of earlier studies, particularly Verba et al. (1971, 1978), in discussing the effect of socio-economic status on the exercise of the franchise, which is only one form of political participation. These authors give equal weight to the three main variables that make up socio-economic status. Wolfinger and Rosenstone maintain that the effects of each of these are not the same, their combined effects are not necessarily cumulative and their correlation is rarely along the same lines. According to Wolfinger and Rosenstone, therefore, it is necessary to isolate each variable and study its individual effects. In light of the data gathered, Wolfinger and Rosenstone conclude that education is the variable that has the greatest effect on the exercise of the franchise. They also weaken the hypothesis that a higher income necessarily means a higher propensity to vote.

Another aspect of the participation and representation of ethnic minorities in the political system discussed by several authors is the concept of "critical mass," that is, the aggregate of converging elements likely to promote political mobilization directly. This is undoubtedly what Lemieux (1986) means when he says that among "the many factors that help establish contacts between ethnic minorities and government through political parties are concentration and geographic density."

Similarly, Moodley (1981) and Wood (1981) each group a number of factors that can influence the participation of an ethnic group during general elections under the term critical mass. The factors are demographic density, economic weight, religious homogeneity, the degree of representativeness of élites perceived by the group's members (legitimacy) and level of education.

This is what Wood found in a study of the electoral behaviour of immigrants from the Indian subcontinent in the riding of Vancouver South. During the 1979 federal election, representatives of the leading parties massively canvassed the Indian vote of this constituency for the first time. The growing socio-economic interaction of a growing ethnic group (such as Indian immigrants in Vancouver South) requires a certain amount of mutual political compromise. As soon as the critical mass is reached, it draws the attention of the politicians and institutions of the dominant group.

The observation made by Anwar (1986) regarding the participation of ethnic minorities in British politics also uses the concept of critical mass. The critical mass of one given ethnic group would not, of course, be enough to explain such a result. One must also consider the distortion caused by Britain's uninominal simple majority ballot system, which is very similar to Canada's.

Integration Policies

Different studies have tried to establish the relevance of integration policies. For example, in D'Arcy (1985), Souchon-Zahn tells us about interesting experiments in France which attempted to establish a link between elected politicians and minority group cultural associations. This involved the law of 31 December 1982, which created district initiative and advisory committees. (The third section will give further details on complementary participation structures.)

Also in D'Arcy (1985), Gilbert and Guillaume state that they do not intend to examine participants' behaviour using rigid and airtight variables to explain the phenomenon of representation. For example, in their article on political commitment or efforts to establish representation, Gilbert and Guillaume explain that attempts to improve representation are often intended only to perpetuate the power representatives hold.

These authors go on to say that the political task of representation "is a constant struggle to avoid the undifferentiated, the unstable and the informal." This involves an intelligible codification of the expectations of those from whom representatives receive their mandate.

Similarly, Murswieck (D'Arcy 1985) maintains that West Germany is undergoing a renewed debate on parliament and parties as central representative institutions. This point of view is echoed by several Canadian analysts in commentary on the Canadian political system. Neo-corporatist or extraparliamentary representation methods offer some possibilities for solving the representation crisis because, according to Weber's premises, "legality and legitimacy" no longer suffice to justify the existence of a representative democratic system.

Thernstrom (1983) advances essentially the same thesis in his article on the right of ethnic minorities to political representation in the United States. He establishes that this goes well beyond the simple right to vote. The right to vote is a formal right, which must be supported by positive action to rectify the electoral distortion that prevents proportional representation of Blacks, Hispanics and Asians in the political system.

Salient Points of the Problems Raised

Our synthesis of these works reveals that several authors have firmly insisted on certain dimensions of the relation between politics and ethnic minorities. The Commission shares their preoccupation with three of these dimensions: integration, state–minority relations and the role of the media. This section summarizes the most pertinent theoretical elements of these three dimensions.

Integration

According to the authors reviewed, ethnic minorities use a variety of integration strategies. Political participation and representation were touched on in the preceding section, but on the evidence, they are measures developed to increase political integration. We will concentrate primarily on the problems raised by two specific types of integration: structural assimilation and acculturation. These two integration strategies generally originate within ethnic minorities and are not always the result of government measures or initiatives.

As Moodley (1981) emphasizes, for the minority group, acculturation consists of adopting the values and lifestyle of the majority, and structural assimilation is integration through the institutions of the majority. Similarly, Kim (1986) treats acculturation and social assimilation as indicators of political participation without, however, defining precisely what he means by "social" assimilation. At another level, the pressures society exerts to impose conformity can induce members of ethnic minorities to adopt the conventions of the majority. Differences do exist, however, in the way society receives ethnic minorities' demands for participation and representation.

Magnusson and Sancton (1983) and Miles and Phizacklea (1979) point out, for example, that the result of the social conformity that exists in England is that large English cities cannot deal with increasing social demands, especially by Afro-Caribbeans and immigrants from Pakistan, India and Bangladesh. English politics are structured to account for the interests of various social classes but not of racial or ethnic groups. Americans, on the other hand, have enormous difficulty meeting Blacks' demands for legal equality and collective recognition, because U.S. political traditions are focused more on individual than on collective rights, as illustrated by the American Constitution and the history of its interpretation by the Supreme Court.

The State and Minorities

Multiculturalism is the most convincing manifestation of a state's willingness to work out its relations with minority groups. The Canadian policy on the subject is a good example of this willingness. Juteau (1986) argues that the Canadian government's official policy of multiculturalism is not exempt from criticism. She points out that by taking over the ethnic issue, the state is helping perpetuate the existing social order, which is clearly advantageous for dominant groups. Zylberberg (1986) states the view that France's state regulation of religious minorities perpetuates the "us–them" distinction that often characterizes relations between majority groups and ethnic minorities.

Further to the discussion of the immigration crisis in France, Courtois and Kepel (1988) maintain that "the nation-state must negotiate the degree of cultural community and sociopolitical cohesiveness with its ethnic minorities." Like Juteau, Courtois and Kepel suggest that the effectiveness of national institutions is measured in terms of their capacity to disseminate dominant values.

In France, the problem is particularly acute because of the "difficult passage from the individual to the collective" (Tramier 1990) when dealing with immigrants. Before the Second World War, the French government dealt with immigrants individually, but today it must adapt to the demands made by members of minority groups that are keenly aware of their ethnic identity. As Verbunt (1984) shows, the novelty of the phenomenon is illustrated by the fact that France did not recognize the right of association of foreigners residing within its borders until the autumn of 1981.

To return to multiculturalism, a criticism we encountered regularly is that multiculturalism confers the perception that the activities of groups that benefit from its programs are "folkloric." Therefore, Peter (1981) sees multiculturalism as a way to limit ethnic minorities' emancipation in the cultural domain and to avoid granting them increased political participation. To support his argument, Peter maintains that ethnic groups were never in the past able to combine their interests and articulate them within the framework of Canadian political parties, with the exception of the Communists, who addressed themselves to a few ethnic groups, mostly in western Canada.

Hawkins (1982) established a parallel between Canada's and Australia's official multiculturalism policies. Since the 1960s, both Canada and Australia have faced floods of immigrants from developing countries. To meet the integration needs of these new populations, both governments developed an official policy of multiculturalism. These policies do not involve massive changes in established political systems, and it is unlikely that they ever will. The author maintains that multiculturalism is essentially a political project with no true popular base. It does not respond to the specific demands of ethnic groups. Rather, it seems to be part of a strategy of the party in power to woo voters in immigrant communities. This would in turn make these ethnic groups dependent on the governing party.

Forrest (1988) makes basically the same argument when he discusses the cultural and social cleavage associated with urbanization and development in Australia. Among other things, he emphasizes that socioeconomic status, ethnic identity and sex are the determining variables. He concludes that immigration policies influence the electoral vote and that efforts by the Australian Workers' Party to promote immigration and win the ethnic vote by easing the current legislation seem to have borne fruit.

The Media

Very few authors have dealt with the question of the media's effectiveness in the mobilization for political action. The main commentators are

Leithner (1988), Raub (1988) and Lecompte and Thomas (1983). According to Leithner, there are two perceptions of the ethnic media's capacity to mobilize immigrants for political action. The first, "integral" perception is that ethnic media familiarize newcomers with the norms of the society and convey the rules of Canadian politics. In the second, "non-integral" perception, ethnic institutions surround immigrants with an information network centred on their own ethnic group, and limit the circulation of information about the new country. In a 1983 Toronto field study, the author leans to the first view.

Raub (1988) refers to the normative and "uninforming" role of publications such as *National Geographic*, which convey stereotypes and clichés about ethnic minorities that contribute to a watered-down perception of ethnic groups. These magazines' social messages substantially reflect the values of other mass media. As an example, she offers the following sentence, which conveys the sense of her article: "The Polish-American doctor or businessman is an 'American', the Polish-American worker remains a 'Polack'." *National Geographic* conveys the ideological assertion that determination and hard work lead to social mobility.

Finally, Toinet (1983) closely examines ethnic groups' access to the media. First, she tackles the problem of the definition of the ethnic media: what confers on a medium its "ethnic" character – property, management, audience, readership, language used or content? Without answering the question precisely, the author says that the large American media are still clearly dominated by a white, Anglo-Saxon Protestant majority. This is probably caused by the indifference of the journalistic environment of the majority and the "integration-advancement" strategy that attracts the most accomplished members of ethnic groups. Thus, the majority group can show that the system is democratic, deprive the minorities by removing their natural leaders, and strengthen itself with new blood. A parallel could be drawn to integration attempts by members of visible minorities in the Quebec and Canadian media.

Problems and Elements of a Solution

Except for certain controversies or differences in points of view among authors about factors of political participation and integration, we singled out several common problems for which researchers have generally agreed on concrete elements of a solution. We sort these problems into two groups: the first concern ethnic minorities' representation difficulties; the second concern obstacles to participation, be they linguistic or linked to political "competence." For these groups, which often overlap, we will first state the problem and then any solutions proposed by the authors.

Representation and Ethnic Minorities

Representation and Political Parties   Most authors who focus on the various aspects of the ethnic minorities' participation in the political system deplore the lack of ethnic candidates and the underrepresentation of ethnic minorities at the governmental decision-making level and in political party hierarchies (Mohl 1986; Rath 1983, 1988). Nevertheless, the fact that a candidate belongs to an ethnic group is not enough to get him or her elected. Anwar (1986), for example, believes that except in rare cases, an elector's choice depends much more on the candidate's affiliation to a political party. On the other hand, Rath (1988) stresses that in the Netherlands, immigrant voters in recent elections have voted for the Social Democratic Party because this party put forward many ethnic candidates. The more progressive the party, the more likely it is to welcome ethnic candidates to its ranks. As for the assertion that ethnic minorities vote in a block and that this vote can swing elections in constituencies with large ethnic populations, several authors have refuted it, particularly Anwar (1986) and Lacroix and Kirschbaum (1986). In Lacroix and Kirschbaum's view, the minority vote in Canada reflects an extension of the Canadian political environment.

It is nonetheless true, as Anwar notes, that regional or local concentration of some ethnic groups can decide whether a seat goes to one party or the other, especially in a simple majority electoral system such as Britain's or Canada's. Moreover, it is often in a constituency dominated by ethnic groups that political parties will open their ranks to an ethnic candidate. As the Canadian author Wood (1981) mentions, as soon as the critical mass has been reached, it draws the attention of the dominant group's politicians and institutions, such as parties and the media. For Le Lohé (1979), two conditions must be met if an ethnic candidate is to get elected, especially if the candidate is not of European descent: the candidate must have a safe seat (that is to say, the party is sure to win in the constituency) to compensate for the loss of the white majority vote, and the candidate must be able to count on the majority vote of nonwhite voters.

In light of this, the proposals made by Anwar seem particularly useful in responding to the objective of promoting greater representation and increased participation by ethnic minorities in Canadian politics. We set out only some of them here:

- Ethnic minorities should join political parties and should be encouraged to do so.
- After joining a political party, members of an ethnic group should

try to occupy positions at the decision-making level.
- Members of ethnic minorities should present candidates for election and see to it that they are elected.
- Candidates belonging to ethnic minorities should run in safe constituencies, as well as in ordinary constituencies.
- Candidates of ethnic origin should not be chosen only in constituencies with a strong ethnic density.
- Candidates of ethnic origin should not be perceived as representatives only of their own communities, but of all citizens in the constituencies in which they live, campaign and win elections.
- Political parties should not present their ethnic candidates only as such but rather, and especially, as party candidates who possess certain qualities and capabilities, as do other candidates.
- Political parties must follow up increased participation in party proceedings by members of ethnic minorities.

As in the British system, Canadian voting does not favour small parties. This supports Anwar's (1986) suggestion that members of ethnic minorities must focus their efforts on increased penetration, representation and participation at the decision-making levels of the leading political parties.

Access to the political system is not necessarily realized at the provincial and federal levels, however. According to Peter (1981), access to these levels is gained gradually, and begins at the municipal level. It is evident that the avenues of access to politics must be broadened so that ethnic groups can grasp other strategic levers or simply so that they can have a say in the decision-making process. In this context two European structures merit attention: orientation advisory committees and district initiative and advisory committees.

Examples of Other Types of Participation Structures Orientation advisory committees for the protection of foreigners are a type of participation structure found at the municipal level in Germany, Belgium and, more recently, the Netherlands. These committees have a twofold mandate: to advise the mayor and city council on all questions concerning foreigners and to manage consultation and cooperation with individuals or institutions that work with immigrants. These committees are made up of volunteers from a variety of ethnic groups, unions, employer organizations and so on.

Rath (1983) carefully examined this system before it was adopted in the Netherlands in 1985. He notes, however, that it has several shortcomings. Chief among these is that the committees are unimportant because they offer only advice, so they cannot meet the high expectations of immigrants. Rath also notes that there are fewer foreigners than Dutch people sitting on the committees. We will return to this issue in the next section.

In 1982, a new institution was founded in the districts of Paris: the district initiative and advisory committee. This new system is also designed as a bridge between representatives and citizens through associations that send delegates to the committee. Thus, the associative mode of representation was added to the traditional mode of representation. Of course, as noted by Souchon-Zahn (D'Arcy 1985), the committee is not immune to the contradictions inherent in political systems, because it is the place where public interest (symbolized by the elected members) and special interests (the associations) constantly confront each other. But an advantage of this committee is that everyday concerns are voiced, not positions of principle, electoral platforms or ideological declarations.

One can see here a fundamental difference between this and the orientation and advisory committee system: the immigrants who sit on this committee already come from representative and mediatory bodies (volunteer or community associations), while anyone sitting on an advisory committee does so strictly *in propria persona*. Beyond this representative aspect, the structure of the district initiative and advisory committee might be useful in Canada, where many community ethnic organizations are supported by the policy of multiculturalism. It would establish closer links with elected representatives, while helping to ensure that they improve their understanding of the issues important to ethnic minorities. Because of their purely advisory function, however, the two systems resemble the ritual participatory structures studied by Parry (1980); immigrants still would lack influence in decision making.

Extending the Franchise to All Immigrants   We cannot remain silent about extending the franchise to immigrants, which, according to Rath (1988), can provide them with a special opportunity to engage in additional political activities and to express interest in the representatives of political parties. The author refers to Dutch legislation, passed in March 1986, that granted the right to vote and eligibility for municipal election to all immigrants. He points out that, although ethnic minorities are still underrepresented, in the 1986 municipal elections many members of ethnic communities took the opportunity to stand for election. Entzinger (1984), who has studied Dutch initiatives on this matter since 1981, praises official willingness to integrate these minorities into the national political system.

As Rath states, the right to vote is a necessary but not a sufficient condition for exerting direct political influence. The franchise is merely a preliminary requirement for participation. In light of the Dutch experience, the extension of the franchise to all permanent residents, regardless of their status, seems to actually increase political mobilization. Saskatchewan's chief electoral officer, K. Lampard, recently supported it in a brief presented to this Commission.

Obstacles to Participation

These proposals have the merit of helping to widen and improve participation at the institutional level, whether it involves political parties or other representative bodies. But, as Anwar (1986) points out, they will not succeed without effective and direct participation by immigrant citizens. Many obstacles now hinder this participation: according to the literature, the most important and most frequently encountered obstacles seem to be the language barrier and "political illiteracy" – the lack of political competence.

Language Barrier   Bilingual or multilingual voting ballots are controversial, especially in California, where nearly half the population belongs to ethnic minorities. Obviously, this question has not become as serious here, but it is of primary importance.

In the United States, the supporters of bilingualism or multilingualism in election campaigns maintain that unilingualism and monoculturalism are undemocratic. They point out in particular that ballots printed only in English prevent thousands of Americans from voting because they have difficulty with that language. These supporters say that Hispanic and Asian Americans find this a barrier to their understanding of electoral issues.

Critics see bilingualism as something that removes immigrants' motivation to learn English and, therefore, hinders their integration. They add that the law requires applicants for citizenship to pass tests in English; furthermore, bilingual ballots would be too costly.

Loo (1985), on the other hand, refutes several of these arguments by basing his analysis on his observations, over several years, of Chinese and other groups. He points out that people develop their language skills unequally, and that many people who can speak English still have difficulty understanding written English. His studies show that Koreans, Chinese, Vietnamese and other Asians seem to be particularly vulnerable to problems in mastering English because it involves such fundamentally different linguistic structures.

Thus, for Loo (1985), language constitutes an undeniable obstacle to political participation, particularly to the understanding of electoral issues and the exercise of the right to vote. Rath (1983) observed the same phenomenon in the Netherlands, where there are many Turks, Surinamese and West Indians. He states that the language barrier prevents immigrants from playing a full role on the advisory committees. This maintains or even reinforces their minority status in relation to the Dutch. Rath and Loo, therefore, recommend translation of ballots, and Loo also suggests that immigrants be helped throughout the electoral process.

Immigrant Citizens' Lack of Political Competence   As mentioned in relation to variables, several authors have concluded that education is the strongest variable in the exercise of voting rights (Wolfinger and Rosenstone 1980; Verba et al. 1978; Olsen 1982). In effect, education can be a factor in citizens' political competence, which Parry (1980) says is a preliminary requirement for participation.

Indeed, these authors explain, to participate, one must accurately understand all the stages of decision making. In other words, Ehrlich and Wootton (1980) maintain that to participate in politics a person must know what kind of decisions are being made and what kind of decision-making methods are involved. Citizens of foreign origin are not, therefore, always "competent"; they do not know enough to understand how electoral processes work or what the electoral issues are. Wolfinger and Rosenstone (1980) believe that older adults, because they have participated in many elections and understand the bureaucracy, know more and are more politically competent than young people who have just reached voting age.

In Canada, where a very complex constitutional debate has been raging for several years, this type of argument takes on special significance, particularly since, as Chan and Lam (1983), who interviewed Southeast Asians in Montreal, have shown, immigrants often have only a rudimentary and extremely stereotyped understanding of the Canadian political system. They could be said to be somewhat "politically illiterate." Similarly, Rath (1983, 1988) points out that immigrants to the Netherlands have a poor understanding of the Dutch electoral system, and their lack of knowledge about the "municipal machine" appears to be a barrier to immigrants who sit on the advisory committees described earlier, and contributes still more to the inequality between them and the Dutch.

Moreover, this political illiteracy, which is both explained and accentuated by language barriers and low levels of education, can be attributed to other factors, such as immigrant voters' perception of their lack of information, their degree of individual motivation or the presumed effectiveness of their contribution to the political system. In certain ethnic groups it can also be made worse by other factors, intrinsic to the groups, such as religious and economic divisions, reflexive identification, and so on. Some immigrants' political pasts and experiences can also condition their political behaviour. This happened to Cuban immigrants to the United States; their experience of the revolution, which made them anticommunists, explains, according to Portes and Mozo (1985), their tendency to vote Republican. Another example is that of the Vietnamese refugees in Montreal interviewed by Chan and Lam (1983). Still haunted by their past, these refugees instinctively resist any sort of nationalism.

Laferrière (1984), who has studied the Canadian political system, raises another issue – that of the perception shared by the two dominant groups in Canadian society: this view of the attitudes of a given ethnic group is homogeneous, and is not traced back to the conditions of the country of origin. Enloe (1986) takes up this question of the perception of the members of majority groups, who continue to see members of ethnic communities as "ethnic first," even when they are elected and ready to give up their ethnic identity. For Enloe these people are being cheated by the system.

Among the many suggestions we received for combatting these various obstacles, or at least minimizing their impact, more and better information seems to emerge as the deciding factor. In Canada and a few other countries, multiculturalism already offers several bases for overcoming this lack of understanding of the political system, but some of these bases still must be strengthened. Hawkins (1982) reports that in Australia, which has a multiculturalism policy resembling our own, and which heavily subsidizes the ethnic media, the 1979 Galbaly Commission recommended using ethnic organizations as relay points between elected representatives and ethnic minorities, as well as strengthening the information function of the Department of Immigration and Ethnic Affairs.

These two factors highlighted by the Australian Commission – the use of ethnic organizations and the strengthening of the information function – seem to be particular nerve centres. Despite the many criticisms of ethnic organizations in the multiculturalism context, one can agree with Fugita and O'Brien (1985) that they make bridge building with the dominant society possible and that during their organizational stage they can shape the local political system (Le Lohé 1979).

Do the ethnic media perform the same function? Opinions differ on this. But although the authors reviewed did not demonstrate that the ethnic media are important to immigrants' political involvement, neither did they formally prove the opposite. In a recent study, Leithner (1988) states that there is no evidence that the ethnic media isolate immigrants from the political arena.

On the other hand, the increasingly important role that the media play in establishing norms, determining values, and creating a collective identity and consciousness is hardly contested by authors such as Richmond (1984). This can work either positively or negatively. As Raub (1988) says about the American media, mass media can present distorted images of social and ethnic problems. Chan and Lam (1983) point out that the Canadian media convey a rudimentary image of the Canadian political system. Kim (1986), an American, went even further in establishing a close correlation between use of the media for information, whether by ethnic or majority groups of society, and political participation. In his view, the more political information people receive from the media, the more likely they are to participate in the political system.

There seems to be a general consensus on the need for more and better information to be provided simultaneously by ethnic organizations, ethnic media and the mass media. Although the methods have not been addressed, it can be assumed that this information should be strengthened by help to immigrants not only during the election process, but from the time of their arrival in Canada and outside regular events such as electoral campaigns.

Conclusion

Ignorance of the political system prior to participation seems to be at the heart of the problems found in our review of articles and monographs on the subject. The authors attribute this ignorance mostly to lack of instruction, language barriers, lack of political competence (political illiteracy) or institutional obstacles such as political parties and the media.

This gap in knowledge about the political system in Canada and elsewhere points to a global solution: more and better information. All aspects of the concrete solutions the authors proposed suggested intervention at the information level. Since, as several authors maintain, education seems to be the strongest among the socio-economic status variables, we can conclude that education represents a starting point for any strategy designed to extend and promote political participation. Education has to be understood as both formal schooling and informal education or awareness of the political system. This could be acquired through intermediary institutions such as voluntary and community associations. The ethnic media can also educate people about politics, just as the mass media do, despite the weaknesses mentioned in their operations and impact.

Other measures could improve the representation of ethnic minorities. It is surprising that researchers paid so little attention to factors such as permanent voters lists and proportional representation. Some steps have already been taken, including the translation of ballots and campaign information, but methods still have to be refined. Some Canadian experiments, such as the multilingual ballots used in Vancouver's 1990 municipal elections and recent elections in the Northwest Territories, can inspire us in the meantime. We will return to this later, especially in our recommendations.

THE INQUIRY: ANALYSIS AND RESULTS

In this second section, we will look in more detail at relations between visible minorities and the Canadian political system, using the results of an inquiry conducted through semi-directed interviews with a sample of Canadians belonging to visible minorities. Our interviewees were, however, in no way representative of the average Canadian; they were generally highly educated and most had a higher annual income than the average Canadian. Some were active in political parties and community associations. In this respect, they were *leaders* in various domains who represented a very wide and diversified range of personal success. Our inquiry must therefore be interpreted with these considerations in mind: it is representative neither of all visible minorities in Canada, nor of all their behaviour and political attitudes. Although it is not exhaustive, our inquiry does make it possible to define some behaviour and to understand its meaning. Our inquiry also makes it possible to identify several problems and to propose some solutions.

It should be noted that our analysis is based on synthesis tables made up from responses to the questionnaire. These synthesis tables, which are complemented by the interview transcripts, are the source of the following analysis of the six communities in the inquiry.

Interview Report: Arabic-speaking Community

Description of the Interviewees
Most of our interviews with members of the Arabic-speaking community took place in Montreal (six out of nine); the rest in Toronto. The expression "Arabic-speaking community" refers to a population of extremely diverse origins, coming from the Maghreb, the Mashrek, Egypt and Iran. We found this diversity among our interviewees. Our respondents came from Morocco, Algeria, Egypt, Jordan, Lebanon

(two people), Syria and Iran. We interviewed roughly the same numbers of Christians (four) and Moslems (five), and of men (five) and women (four). The average age was 43; six were between 31 (the youngest) and 41 years old, and the oldest respondent was 66 years old. The interviewees had similarly wide-ranging terms of Canadian citizenship; the average was 18 years, the minimum 1 year, the maximum 60 years, and one had received landed immigrant status during the previous year. Three respondents had spent some time in France before coming to settle in Canada. Most interviewees had spent their youth in their countries of origin, approximately until adulthood and on the average until 24 years of age (here we are not counting the time some respondents spent in France). One person had lived only a few months in his country of origin. Most of our respondents were highly educated. Three held doctorates, two held masters' degrees, three held bachelors' degrees (one received in France), and one person had left school after 10 years of study, ending with night classes. All knew three or four different languages, and most spoke Arabic, English and French. Almost all worked in the service sector; they were teachers, journalists or public servants. Their average salary was $30 000, but as most respondents did not divulge their incomes, that figure is only an indication. Eight respondents were active in associations, six of them in community associations.

Electoral Behaviour, Pressure and Political Action
It is difficult to explain the electoral and political behaviour of our Arabic-speaking respondents. In fact, each had a unique attitude and did not follow any major trend, so overall it is almost impossible to construct a profile from these respondents.

We did, however, find one practical characteristic of their electoral behaviour: most of our interviewees did not belong to political parties, but they did make financial commitments. Four respondents had contributed to federal election campaigns, four to provincial campaigns and three at both levels. We found these results similar to their pattern of donating to political parties, with five having made contributions, two at the federal level and four at the provincial level. Most respondents who belonged to parties had also donated money to election campaigns or to political parties. On the other hand, out of six who did not belong to political parties, four had donated to a political party or an election campaign, all at the provincial level and three also at the federal level.

Most of the people we interviewed voted in all elections (except the one who did not have the right to vote); we note, however, that one person did not yet know whether she would vote at the next election, another did not vote in Toronto municipal elections because she lacked information on candidates, and another refused to vote at any level because "They are not interested in us. What use would it be for us to be interested in the political system? Maghrebian immigration ... does not carry any weight on the Canadian political scene, therefore I do not feel involved."

In general, Arabic-speaking interviewees remained faithful to their political allegiances; five out of seven said that they were satisfied with their choice; three had already changed party affiliation, two at the provincial level (in Quebec), one at the federal level but not at the provincial level (this person therefore belonged to different parties at the provincial and federal levels). Finally, two people had no political affiliation, which conformed with the above result in that these people did not vote.

The interviewees described similar priorities for the criteria that they used in choosing a candidate during an election. All the respondents gave high priority to the candidate's personality (five considered it most important, three placed it second) and to the candidate's election platform (three placed it first, six placed it second); the political party came in third (for seven people), followed by ethnic origin and sex, which was clearly last. This order confirms the interviewees' replies on the importance they placed on a candidate's ethnic origin when voting; all said they decided first on the basis of the candidate's competence. For half our respondents, ethnic origin was not relevant; for the other half it was not a determining factor but they paid more attention to ethnic candidates and supported them if they were as competent as the others.

In identifying the types of political pressure and action favoured by our interviewees, we again found an interpretation problem like that found in the preceding section. In fact, it seems very clear that our interviewees did not all have the same idea of political action, because some who had comparable experiences and activities gave us opposite replies. The result was considerable confusion. Four respondents said they were politically active, but only one had participated in an election campaign and in the political activities of a riding association. Another had worked with René Lévesque. Two interviewees were professionally involved in politics as media commentators; one was active while the other was not. Also, four respondents said they were not politically active and only one expected to stand as a candidate some time in the future.

All our respondents had exercised pressure on the government, especially by signing petitions, by joining or organizing demonstrations, or even by direct intervention. Most of the time, this pressure was used to help their community in Canada and abroad. We noted, however, that global questions such as human rights, development aid, or the general situation in the Arab world[2] were important to our interviewees. All discussed Canadian politics regularly with their neighbours and colleagues, and two were specifically interested in Quebec politics.

Most of the interviewees (seven) knew some community figures who were politically active, either in community associations or in other types of associations.

Representativeness of the Political System and of Politicians

Although the interviewees had little in common in terms of political behaviour, their points of view converged regarding the representativeness of the political system and politicians. Most of the interviewees believed that a politician should serve the people. Two different ideas, however, could be identified. For four people, it was service to the community that was most important. Members of Parliament must, they said, know their base very well; they must be interested in the public and in their constituencies, not only during the few months before the elections but throughout the entire year. Politicians must listen to citizens and defend their interests. Three others said they were very concerned with Canada's international position. They wanted politicians to defend Canadian interests by having a good knowledge of international issues.

According to our interviewees, politicians have an obligation to rise above their personal interests. Some said they must be honest, benevolent and moderate; they must also tell the truth and keep their promises. The prime minister must meet the same criteria, but some interviewees added "he is the first servant of the country"; as such, he must represent all citizens, not only the members of his party.

Their judgements of Canadian politicians varied greatly. Only one person said they were good and that "this is the least corrupt country" that she knew. On the other hand, three more critical respondents said that politicians did not represent the people because they were too remote from the concrete realities of the country.

But most of our respondents (five) had a view in between. For one interviewee, politicians were better here than elsewhere, especially better than the politicians of his country of origin. For the others, there were good and bad politicians. Some were representative; others were opportunist, chasing after votes, using "clichés" or "expedients" to seduce and favour some groups more than others. One person described parliamentarians as incompetent on international issues: "I find it very serious," she told us, "that a member who sits in the Canadian Parliament does not know the difference between Lebanon and Libya." More pointedly, another said: "Eighty percent of them are bad." Some interviewees were disappointed in, if not frustrated by, Canadian politicians because they had had high expectations of them when they were still in their countries of origin. Thus, their perception of the political system was not always very positive. They called it "acceptable," "not bad" or "correct." Several emphasized that it was not accessible to everyone, nor was it representative.

Interest in Canadian Politics

All our respondents followed Canadian politics. The majority, that is six persons, were interested mainly in Canada's foreign policy, image and role on the international scene. According to almost all the interviewees, Canada's foreign policy is too dependent on that of the United States. One said that Canada does not sit on the United Nations Security Council and does not hold a position worthy of a great nation. On the other hand, slightly fewer (five) were concerned with internal policy issues. They were interested in the concept of democracy and the democratic process, the Constitution, the federal structure, and (for only two people) relations between government and visible minorities. They had expectations which matched their interests. Most interviewees said that Canadian foreign policy should be coherent and independent. The wish of one interviewee was indicative of this view: "I would like to be a Canadian," she said, "and not an American."

On domestic policy, hopes were more varied. They looked forward to the day when politicians would be more vigilant. One interviewee talked about Quebec independence. Another noted that democracy functions poorly because the opinions of the different ethnic groups are not taken into consideration. She believed that the government should be urgently concerned with this. Finally, one person stressed the importance of the government's maintaining its social policies.

Three respondents said they were interested in politics before they arrived in Canada, and that they were already politicized in their country of origin. The other five[3] found their interest had increased over the years. All interviewees said they understood the main problems of Canadian society better. One said that he understood that Canadian society is not homogeneous. He believed that problems are perceived differently by people with a different past and present, which implies that the consensual view of Canada is now a thing of the past.

Canadian Politics and Visible Minorities

The respondents agreed that the Canadian political system is not at all representative of the population because it excludes women, Aboriginal people and visible minorities. This unanimity hides differing feelings and nuances, however. One interviewee admitted the system is no worse than any other and that it represents the majority; he noted that the presence of massive ethnic groups in large cities has forced politicians to pay attention to them. Others said that reality contradicts the principle that everyone should have access to the system: "Officially," some said, "politics makes room for visible minorities, but not in reality."

Criticism was sometimes more virulent: "There is a vice in the system," one told us, "much discrimination, such as in the Bélanger-Campeau Commission where there are no ethnic representatives." Some felt they were manipulated by the system: "I believe that ethnic minorities are used as a sort of exchange currency in the great debate between anglophones and francophones." More generally, it was thought that visible minorities' opinions are sought only at election time. Several stressed that the right to be different is not respected and one person assured us that there is racism at the political level.

According to most of our interviewees, these problems are created by "psychological reasons," "invisible barriers," "doors" that are closed. In fact, there were two explanations possible. Some respondents believed that the reasons for these difficulties must be sought within the community itself, saying members of ethnic communities "do not feel involved, because at the same time they feel that socially speaking they are the last of the last, because they are never consulted, and because they suffer discrimination and racism." Another said, "They feel marginalized compared with the white Anglo-Saxon majority that controls the system." Other interviewees said that society is responsible for excluding members of visible minorities believing that visible minorities are not well accepted and society does not trust them. The fact that during the recent municipal elections in Montreal several candidates of ethnic origin stood for election and none of them won reinforced this belief. Some also insisted that political parties did not support candidates of ethnic origin.

Several respondents complained of the lack of information, reproaching the political parties: "We do not necessarily know their objectives, nor their programs," they explained. Although they said that they were treated differently by the political system, they had not always experienced this personally. Several stressed that some communities, such as the Jewish, Italian or Greek communities, were more privileged than others. More visible minorities, they told us, such as the Black communities, always faced more problems. In other respects, however, the Quebec Arabic-speaking community's knowledge of French was seen as an advantage and a means of integration.

Finally, from most respondents' point of view, the interests of the Arabic-speaking community are not very well championed in Canada. Here too, there were several explanations possible. Two people believed that in this, pressure groups were more effective than politicians. For three others, it was up to the community itself to support its positions and consequently to organize, which was not always the case. In the final analysis, the view was that divisions within the Arabic-speaking community that reflect conflicts between Arabic countries were partly responsible for this state of affairs. It should be noted that many of our Arabic-speaking respondents, particularly the Lebanese, expect Canada to become more interested in the problems of their countries of origin.

Of course, the solutions contemplated depended on the obstacles our interviewees had identified. Barriers must be lowered, they said, and doors to the system must be opened. Not only must new citizens be told how the political system works, but visible minorities must also be encouraged to get out and vote to support ethnic candidates. For some interviewees, the effort must come from the communities themselves, which must demonstrate their interest by fielding good candidates. Participation, they told us, must be at all levels: economic and social, as well as political. For political participation, one interviewee suggested that participation must take place at the municipal level first, and then at the provincial and federal levels.

Our interviewees wanted to be treated as full Canadians; in this sense they did not think they had a special role to play politically, but they did say they wanted to occupy the position they deserved as citizens of this country. For some, however, this did not mean losing their identity or denying their diversity. Similarly, they believed it was necessary to encourage participation rather than stress integration. One respondent emphasized: "I hate it when I am told 'You are in our house now, so you must act this way.'" In the opinion of many people, however, ethnic groups have a particular role to play. Some said ethnic groups contribute to a welcoming society; for others, society absolutely must specify the role it intends for new arrivals. "Are they a labour force, full citizens in their own rights, or investors? Because there is some confusion about this," they told us.

Our interviewees were not at all optimistic about their participation in the future. Three said increased participation by visible minorities would renew Canadian politics; elected representatives would gain legitimacy and communities would have more influence. For the others, however, the outlook was grimmer. Because nothing was really being done to change the situation, some believed that the communities' role would be limited to the economic level. Others said that because the

Canadian government wanted to increase immigration quotas, it was "absolutely urgent for them to get politically interested in the life of ethno-cultural communities." Some even had an apocalyptic view of the future; one interviewee pointed out that fear could easily degenerate into hate, if not into outright discrimination and racism. "It is as if the sword of Damocles were over the head of Canadian society," he said. Another went even further; in his opinion, "without the total and full participation of the ethnic communities, the country will fall apart." In both cases, France was cited as the example not to follow (both the respondents having lived there). The government must act quickly and sensitively, they said, because visible minorities constitute an increasingly large segment of society; they can no longer be ignored.

The Community and the Media

According to almost all respondents, the media do not give the Arabic-speaking community of Canada enough coverage. When they do cover it, they explained, it is with clichés, such as "Arabs are all terrorists, or they have 50 women or something degrading like that." And, like other communities, the Arabic-speaking community objects to routine mentions of the ethnic origin of criminals. Explanations given for what they consider negative media coverage differed from person to person. For some, it showed journalists' ignorance and misunderstanding; others saw it as the result of pressure from anti-Arab groups.

The respondents followed political events closely and were especially interested in the news. They listened to a variety of networks such as the CBC, Radio-Canada and Radio-Québec, of course, but also French, American and community networks. They read several newspapers. Most interviewees read not only the Canadian newspapers – for anglophones the *Toronto Star*, the *Globe and Mail*, the Montreal *Gazette;* for francophones *Le Devoir* and *La Presse* – but also several foreign dailies and magazines such as the *New York Times, Time, Newsweek*, the *Guardian,* the *Financial Times, Le Monde, Libération* and *Le Monde Diplomatique*. The radio programs most listened to were on the CBC and Radio-Canada.

Interview Report: Chinese Community

Description of the Interviewees

Because Canadians of Chinese origin are concentrated in a few large cities, especially Vancouver, we conducted four out of eight interviews there; the others were held in Montreal. Only one interview was conducted in French. On average, our interviewees had been Canadian citizens for approximately 12.5 years. The number varied between

5 and 21 years. One interviewee was born in Canada and another was not yet a Canadian citizen. The average stay in Canada was 19 years, ranging from 5 to 38 years. Six interviewees were married, and six of the eight were men. One interviewee was Protestant, two were Catholic, the others described themselves as atheists. Their average age was 39, with ages ranging from 34 to 45. Finally, their average annual income was $37 000, ranging between $20 000 and $50 000 annually.

Except for one respondent who was born in Canada, our interviewees' immigration route was directly from Hong Kong; five of them settled in Vancouver and two in Montreal. Each of our interviewees was well educated, and held a university degree. For the most part, they worked in the service sector, the public service or the community sector. Slightly less than half spoke three or more languages.

Some spoke French, English and Cantonese; others spoke English, Cantonese and Mandarin. The rest were bilingual and spoke English and Cantonese, or French and Cantonese. Our interviewees were active in Chinese community associations and some said they belonged to other organizations.

Electoral Behaviour, Pressure and Political Action

Half the interviewees of Chinese origin in our study were active in political parties. Their activism, however, was limited to municipal politics, since all those who said they are members of a political party belonged only at the municipal level.[4] As well, most contributed financially to election campaigns or political parties. Six respondents said they had donated, most at all three – municipal, provincial and federal – levels. All our interviewees said that they voted in the last election. Here again, they voted more in municipal elections and slightly less in federal elections. At the provincial level, half the interviewees said they did participate.

Compared with the Vietnamese community, which shows a certain amount of political conservatism, we noted that four of our interviewees had changed their party affiliation since their arrival in Canada. Some did so at both the federal and provincial level because, they told us, "the party policy changes with time." More than half our interviewees said they were politically active. Compared with the Vietnamese community, where politics takes place mainly through community organizations, when our interviewees of Chinese origin were politically active, they operated mainly within the institutions of the host community. While one "got involved in a municipal election campaign to support a Chinese candidate," another told us that he was elected to the Vancouver city council "although he was just beginning to be politically active." They also intended to engage in active politics. One person added that if she were to be politically active, she would concentrate her energy mainly on defending the interests of the Chinese community. During an election campaign, several interviewees said that they were ready to get involved to work for a candidate from their community. However, ethnic origin was not enough, because, in an election, our interviewees placed greater emphasis on the party platform and the candidate's personality, the two being equally important, while the political party came next.

We found that most of our interviewees had lobbied the government and engaged in political action in areas as diverse as grants, zoning in Montreal's Chinese neighbourhood, Chinese refugees and the head tax. For the most part, this pressure was exerted through Chinese community organizations, in which half of our interviewees were active.

All our interviewees discussed Canadian politics within their families and at work, with the proviso that "Canadian political issues are very often discussed with colleagues because close friends and relatives are either uninterested in politics or interested only in Chinese politics." Most respondents also said they knew people in the community who had political experience.

Representativeness of the Political System and of Politicians
Our interviewees said the Canadian political system was fair and democratic and that many Chinese chose Canada as their adopted country because it was reputed to be a democratic country. They said that, on the whole, politicians were representative. Some interviewees added, however, that "it is unfortunate to note that some politicians have been co-opted by the system, they are sometimes remote from the people, and they do not keep their promises." From their point of view, a good politician was one who "knows both of Canada's official languages, defends the interests of the people rather than his personal interests, has the potential to develop the Canadian economy, listens to people from his or her constituency and knows how to promote Canada abroad."

Interest in Canadian Politics
As stated earlier, our interviewees of Chinese origin showed a marked interest in Canadian politics, particularly in the constitutional debate, multiculturalism, immigration, international relations, the Canadian economy, the affirmative action program and the Goods and Services Tax. They hoped that the government would be able to create a multicultural society, intensify affirmative action and employment equity programs, promote the social, linguistic and economic integration of

all groups and preserve original cultures. Finally, our interviewees said that, since their arrival in Canada, they had become more interested in politics and better able to understand the problems facing Canadian society.

Canadian Politics and Visible Minorities

It appears from our study that the Canadian political system is not considered representative of Canadian society. We were told, among other things, that people from visible minorities must fight to climb the social ladder. As far as all the interviewees were concerned, politics, as practised in Canada, does not really make room for members of various ethnic communities. Many cases were cited as examples during the interviews. It was pointed out that "there are only two federal MPs of Chinese origin." It was also mentioned that "political parties have the unfortunate habit of recruiting ethnic candidates only when a 'critical mass' has been reached. Such responses are increasingly common in Vancouver where members of the Chinese community are beginning to have more influence in constituencies." Our interviewees from Vancouver also made it a point to mention that the municipal scene gave higher priority to members of the various ethnic communities; therefore, "at the municipal level, for several years now, there have been individuals of Chinese origin on council."

Of course, there were real obstacles to greater participation in political life. Language problems were seen as the most difficult to overcome, especially in Montreal. Another important obstacle was their lack of practical experience in political life in a democracy. "Some have never experienced a democratic system. I am thinking especially of those coming from Hong Kong. Those who were educated in such an environment have practically never exercised the right to vote." Culture was also a barrier, since political involvement assumes a distancing from the family, and "family life is very important among people of Chinese origin." Some mentioned a fear that politics was likely to cause difficulties. Finally, the lack of training, information and relevant experience were other problems that our interviewees told us about. These difficulties seemed to matter more to the first generation: "It is understandable that the first generation will have problems with training and education. We must wait for the second and third generations before ethnic communities become more involved."

When asked what solutions they proposed for overcoming these obstacles and increasing their community's participation, our interviewees first mentioned the importance of good information which would encourage people to enter their names on the voters list, help them get out to vote, and get them interested in the political parties. They believed that the ethnic media and community organizations were important in this: "Organizations such as ours play a crucial role in the electoral process. At SUCCESS, for example, we organize election evenings, educate the public about elections, help them enter their names on the voters list and vote."

At another level, and in contrast to the Vietnamese community, our interviewees believed that ethnic groups had a special role to play in politics. They were emphatic in saying that the diversity of cultures enriched Canadian society, and that candidates from ethnic communities were more sensitive to the particular needs of those communities. They maintained that immigrants make important economic, cultural and industrial contributions to Canada and that it was important for the society to recognize that.

Six of the eight interviewees in our study believed they were treated differently by the political system. However, they believed that over the years this different treatment would decrease. On the other hand, for some, "what one receives in a situation depends on what one has invested in it ... It is so easy for people who have been 'disadvantaged' to say that they have not been well treated by the majority." However, all our interviewees acknowledged that there were differences among the nationalities: "If there are differences, they are based on the degree of integration of the various ethnic communities. The Jewish and Italian communities have integrated well in Quebec and they participate actively in the affairs of the province." Our interviewees suspected, therefore, that the society favours some communities to the detriment of others.

In their relations with institutions and political personnel, three people wanted to be treated as members of the Chinese community, three others as Canadians and two as Canadians and citizens of Chinese origin at the same time: "I prefer to identify myself as a Canadian of Chinese origin. I am first of all a Canadian, but of Chinese origin." There was the same diversity in their answers on the defence of their interests. Pressure groups come first, followed by political parties, governments and MPs.

The Community and the Media

Our interviewees reproached the media for not giving the Chinese community enough coverage and for giving only negative coverage when they happened to be interested: "They write about 'the invasion from Hong Kong,' they accuse them of building over-large buildings and causing housing prices to rise. They also talk about Chinese youth gangs and crime, and present us all as restaurant owners."

Finally, our interviewees from Quebec read *La Presse*, *Le Devoir* and the Montreal *Gazette* as well as ethnic newspapers. In Vancouver, they read the Vancouver *Sun* and the *Globe and Mail* as well as ethnic newspapers. News broadcasts were listened to as intently in Vancouver as in Montreal.

Interview Report: Haitian Community

Description of the Interviewees

Ten semi-directed interviews were held in Montreal, where most Haitian immigrants to Canada have settled. All the interviews were conducted in French. On the average, our interviewees had been Canadian citizens for 13 years, the number varying from 5 to 26 years. The average length of stay in Canada was 18.5 years, ranging from 7 to 22 years. Six of our interviewees were married, three were single, and one was divorced. Six of the ten were men. The religion of all our interviewees was Roman Catholic. Their average age was 41, with ages ranging from 26 to 53. Their average annual income was $35 000, ranging from $25 000 to $55 000.

Six of the ten interviewees came directly to Montreal. One lived in Toronto before settling in Montreal, two others lived elsewhere in Quebec – in Mont-Laurier and Thetford Mines, Saint-Hyacinthe, and in Quebec. One last respondent settled first in Miami and New York.

Nine of our interviewees held university degrees. Two were in business, five were in the public service, two were in community organizations and one was in journalism. Four of the ten spoke more than three languages: French, English, Creole and Spanish; or French, English, Spanish and Italian. Four spoke three languages: French, English and Creole. The others were bilingual in French and Creole. All but one of our interviewees were active in at least one Haitian community organization and five of the ten belonged to other associations.

Electoral Behaviour, Pressure and Political Action

The Canadians of Haitian origin in our study were active mainly at the provincial level and contributed primarily to Quebec election campaigns. Seven of the ten contributed to political parties but, again, they supported provincial parties rather than federal or municipal parties. Their interest in politics was stable, with nine of the ten stating their intention to enter active politics some day. All voted in the last election; eight of the ten had voted in municipal, provincial and federal elections, and two in provincial and federal elections. All the interviewees also intended to vote in the next municipal, provincial and federal elections. Six of the ten interviewees said they had not changed political affiliation since they arrived in Canada, because "most of the political parties haven't given me the impression that they can do better than the others – than the one I vote for." Those who said that they had changed political affiliation, mainly at the provincial level, explained it by "a new awareness of the cultural communities under René Lévesque, who was in power when I arrived, something that definitely influenced me."

More than half of our interviewees said they had already been politically active. During municipal elections, some had supported a candidate, others had exerted pressure on the political parties, and still others had been committee chairpersons or candidates in a constituency. Finally, two said they had been involved in school board election campaigns. Although our interviewees placed some importance on candidates' ethnic origin, they nevertheless voted for the party and its platform.

All but one of our interviewees had lobbied various governments. These activities were as diverse as signing petitions, lobbying municipal authorities to get a housing cooperative built for the poor and requesting subsidies. They had also exerted pressure on the Quebec Human Rights Commission in connection with the Haitian taxi drivers' case. The problem of Haitian refugees also preoccupied some of our respondents. It should be emphasized that this pressure was exerted through Haitian community networks. Briefly, they were interested in politics, they discussed it, they participated in it and they personally knew one or more people active in politics.

Representativeness of the Political System and of Politicians

Our interviewees said the system of political representation in Canada was more or less adequate. They judged it equitable, but some hoped for an elected Senate. Some emphasized that "the system of representation should be revised and moved toward proportional representation since the percentage of votes do not correspond to the number of members elected to Parliament." For others, the system of political representation needed to be revised, because "to run for election, one needs to be equipped with resources that are not necessarily available to all levels of society."

Our respondents judged that politicians were representative of the population and wanted them to respect their electoral commitments, to be sensitive to the needs of cultural communities, to be good administrators, and to listen to people's needs and claims, especially those expressed by voters in their constituencies. Nearly all deplored how few ethnic members of Parliament there are.

Interest in Canadian Politics

At this stage in our analysis, we note that four of our interviewees indicated that they were more interested in Quebec politics because "the dynamics in Quebec are more interesting. The politicians are closer to the electorate than federal politicians." The rest followed both Canadian and Quebec politics, especially the debates on the Constitution, international relations, immigration, the Goods and Services Tax and the educational system. They were all more interested in politics now than when they had arrived in this country and now that they understood Canada's problems better.

Several interviewees said that things were going badly in this country and hoped for better communication among the different regions. Some frankly declared themselves sovereigntists and doubted that Canada was interested in keeping Quebec in Confederation.

Canadian Politics and Visible Minorities

From our interviewees' point of view, the main obstacle to political involvement by ethnic communities was that the Canadian political system was not very accessible: "One could say that some political parties show little interest in the ethnic communities, except at election time," some said. This situation is reinforced by the fact that in Haiti, the people do not vote and those who control politics belong to a corrupt clique. In sum, they lack democratic experience and models because practising politics tends to be dangerous in Haiti.

Information about the political system was sometimes lacking because "the cultural communities are not really up to date with politics. Members of these communities do not see to it that their names are entered on the voters lists." Finally, our respondents reported having had difficulty identifying with "speeches made by political parties that do not make room for new clientele ... and also the parties' attitude, which makes getting along in their organizations less comfortable than you might imagine."

All our interviewees believed that the number of candidates of ethnic origin must absolutely be increased. This, they said, was a first step to overcoming the obstacles discussed previously, but these candidates would need to run in safe constituencies. At another level, they emphasized that training and information would increase participation: "There needs to be some work on educating the public: what an election is about, why vote, an explanation of which levels of government are responsible for which activities in community life. When the census is taken, there should be better publicity in different languages, not only in *La Presse* and *Le Devoir*, but also in the ethnic newspapers and on community radio and television. Information should be the responsibility not only of community organizations but also of the host society."

Many hoped that, in the future, the leading political parties would be much more interested in their community and their leaders. They hoped that close relations with political parties could be maintained, even after elections. For many this phrase had considerable meaning, "as long as an effort is being made to cultivate the generations that have been left out, the underprivileged economic classes that feel they have no place in society. If they are not represented in the media, in the public service, at the decision-making level, one cannot expect these people to participate."

Nearly all our interviewees believed that members of their community had a special role to play in politics, particularly "in promoting the integration of immigrants when they arrive in this country." Several also believed that "the participation of different communities is essential because it makes it possible to make more enlightened decisions." A few respondents disagreed with this because "one does not elect an Italian for Italians, a Haitian for Haitians." That being the case, our interviewees were quite optimistic about their future and hoped ethnic candidacies would increase. This optimism was also caused by the perception of seven of the ten interviewees that they had been treated the same as native-born Canadians by the political system. Some said that this had improved in recent years, while others insisted that "being Black and poor means that one is already doubly a minority. If one is female, this minority situation is tripled." "Visible minorities are not treated very well because policies put forward to help them participate are not respected." As for differences in the way nationalities are treated, most of our respondents acknowledged that these differences exist and stressed that they mirror the communities' economic status. Despite this, all wanted to be treated as Canadians or Québécois by political institutions and people.

Finally, our interviewees believed that their community's interests were protected better by pressure groups, although several made it a point to recall that the "Parti québécois has often taken up our cause, I know, and I think that we have been generally well supported. Perhaps, in return, we are not doing the same for others."

The Community and the Media
Media coverage of the Haitian community was judged very negatively and some of our respondents stressed the need to go beyond generalizations and folklore. Some respondents insisted, however, that media coverage had improved in the past few years. Mainly, our interviewees

read *La Presse* and *Le Devoir* and, to a lesser degree, *Le Journal de Montréal* and the Montreal *Gazette*. Some also read ethnic newspapers. Television and radio news broadcasts were widely listened to, community radio rather less.

Interview Report: Indian Community

Description of the Interviewees
Most Canadians of Indian origin are concentrated in the large cities of Vancouver, Toronto and, to a lesser extent, Montreal. We found this distribution in our interviewees' places of residence. In fact, we met four people in Vancouver, three in Toronto and three in Montreal. All but one of the interviews were held in English. Three respondents in Montreal knew French but only one knew it perfectly; the other two spoke it with difficulty. Without exception, all our respondents spoke English and several Indian languages; most spoke Hindi (eight of the ten) and Punjabi (six of the ten).

The average age of our respondents was 48.5, but the interviewees from Vancouver were on the average younger (46) than those from Montreal (49.5) and Toronto (51). The youngest respondent was 40; the oldest, 56. The group was fairly homogeneous in age because seven people were between 44 and 54. Of the ten people we interviewed, only two were women.

The respondents were mostly of the Hindu religion (four people) or Sikh (four people, three of whom lived in Vancouver); one was Moslem and the last Christian. Our respondents' level of education was high; all were university graduates. Three held doctorates, five, masters' degrees and two, bachelors' degrees. The respondents' professions were in keeping with this high level of education: three worked in business, three were university professors, two were social workers connected with visible minorities, one was a journalist and one was a lawyer. The respondents' average annual income was remarkably high, exceeding $183 000, but if we exclude the highest income ($1 million) and the lowest salary ($25 000), we obtain an average annual income of $73 000.

Our respondents had spent an average of 20 years in Canada; seven of the ten had stayed between 18 and 22 years, which indicates that most of the interviewees arrived during the great wave of immigration from India in the late 1960s and early 1970s. The shortest length of stay among our respondents was 10 years, the longest 35 years. On average, our respondents had been Canadian citizens for 14.5 years. (This average excludes one landed immigrant who had just applied for citizenship at the time of the interview.) Among the other respondents, the first to obtain Canadian citizenship did so 28 years ago and the one who received citizenship most recently did so eight years ago. On the average, seven years passed between the respondents' arrival and their receipt of Canadian citizenship. All but one respondent, who was Pakistani, came from India,[5] but they did not all follow the same route; five interviewees came directly to Canada from southern Asia, the others spent some time in Asia (Java, Hong Kong), Europe (Great Britain), East Africa (Malawi) and North America (Mexico, the United States).

We were therefore dealing with a remarkably homogeneous group of interviewees; they belonged to the same generation, had a comparable level of education, came from a similar socioprofessional background, and had lived in Canada for much the same length of time. In the dimension of religion they were diverse, and probably also in their geographic origin in India,[6] as well as their itineraries after leaving the Indian subcontinent.

Electoral Behaviour, Pressure and Political Action

The electoral behaviour of the respondents who were Canadian citizens (one was a landed immigrant) had the following characteristics: they had voted in all elections and all said they intended to vote in the next election. Seven of the ten interviewees had donated money to an election campaign, five at all three levels: municipal, provincial and federal. A minority of the interviewees had not changed political affiliation; one claimed no affiliation and four said they had changed affiliation.

Nine of the respondents said that they based their vote on the candidate's personality. They valued a candidate's competence above all, but for most of the interviewees, the candidate's ethnic origin could influence their vote because, with equally competent candidates, six of the respondents would choose an ethnic candidate over a native-born Canadian. Most justified their choice by their conviction that visible minorities were underrepresented in the Canadian political system. One interviewee said: "Given equal abilities, I would choose the candidate from the ethnic group because I think ethnic groups are not properly represented, and I would do anything to improve that. But I would not do so if I thought the ethnic candidate was not as good as the other candidate." On the other hand, religious affiliation did not influence our respondents' votes; for them religion was a private matter that had nothing to do with politics. However, religion could play a role if the candidate showed any religious intolerance.

To sum up, our respondents performed their civic duty by voting regularly; most contributed to election campaigns and had no political affiliation because they voted mainly on the basis of candidates' personal qualifications.

Half of the interviewees belonged to political parties, four at the federal level, three at the provincial level and two at the municipal level. One belonged to a party at all three levels. The number who contributed to political parties was slightly lower than the number who contributed to election campaigns; only six donated to a political party but seven contributed to campaigns. The result was that half the interviewees were financially involved in politics, and eight of the ten participated in financing either a political party or an election campaign, four donating at two levels. Half the people we interviewed said, however, that they were not politically active. We noted a hierarchy among those who said they were active. One had been a parliamentary secretary for a political party in India and was no longer active because she had become a journalist; another had participated in Quebec election campaigns, especially organizing candidates' meetings with the Indian community and participating in financing workshops. A third was very active on committees of his riding association, of which he was executive vice-president. Two others had been active for many years and had run in several elections under the New Democratic Party banner.

Half the interviewees said it was very unlikely that they would be politically committed in the future. They generally mentioned professional reasons; for one, however, the reason was his difficulty in mastering French, which limited his involvement. Among the other five respondents, three foresaw being politically committed while the other two would be candidates in the next election, one at the provincial level and the other at the federal level. All the interviewees said they personally knew politically active people in their community, and discussed politics with their neighbours. Nine interviewees were active in associations, eight in their ethnic community, and four were also active in professional, humanitarian, multicultural or social areas. It can be said, therefore, that most of the interviewees were involved in political life and in community associations, that half were politically active or expected to be active in the future, and the other half wanted to devote themselves to their professional lives.

Representativeness of the Political System and of Politicians

The interviewees' expectations of politicians varied, and these expectations were not all at the same level. Some placed greater emphasis on the qualities that politicians ought to have, while others were more interested in their role or tasks. This diversity, far from constituting a divergence, painted a composite portrait of the ideal politician.

The interviewees insisted on certain character traits and qualities that ideal politicians ought to possess: according to them politicians must be flexible, upright, open, honest and neither egotistical nor untruthful. The interviewees described the politicians' function essentially as that of the nation's representatives, mediators between different members of society, various interest groups and the Canadian provinces and regions. One said politicians must know how to listen to everyone while defending the interests of all, and they must also be leaders capable of defending fundamental principles such as human rights, equal rights or opposition to racism, even if this might sometimes harm their popularity. They thought that to do this, politicians must not be prisoners of public opinion or interest groups. Our respondents considered politicians to have very heavy national and international responsibilities, especially national tasks: ideal politicians, they said, must focus on social and community problems, deal with economic issues, create jobs and be interested in training, particularly in advanced technology. Finally, they must know how to plan and keep within their budgets. For most of our respondents, Canadian politicians fall well short of this ideal.

Most of the people we interviewed had rather negative views of Canadian politicians; their judgement was not uniform and some were more moderate than others. The most balanced opinion came from a minority who distinguished between good and bad politicians. On the whole, politicians were criticized for making promises that they knew they couldn't keep if elected, and for thinking more about poll results and "what people will say" than about fundamental principles, the country's interests or political rights. Paradoxically, the respondents believed both that politicians lacked contact with the people and that they followed public opinion too often. Politicians were suspected of thinking mainly of their personal interests and of seeking power and money. There was less of the most severe criticism in this group of respondents. Some reproached Canadian politicians for "a chronic lack of ideas," for using the country's divisions to their own advantage, for being "mediocre," for being "bureaucrats" and for lying.

The majority of the interviewees thought that Canadian politicians were not really representatives of all members of society, more specifically that they did not represent visible minorities, women or Aboriginal people. However, a few interviewees saw them as representative, but said they were representative in their very mediocrity: "Canadians are not interested in problems, they do not take initiative. In this respect politicians are representative, they do not make firm decisions on issues." For another "they are obviously representative."

The image of the political system was scarcely better for the interviewees. For one it was "a very good system, one of the best." Another shared this view but was more specific: "It happens that a party with 35 or 40 percent of the vote obtains the majority of the seats in parliament; as in all systems, there are limits." Two-thirds of the respondents, however, were more critical: among these, some criticized the system particularly for not being representative of all social categories, explaining that elections by their very nature exclude those who cannot bear the cost. Others questioned the concept of democracy: "What sort of democracy should we have in a multi-ethnic society? Will we build a democracy in which the majority squelches the minority, one in which there would be no social contract, or a democracy that has mechanisms that permit minorities to participate?" We were also told that a true democracy has the duty to defend and protect minorities, that it must represent all groups, which one interviewee claimed was not the case in Canada because "the fundamental characteristic of the system is a hierarchy based on race and language ... with the English at the top, then the French, then white Europeans and below that come the other immigrants." Most of our respondents, therefore, perceived the system and politicians quite negatively and critically.

Interest in Canadian Politics

All but one of our respondents said they were keenly interested in Canadian politics. The other was interested in democracy but "tired of politics." For most of the interviewees this interest in politics was not something new; for two-thirds of them, it dated from before their arrival in Canada, when they were still in India. For most of the interviewees, it was a citizen's duty to be interested in politics: "I think it is my duty to become involved and to be active in politics. We must pave the way for the next generation, we must help define the system. I think it is our responsibility."

Respondents' spheres of interest varied, but nine of the ten were most concerned about community questions, such as the place of visible minorities in society, multiculturalism, intercommunity relations, and fairness and equality in professional, economic and social conditions as well as immigration. The question of multiculturalism was mainly raised by the interviewees from Vancouver. Their views were varied, but criticism of the current policy dominated the different interpretations. In effect, they said: "The federal policy makes no sense. For the federal government, multiculturalism exists only for ethnic communities. Does that mean that 90 percent of Canadians have no culture and only 10 percent, the ethnic minorities, have one? There will be multiculturalism only when all the people believe in it."

Other areas of interest varied with the interviewees. Nearly half were interested in social issues, especially "social welfare and health services," and in how the system operates; for example, political institutions, the question of federalism and distribution of power between the central government and the provinces, and the democratic process. To a lesser extent, they also referred to economic issues, such as productivity and competitiveness; international issues, especially Canada's foreign policy; the make-up of Europe in 1992; free trade between Mexico and the United States; and global issues such as the environment. All those interviewed said that they understood the problems that concern Canadian society, mentioning the economy and Quebec sovereignty. One person also mentioned problems that to him seemed secondary to the issues already listed: integration, employment and violence.

Our respondents' expectations varied considerably concerning four different subjects: democracy, federalism, immigration and politicians. They hoped democracy would be integrated into the operation of the system and political practice. Some especially wanted to see minority groups taken into account, so they could have real equal rights and a larger presence at the political level, thus improving their representation in the system.

On the subject of federalism, expectations were different, and Canadian unity was essential for most: "We must not end up breaking with Quebec." For one (this was a minority point of view), "Quebec has certain rights and needs mechanisms to administer these rights."

On the question of immigration there were different points of view. For one person, the policy must be egalitarian, and members of ethnic groups (southern Asians especially) should have the same rights as Europeans on issues such as family reunion.[7] For another, the immigration policy was "really an unreasonable policy" because without adequate financial means it is "unfair to have people come and then leave them to themselves," adding that they would be "a handicap rather than an asset to society." Another interviewee had a radically different view on this question and proposed instead the "doubling of Canadian society in the next 10 years"; this, he said, is "a major prerequisite" for the country's development. He maintained that immigrants constitute a considerable labour force because "they work harder" and have "the lowest unemployment rate."

At another level, several respondents expected politicians to devote themselves more sincerely and honestly to constituency, provincial and national problems, taking into account changes in the population.

Finally, they expected politicians to deal with the problems that face each individual, not only those that face the majority of citizens. We will return to these issues in the next section.

Canadian Politics and Visible Minorities

Most of our respondents believed they were treated differently by the political system and emphasized especially that visible minorities in general, and the Indian community in particular, were not accurately represented at the political level and that their interests were not protected. Most of the interviewees thought that visible minorities were excluded from the political system for various reasons, some originating from within the community itself, others from outside, which are all intrinsic to the system or society.

The "fundamental problem" behind the external reasons lies in the democratic process itself, an interviewee told us, because the democratic process in Canada protects "the interests of the majority" and the law of numbers explains the exclusion of minority groups. Some advanced historical reasons to explain "the domination of politics by the Anglo-Saxon majority" and the "stratification of society by race and language," which explains the exclusion of minority groups. "When someone does not belong to the system he has trouble integrating with it," and consequently, "there are groups in the system and groups outside the system. Visible minorities are outsiders, excluded from politics." One interviewee added that this exclusion was flagrant in the Spicer and Bélanger-Campeau commissions, with visible minorities largely excluded.

For some individuals, the political parties had an important responsibility. The satellite organizations launched by some political parties were generally criticized by our respondents, who thought them "discriminatory." By making ethnic minorities half-members, they said, parties create political "ghettoes" that institutionalize segregation. Some added that these practices have negative consequences because they create intermediaries between the communities and the leaders of political parties, and suppress direct contact. One of our respondents stressed that political parties choose "some ethnic candidates across the country to show their links with the community" and that "these candidates become colonial masters and the communities become flocks governed by lords ... There is no longer any direct communication with the community."

Political parties were also reproached for not being open enough to ethnic communities and visible minorities. Equality of race and sex, we were told, has not yet been reached. The main reason given by the interviewees to explain political parties' reluctance to select ethnic candidates was racism. Racism, one interviewee explained, affects "society and the political parties at the same time." The members of riding associations are not exempt from racism and, he added, "even if they escape, they would think of their electorate and tend to think that a candidate from the majority community will have a better chance of winning." Another also stressed that not everyone is prepared to accept an ethnic representative because, he said, "there are still people who think that members of ethnic communities should not run ... and that perhaps the second generation will be able to." In our respondents' opinion, this rejection is caused by the real separation between society's mainstream and the visible minorities; there is, one said, a problem of ignorance and perception, and he added that "in cities, people are more educated, less narrow-minded," and therefore less hesitant to vote for ethnic candidates.

The respondents proposed a second way of looking at our analysis, at the community level. The reason given most often to explain the lack of participation by ethnic communities in the political process was the need for new arrivals to build up their stability and economic independence; they must first fight for "bread and butter." According to our respondents, there were other economic limits to their participation, such as the high cost of elections and the standing a politician needs. Recent arrivals had not yet amassed the large sums of money that were needed, or established financing networks. According to one interviewee, it is easier for an Anglo-Saxon than for a person of other ethnic origin to raise funds from businesspeople and unions: "Ethnic candidates are underfunded" and they cannot buy advertising space in the media. Language is another problem in the community; whether it is French for residents of Quebec or English for other Canadians, our respondents said that the language barrier limits the participation of ethnic groups. Some interviewees noted the difficulties their compatriots had in learning English, particularly those with little education or a strong accent. They also mentioned how difficult adults find it to learn a new language while working and added that adolescents "even if they attend school and then university, do not necessarily become bilingual."

Some of our respondents stressed how difficult it is for members of ethnic communities to understand the political system; it is a matter of "political culture," they said. One person said, "Indo-Canadians do not know what it means to be a Canadian ... There is perhaps a formal procedure when they receive citizenship, but people have still not adapted to it." They emphasized that members of ethnic communities do not understand the system, that they lack experience and information. They do not understand, one interviewee told us, "that they can and must expect answers to their concerns from politicians" because "people in India do not expect that a politician will do anything for them without a favour." They also said that the lack of representation in the political system reinforces ethnic communities' sense of exclusion and discourages participation. Some offered social explanations for Indo-Canadians' lack of participation. They told us that "the first concern of ethnic communities on arrival in Canada is to consolidate their cultural and religious position, because they think that is the first threat they face as a community." Others explained that Indo-Canadians had extensive family lives that left them little time for social or political activities. One person stressed that Canadians of Indian origin have particular problems communicating. She said, "the members of my community are very quiet, they do not make any noise, they do not speak with their neighbours, and they even encourage their children to stay in the house."

Finally, others added that the community must protect its own interests. We were told that these difficulties derived from the "diversity of the community," created by the diversity of language, religion and internal divisions, transposed from problems existing between various ethnic and religious communities in India.

The solution to these problems implied a change in the behaviour of Canadian-born citizens: our respondents said they wanted to be treated as Canadians and not as members of their community. But they emphasized that their feeling of being Canadians first and foremost did not exclude their attachment to their specific culture, and some deplored having to defend their rights as a visible minority. This was why half of the interviewees did not want Indo-Canadians to play a special role in politics. They thought the only role for them was that which any Canadian citizen plays. One asked: "Why should we speak of ethnics and non-ethnics? We are all Canadians." Besides, some thought that assigning a specific role to visible minorities would merely exacerbate existing divisions and antagonisms.

For the other interviewees, there was no doubt that ethnic groups had special roles in Canadian society, although respondents defined it in their own ways. For some, it was to enrich the political debate by introducing a new point of view, another way of looking at things. One respondent compared this to the political "revolution" women have fought, which has "obliged political parties to see things in terms other than white and male." Another believed that visible minorities can help defend the concept of "one Canada." According to her, "people who experienced serious political problems in their country of origin ... had a vision of one Canada, which was peaceful, calm and prosperous. They have developed a strong attachment to this country." And because of this attachment, "minority communities have a role to play in bridging the gap between anglophones and francophones."

According to most of our respondents, visible minorities all have something to gain from greater involvement in politics: "The only way to be represented is to be involved," one said. Another interviewee said: "Ethnic leaders must encourage members of their communities to participate actively at all levels of the political process, especially to get involved in parties." For this involvement to be real and possible, the interviewees looked forward to genuine support from government and political parties. Several thought that the government has a special responsibility to help visible minorities integrate into the system. Some suggested that the government establish basic assistance programs, both financial – for associations, for example – and educational. Several respondents hoped that the government would finance "language training programs in a sociocultural context," and produce television programs to increase political awareness for the ethnic media and the traditional networks. One respondent saw education as the key to equality; she suggested free training at all levels from elementary school to university. Because tolerance is acquired with knowledge, one interviewee suggested introducing cultural programs on television and in the schools so everyone could become familiar with different cultures and multiculturalism could become a reality. The government must promote fairness. One interviewee told us: "We expect the government to offer us the same opportunities in school, business and employment," while another proposed that an ethnic group member participate in employee selection and promotion committees to ensure the application of equal opportunity measures. Several people thought that minorities should be better represented in institutions, the public service and the courts, so that all may feel they really belong to Canadian society.

Most of our interviewees thought that ethnic groups should be encouraged to join and get active in political parties. They believed that "if election platforms had more room for ethnic content, people might perhaps feel more welcome and would join the parties," or that "parties should be living institutions ... they must move with changes in the country and the people." One respondent added that parties must take into consideration the new face of the cities, where ethnic groups are becoming an important component. Parties must encourage their participation: "This could be done through financial help or political training,

and sometimes they should be able to nominate people in parallel political activities, to give them confidence and prove that they can participate in the system." According to others, political parties must encourage
ethnic candidates and "one of the means for doing this is to provide the
necessary funding." The government, some said, like politicians, "must
reduce intercultural conflicts" by defending racial equality at the political level and promoting it among the non-ethnic population.

Most of our respondents were optimistic about the future; they
hoped that visible minorities would become more and more involved
in politics, and consequently become more important in influencing
decisions and promoting change. For some, this change will "be only
a reflection of reality"; it will allow "more harmonious, more open relations between the various components of society," and "the reward as
a result of this will be to reinforce our commitment as a multi-ethnic
nation."

The Community and the Media

Most of our interviewees thought that the media do not give enough
coverage to the Indian community. One person pointed out that this
generally reflects the attitude to all visible minorities. Only the Jewish
and Black communities get wide coverage, she said, the former because
they are powerful in Canada and the Blacks because of the violence of
their relations with the police. Only one person thought that the Indian
community, like the Chinese or Japanese communities, enjoys prestige
because of the ancient character of Asian civilizations. According to
this person, the Canadian media present quite a positive image of the
community. But this point of view was an exception; the other respondents all agreed that the image the media present of the Indo-Canadian
community is negative. For example, they cited the fact that the media
have no interest in Indian culture unless a problem such as the wearing
of turbans by Sikh RCMP officers gives rise to a national debate. This
tendency to give a negative image of the community also comes from
the practice of identifying the origin of a criminal who belongs to an
ethnic group, and not doing so when an Anglo-Saxon or French
Canadian is involved. Our respondents advanced a variety of reasons
to explain this. Some said the issue must be seen from the community's
perspective and others said the fault lay with journalists: "If we can't
get their attention it may be because we can't raise issues that interest
them." Their view was that journalists only report spectacular events;
one interviewee said an Indian woman who immolates herself is more
newsworthy than a meeting about problems faced by visible minorities.
Some respondents spoke of "mental colonialism," which they attributed

to the superficiality of journalists' knowledge of visible minorities and to their lack of appropriate research. Others advanced the view that "the situation that now prevails in India" has a negative influence on Canadians of Indian origin. One person explained that the Sikhs' struggle for independence from India and the outrages that have arisen from it ensure "that [Sikh Canadians] will be criticized when they fight for their rights." Another stressed that the media have a pernicious influence because they "justify prejudice and racism." They should, instead, promote multiculturalism. Two other respondents believed this situation would improve as the Indian community increased its participation in politics and society and its representation in all Canadian institutions, including the media.

Our interviewees read a very wide range of newspapers regularly, because of the regional and linguistic disparity of our sample. All read ethnic papers, such as *India Abroad*. The francophone papers were little read; one respondent read *La Presse* from time to time and another had replaced this newspaper with *Le Devoir*. English-language dailies were mentioned most, specifically the *Toronto Star*, the *Globe and Mail*, the Montreal *Gazette* and the Vancouver *Sun*, as well as magazines. The most-read magazine was *Time*; also mentioned were *Business Magazine*, *Business Week*, *Fortune* and *Maclean's*. Two-thirds of our interviewees watched CBC television, especially its news broadcasts, but several flipped through the various Canadian and American networks "to get full coverage of events." Our respondents listened to the radio very little, except for one who said that he listened to it and watched little television. The stations most listened to were on the CBC Radio network.

Interview Report: Jamaican Community

Description of the Interviewees
Most of our interviews (seven of ten) with members of the Jamaican community were held in Toronto, where 49 percent of the total Canadian community is concentrated; the other three were held in Montreal. All the interviews were in English. The average age of the respondents was 51, with the minimum 32 and the maximum 65. Outside the two extremes, all belonged to the generation born during the 1940s.

All the respondents were Christians. Eight of the ten specified that they were Protestants; of these, three were Anglican and one Presbyterian.

Six of the ten respondents were university graduates (four held masters' degrees), two had college training, and two others did not finish their secondary education. Three were teachers, one was a journalist, three were managers, one was a provincial public servant and one was a retired blue-collar worker (the tenth did not indicate type of job). Their average annual salary was $53 220, with a maximum of $85 000 and a minimum of $19 200. Our respondents, therefore, were for the most part white collar, middle class and had a high level of training.

The majority – seven of the ten – came directly from Jamaica. The other three lived first in Great Britain, the United States or both countries. On average, the interviewees had been in Canada 21 years (maximum 28, minimum 14) – six of them arrived between 1962 and 1969 – and they had been Canadian citizens for an average of 14.5 years (maximum 23, minimum 4).

Electoral Behaviour, Pressure and Political Action
The Jamaicans we interviewed were generally politically involved, seven of them as members of political parties; only one person was involved at the municipal level (there are no municipal parties in Ontario), four at the provincial level (but none in Quebec), and three at the federal level.

Election campaign financing brought out behaviour that was completely different in Quebec and Ontario; the study of the Jamaican community revealed political behaviour that differed greatly from one province to the other. None of the Montreal respondents had contributed to an election campaign or a political party. In Toronto, political commitment was accompanied by financial support: all the Toronto respondents had contributed to campaigns. All donated at the provincial level,[8] seven at the federal level and four at the municipal level; four had contributed to campaigns at all three levels, and three had contributed at the provincial and federal levels. In Toronto, five out of seven respondents also donated to provincial political parties, and four to federal parties. We note that the respondents who had never donated to a political party did not belong to any party and did not trust them.

All our Toronto respondents had voted in all elections, except one who was unable to vote in the last provincial election because she was on a business trip. Our Montreal respondents didn't show such constancy; none had voted at all three levels. Of the three Montreal respondents, two voted at the municipal level, one at the provincial level and two at the federal level; one voted only at the federal level. On the other hand, all the interviewees, in both Toronto and Montreal, said they intended to vote in the next election.

The Jamaicans cannot be described as conservative; in fact, only three had never changed political affiliation. One had not changed since joining a party, two had changed at least once, and four said that they had no political affiliation and based their choices on the candidate.

The interviewees from Montreal affirmed that a candidate's ethnic origin did not influence their vote; they chose the candidate that represented them best. In Toronto, the response was completely different – almost the opposite. Only one person gave the same reply as the Montreal interviewees, and another was quite close but noted that he chose candidates for their personal worth and because they seemed most able to defend ethnic groups. Another said that candidates' ethnic origins did not influence his vote, though he always supported Jamaican candidates (sometimes without voting for them – with money, for example). All the others (four of seven) said they would choose, given two candidates of equal quality, an ethnic candidate over candidates of French or English origin. Two interviewees added that they were more demanding of ethnic candidates because, as one of them explained, an incompetent ethnic candidate means that the whole community will suffer; "that is why one must choose only people who will win."

Although respondents in Montreal and Toronto alike emphasized the candidates' personal qualifications, in Toronto, given equally qualified candidates of ethnic or non-ethnic origin, they would choose the former. This is one way they fight the community's underrepresentation in the system, an interviewee told us.

Religious affiliation played no role. The same pattern was found in the priorities the interviewees chose to explain their votes: five thought the election platform counted most, four thought it was the candidate's party; the candidate's personality only came in third place, followed by ethnic origin. The candidate's sex was least important.

Seven respondents described themselves as politically active; the other three said they were not active. However, we must make a correction for one respondent who described herself as "non-active." She had a very narrow idea of "active politics"; she limited political activism to candidacy in elections. This person was, however, very active in political action groups; she had also helped candidates by campaigning door to door. Counting her, eight respondents were active, with two inactive. We should note that the inactive interviewees were Jamaicans from Montreal. One had no intention of becoming active, but the other wanted to be.

On the other hand, all the active respondents intended to continue. Thus 90 percent of the interviewees expressed the wish to be politically active. Among these nine, three did not wish to stand for election, three had already stood for election and hoped to do so again, and two thought this not very likely, unless new parties were to appear. It should be noted that this was the attitude of those who showed hostility toward political parties in general, explaining this reaction by their attachment to freedom of individual action, regarding political parties as a prison.

We found the same overall result for political lobbying: that is, two respondents had never exerted political pressure (people in Montreal) and eight had exerted such pressure (one person said she had not personally done so). We also noted the pessimistic attitude of the Montreal respondents, for whom pressure "serves no purpose." On the other hand, in Toronto, pressure was exerted on many issues, whether directly linked to the community or not: fairness in employment, housing, education, immigration, human rights and literacy. Generally, they considered political pressure efficient; several said they expected to use it again. All the interviewees said they personally knew someone who was politically active. All were active in at least one community, cultural or professional association and six of the ten belonged to at least two associations. Six also held office in associations as president or vice-president. Finally, two respondents said they did not participate politically through associations; one always did; and the other five respondents said they participated in different ways depending on the circumstances. (Montreal respondents did not answer this question.)

Thus it appears that all our Toronto respondents were politically active; most of them could even be described as experienced activists. They were not all politically active through the same channels; two distrusted political parties, others preferred individual to collective action and still others acted through groups or in isolation. This shows that most of these people trusted their networks. They voted in all elections and their activism was accompanied by financial commitment. By comparison, the interviewees from Montreal were much less politically committed, and there was a varying degree of commitment among the three people interviewed. The first stood out as militant, without always making financial commitments, the second was so politically uncommitted that she could be described as apolitical, and the third held a position between the other two. This difference between the two groups can be explained by several factors, especially the length of their stay in Canada. In fact, the Montreal Jamaicans had only been in Canada for 15 or 16 years, while the Toronto average was 23.5 years; they had been Canadian citizens for a shorter time, an average of slightly more than 8.5 years, less than half the corresponding average for Toronto of 17 years. The factor of time seems essential to us, because it is often cited as an obstacle to participation – see the excellent example of the Vietnamese community on this point. We suspect that context is also significant, since the two communities have neither the same history nor the same problems.

Representativeness of the Political System and of Politicians
On the whole, the interviewees had a fairly positive view of the political system. A minority said that the system was quite good or that
Canada was a democratic country. The others qualified their comments,
using phrases like "relatively democratic" and "relatively good." Some
respondents' remarks were negative: "The system is poor." Their main
criticism was of the system of representation; they said large segments
of the population were excluded from the political system: ethnic groups,
women, Aboriginal people (the most often mentioned) and the poor. The
other criticisms of the system were as varied as the respondents: for
one, the nomination system was corrupt; for another, citizenship should
be widened; for still another, the problem was the distribution of legislative seats – he hoped for a system of representation in which the number
of seats a party holds is directly proportional to the number of votes it
gets; and last, for another, it was provincial representation in the federal
structure that was important. In the end, despite these criticisms, the
interviewees seemed to have a generally positive view of the political
system.

As for politicians, the most frequent comment was that they were
certainly no worse than elsewhere, and that among them, as every-
where, there were good and bad. Some were judged honest, devoted,
hardworking, sincere, generous, responsible or reasonable. However,
in general they were criticized as lacking openness and a vision of the
future of Canada. The respondents noted that politicians make more
promises than they can keep, sometimes even verging on incoherence,
according to some. Demagogy, lack of integrity, ineffectiveness, dishon-
esty – these were some of the faults our interviewees found in politicians, whom they accused of thinking mainly of their personal interests.
Respondents said politicians are not representative of the Canadian
population; only two of ten thought they are representative, and one
of these two was guarded: she "thinks" they are representative. They
emphasized the fact that Canadian politicians are white Anglo-Saxon
men from privileged classes, although "this country consists of more
than white men from the well-to-do middle class."

Several respondents also stressed that Canada has a problem
defining itself. "One of these definitions," they said, "which has survived
even though it is no longer appropriate, is that of the duality of Canada,
the concept of two founding nations ... from the beginning this immediately excluded the Aboriginal peoples ... I think that, in the same
way, this definition excludes the multiplicity of people from different
cultures."

There was no typical portrait of the ideal prime minister; for some it was Charles de Gaulle, for others it was not Brian Mulroney. They painted two different pictures at the same time in their comments. One saw the prime minister's role as complex and difficult – an arbiter, an intermediary who must promote equilibrium among provinces, cultures, groups and peoples. The prime minister must, therefore, listen to needs, inspire trust, and demonstrate openness and tolerance. The other said prime ministers must be respected leaders capable of making important decisions, with clear ideas of what Canada is now and what it will be in the future. They must, therefore, be courageous and free of the whims of the electorate – that is to say, not constantly studying polls and adjusting their speeches to popularity levels. They must be able to bring people together. The Jamaican community, like other visible minorities, takes Pierre Trudeau as a reference; it is the present prime minister who is under critical fire. Not all mentioned Pierre Trudeau, but his name came up repeatedly. Similarly, Brian Mulroney was not always the target of disparaging remarks. Of the four respondents who mentioned him, one described him as a good prime minister, another supported him because he fulfilled the vision of a prime minister capable of making difficult decisions and standing by them without seeking consensus (this referred to Mulroney's attitude toward the Goods and Services Tax). The other two respondents were very critical; for one, Mulroney is not a good leader; he lacks ideas, vision and concepts. The other respondent was even more scathing, seeing him as divisive, dishonest and antidemocratic.

In sum, the Jamaican interviewees had a critical but positive view of the Canadian political system, and an equally critical – if more negative – perception of politicians.

Interest in Canadian Politics
The Jamaicans were extremely interested in Canadian politics and generally very militant. Only one said that she was not interested in politics, though she followed developments. This person was no more interested at the present than she had been in the past, and it was likely that she would not be more interested in the future. This was an exception among the interviewees from that community. This interest in politics was not new; it was almost natural for Jamaicans. As one interviewee explained: "In Jamaica, politics is an integral part of life, like the Church, and school; all three are equally important … It is as natural as religion and music." Almost all the interviewees mentioned this Jamaican experience. Some also believed that they are more aware now of the importance of politics in the Canadian context. They thought they understood the problems well, sometimes with considerable humility in view of

the complexity of Canadian society and dynamic change; they did not claim to understand the problems totally or perfectly. Finally, we noted that some had an ideal image of Canada before arriving, which is not rare among immigrants. Several had had the opportunity to travel across Canada and were aware of Canada's diversity, the concept of the two founding nations and the problems between francophones and anglophones, the special character of Quebec and its aspirations, and the changes brought about by immigration.

The respondents' range of interests was as varied as they themselves. However, the question of visible minorities' place in the Canadian system preoccupied all the Jamaicans interviewed, followed by multiculturalism, race relations, human rights, immigration and equity in employment, salaries, education and housing. For our interviewees, education was a vehicle of progress, a tool for change; they were interested in literacy problems – they compared the Canadian situation, where they said there was a 25 percent rate of functional illiteracy, with small countries like Cuba and Sri Lanka, which had literacy rates around 90 percent. The economic situation was a secondary preoccupation, which they approached in sociopolitical terms (social effects on the community, distribution of wealth). Finally, they were concerned with foreign relations, Canada's role in providing aid to poor countries. They deemed Canadian foreign policy to be too closely aligned with that of the United States, especially during the Persian Gulf crisis.

The interviewees' expectations corresponded to their preoccupations. One wanted a political system that is much more open to visible minorities. Some seemed pessimistic about the present situation (the recession, the Goods and Services Tax and the possible secession of Quebec), and all saw these events as signs that we need to think about change. Finally, we can say that most of our Jamaican interviewees were very interested in politics, knew a great deal about Canadian affairs and thought the political system must be opened wider.

Canadian Politics and Visible Minorities

The Montreal Jamaicans, like those of Toronto, felt generally excluded from the political system; they did not feel represented in the legislature, on boards and commissions or in political and administrative institutions. Some interviewees attributed this to communication problems, lack of experience (some refugees never having voted) and to distrust of politicians rooted in negative experiences in their country of origin. These explanations contradict the dominant tone of our interviews and seem more like generalizations about visible minorities. Some interviewees had another point of view, also totally opposed to the interviews as a whole, that there was no specific obstacle facing visible minorities. Their evidence for this was that some groups participate very actively in political life. Some said that if members of ethnic communities are not involved in politics, it is because they do not want to be. Such an opinion was extremely rare among our interviewees, who ascribed their exclusion to obstacles inherent in their community, and obstacles outside the community, which are far more numerous. One told us that if the Montreal Jamaican community, like that of Toronto, has little electoral weight, it is essentially because it is dispersed and has no critical mass; as a result, no leader can mobilize the Jamaican vote. The community thinks it has little influence, that it is not very rich and is of no interest to politicians. This gives rise to feelings of discouragement, frustration or indifference to the process; they feel excluded and therefore do not become involved. What good is it, they say, if they will not be listened to? Among obstacles inherent in the system, the lack of information or training was often mentioned. Citizens of foreign origin do not know their rights or how to exercise them. They feel that they exist in the eyes of politicians only at election time. It must be noted that these arguments were advanced in Montreal; the dominant view in Toronto was altogether different – much more hostile, stressing mainly exclusion, the different treatment of Blacks and racism.

The main obstacle, they said, is the mentality of the Canadian people, a population that identifies Canada as a white society and does not accept people who are different. Society is divided arbitrarily into us and them, Anglo-Saxons and the rest, whites and the rest, Canadians and the rest, and in these circumstances ethnic groups are not accepted as full Canadians. In Canada, there is a perception that there is a dominant race, and this closes the door to ethnic representation and prevents candidates of ethnic origin from representing native-born Canadians. It was said that this attitude is found in riding associations, where Canadians of ethnic origin are accepted only very rarely. Neither does the environment encourage participation, and our respondents referred to latent racism and intimidation attempts. The feeling that they were treated differently by the system because they belong to an ethnic group was very strong, although five of our ten respondents had not experienced it personally.

Nevertheless, all agreed that there are differences that depend on nationality and that least account is taken of visible minorities. They noted a hierarchy of nationalities, with the Anglo-Saxon majority at the top, then French Canadians, then other people of European descent, then Aboriginal peoples and visible minorities. But there were also other criteria, such as the numerical or financial strength of the community.

The Jewish and Italian communities were often cited as examples of communities with more influence, given their electoral weight. Our respondents explained that politicians are interested in ethnic communities only for opportunistic reasons, at election time. In this respect, the Jamaican community cannot compete. Coming from a developing country to start with, Jamaicans do not have the economic clout to finance election campaigns. The cost of elections, therefore, remains a major obstacle to greater participation in the system.

All the interviewees said they wanted to be treated as Canadians. According to them, the dichotomy between being Canadian and being of Jamaican origin exists only in the minds of native-born Canadians. As Canadians of foreign origin, they are not treated as Canadians and said they are required to defend their difference. Of course, they are Canadians but they do not forget that they also have special interests to promote. The Jamaicans interviewed experienced a strong sense of exclusion because they have neither electoral weight nor economic resources. Some noted an improvement and believed that efforts were being made to encourage people to take citizenship, promote multiculturalism and repair divisions. But on the whole, the interviewees thought that only pressure groups could defend the interests of the community. They were divided in their opinion of local Liberal and NDP organizations. For some, local organizations were effective in attracting people to parties and encouraging them to participate. People can meet politicians and get familiar with the system; they feel welcome and needed by the party. But respondents' dominant attitude toward these organizations was critical. Some said they are labour pools to be used only at election time (to lick stamps, said one interviewee). Outside the party, these structures have no real power; the respondents believed that visible minorities are still marginalized in the political system.

In trying to find a solution to these problems, we must differentiate between the Jamaicans in Montreal and those in Toronto. The problems identified were different, and so were the solutions recommended. It should be remembered that the main problem for the Montreal Jamaicans was a lack of information about the system and its operation. The obvious solution is information. "People should be informed about their rights and the exercise of their rights," said one interviewee. And the vehicles for this information are the media or the community's own leaders.

In Montreal, it was believed that, to understand how the wheels turn, it is necessary to educate yourself and others, meet political leaders and participate in politics. Therefore, people have to be encouraged to go out and vote.

The Torontonians, on the other hand, saw the problem in terms of exclusion and marginalization. According to them, the solution lies in a genuine participation at all stages of the process. They said it is the responsibility of political parties to involve visible minorities and to recruit them at all stages, including when candidates are nominated. They also wanted changes to be made in local organizations and for them to be considered as a source of political activists. They expected political parties to increase access by ethnic groups to decision-making structures. Some thought it could become necessary to consider setting quotas in riding associations to increase ethnic representation. They hoped that more elected representatives would come from the Jamaican community to defend it and have its problems understood. But the community must not only become active itself; it must also form interest groups to examine every law and make its position known to Parliament. The community hopes for this kind of change; it wants to promote a more open and pluralistic Canada comprising different but equal people. It believes its contribution will enrich Canada.

The Community and the Media

Except for one cautious person ("I don't want to accuse the media"), the judgement was unanimous: the media do not give enough positive coverage to the community, and they give it too much negative coverage. According to our interviewees, journalists stereotype the Black anglophone community. A successful Jamaican, journalists say, is a Canadian (but they practically never talk about that); but a criminal (and there are few questions asked about this) is certainly a Jamaican. Like other communities, the Jamaican community complains that the ethnic origin of criminals is systematically mentioned. Because the media cover only sensational events, our respondents were afraid that the public receives an essentially negative image of the community, which is too often identified as a community of criminals.

The respondents were conventional in their choice of newspapers or television programs. All the interviewees from Toronto read the *Toronto Star*, the *Globe and Mail* and the two West Indian community newspapers, *Share* and *Contrast*. Some read the *Toronto Sun* for professional reasons, the *Sun* being viewed as a rather bad, often racist, newspaper. The readers' reaction to the *Sun* expressed the general feeling clearly: "May God forgive me, I also read the *Sun*." One interviewee also read several foreign newspapers, American or British, as well as magazines. The most-watched television network was the CBC, especially *The National* and *The Journal*. In Montreal, they read the *Gazette*, and they watched the CBC, CJAD, CKVT or CFCF. As a general rule, they did not listen regularly to the radio.

Interview Report: Vietnamese Community

Description of the Interviewees

Since the Vietnamese community is mainly concentrated in Montreal and Toronto, six of the ten interviews were held in Montreal and the others were held in Toronto, where three of four interviews were in English. On average, our interviewees had been Canadian citizens for approximately 10.5 years, the number varying between 3 and 19 years. Their average stay in Canada was 13 years, ranging from 6 to 27 years. Seven interviewees were married and seven were males. As for religion, six were Roman Catholic and the other four were Buddhist. Their average age was 42, the youngest was 27 and the oldest, 59. Finally, their average annual income was $55 000, with salaries ranging between $26 000 and $100 000.

Five of our interviewees immigrated directly to Montreal and two to Toronto. Each of the other three lived for several years in the United States, Malaysia or Thailand before coming to Canada. Of these three, one chose Toronto and two chose Montreal.

All our interviewees were well educated, holding university degrees. Two of them worked in the public service, four were professionals – dentist, engineer or doctor – and two were teachers. Finally, one worked in the service sector and another was a writer.

One interviewee spoke more than three languages (Vietnamese, Chinese, English and French), and five were bilingual in Vietnamese and English or Vietnamese and French; the other four were unilingual in English or French. Finally, as to the extent of their participation in community organizations, six of our interviewees were active in Vietnamese associations and two belonged to other organizations.

Electoral Behaviour, Pressure and Political Action

Our interviewees were not very active in political parties (only one person) and this was reflected in their contributions to election campaigns and political parties. In fact, only one interviewee had donated money to a federal election campaign, and two had donated to political parties.

Our interviewees might stay on the sidelines of the political parties, but their participation at election time was a different story. We found that all had voted in the last election. Federal and provincial elections interested them most; municipal elections often seemed to be left out. They found it important to go out and vote; our interviewees said they intended to exercise their franchise in the next elections, particularly at the next federal and provincial elections.

Our interviewees can be seen as relatively conservative about their choice of political party. Almost all had not changed political affiliation since arriving in Canada, and the provincial and federal Liberal parties seemed to appeal to them most. Undoubtedly, fear of communism partly explains our interviewees' electoral loyalty and their great distrust of more left-wing political parties. Our interviewees in Quebec were concerned about sovereignty. In fact, anything that threatens to upset the status quo is likely to meet opposition. There were certainly exceptions; some supported the New Democratic Party or the Parti québécois. The interviewees in our inquiry worked mainly in Vietnamese community associations to defend Vietnamese rights both in Vietnam and Canada. In the interviews, they reminded us that "on their arrival in Canada, several community members decided to contribute and fight for liberty, happiness and democracy in Vietnam."

As for their intentions to become politically active in the future, there were a variety of opinions. While half the respondents said they intended to become politically involved, their aim was to promote democracy in Vietnam. On the other hand, those who said they were not very interested in becoming politically involved "believe that this situation will change over the years, with the arrival of new generations."

For our interviewees, the ethnic origin of a candidate in an election was certainly very important, but several said that it was not enough. They said they voted first for the political party and its election platform. The candidate's personality came next. At another level, our inquiry revealed that most (seven of the ten) had exerted pressure on governments, both about establishing democracy for Vietnamese living in Vietnam and about Vietnamese immigration and integration of Vietnamese living in Canada. They generally exerted this pressure through Vietnamese community organizations.

Finally, although the Vietnamese in our inquiry frequently discussed Canadian politics among themselves and with colleagues, few of them personally knew people active in politics at any level – municipal, provincial or federal.

Representativeness of the Political System and of Politicians

From our interviews, it seems that the Canadian political system was seen as representative and democratic since, the interviewees said, its representatives are elected by universal suffrage. They deplored, however, some flaws in the system: the right of the prime minister of Canada to appoint senators to ensure the passage of a bill was raised. They also deplored how the balance of power between the Senate and the prime minister favours the latter, something that does not exist, they emphasized, between the president of the United States and Congress. On the whole, they thought politicians were representative. A good politician listens to public opinion, keeps his promises and, above all, has enough judgement to make decisions that do not follow the "party line." All our interviewees noted that there are very few politicians from ethnic communities.

Interest in Canadian Politics

Our interviewees expressed very little interest in Canadian politics, but when they were interested, it was because of their concern about the economy and immigration. It seems, however, that (with some variation) the longer they had lived in Canada, the more concern they showed for political issues such as the deficit, the recession, the reduction of the income differential between the rich and the poor, the special situation of Quebec and the issue of Canadian unity. They expected Canadian politics to show a better understanding of the needs of all Canadian communities, by promoting their economic and linguistic integration, especially in Quebec, by stimulating affirmative action programs on their behalf and by encouraging immigration, among other possibilities.

Canadian Politics and Visible Minorities

Our interviewees believed the Canadian political system does not make enough room for ethnic groups and Aboriginal peoples. Moreover, they found it "funny, sometimes, to see questions concerning ethnic groups discussed by 'commissions' that do not include any members of ethnic communities." In the opinion of some respondents, the absence of ethnic groups can be an obstacle to greater participation in political life by the members of the Vietnamese community. But this is not the only obstacle; our inquiry showed that language further restricts political participation. As our respondents explained, they have to communicate with the society and "if we cannot master one of the two official languages of Canada, it becomes very difficult to make ourselves understood and known." They also said that ignorance of language sometimes makes it impossible to understand the different parties' election platforms. The cultural origins of Canadians who came from Vietnam and their experience of politics as practised in Vietnam are also obstacles to political participation, although to a lesser degree. According to the Confucian tradition, "one does not act, one waits." Furthermore, as most Vietnamese who come to Canada have never known democracy, the result is "we don't have the habit of viewing ourselves as equals, nor do we see how we can use politics to help us." Age is another factor, as older Vietnamese tend to be intensely frightened of politics. Finally, our interviewees cited adaptation problems in the larger economic, sociocultural, educational and linguistic sense as factors that help explain why this community participates less in political life than they might wish.

Our survey gave our interviewees an opportunity to suggest solutions to their situation. First, they proposed increasing the number of ethnic candidates for election. They stressed that political parties should make the effort to nominate ethnic candidates in winnable electoral constituencies.

They also emphasized that political parties must be mobilized to inform community members about their programs and what they have to offer. They expected political parties to become aware of the ethnic reality of Canada and to defend the interests of the Vietnamese community. Finally, they believed that community organizations, in cooperation with political parties, can be important in helping the Vietnamese community exercise all its political rights.

The interviewees remained divided on the function of ethnic groups in politics. Some said that the specific cultures of ethnic groups can enrich government organizations and cultural, social and economic life. Others maintained that members of the Vietnamese community are full Canadians who have no special role to play. In brief, the question is difficult and several interviewees emphasized this. That being said, all earnestly hoped their community would be more involved in the future, which will be made easier by the fact that "future generations will have adapted more and members of these generations will, therefore, be able to participate in the political system."

Although recognizing that everyone is equal before the law in Canada, five of our ten interviewees believed they were treated differently by the political system. Some maintained that "if members of the community should want to nominate a candidate they would inevitably encounter difficulties." As for different treatment because of nationality, most of our interviewees had not seen any. For others, it was visible minorities, especially Blacks, who continue to be treated worst in Canada.

In their relationships with political institutions and political personnel, four of our ten interviewees wanted to be treated as both Canadians and Vietnamese: "We want to be treated as members of our community, but on the same footing as native-born Canadians." Two others called themselves Canadian and refused special measures: "If people treat us as members of a visible minority, they can in fact give us privileges, but they can also discriminate against us." The other respondents said they preferred to be treated as members of the Vietnamese community.

Finally, our interviewees were divided in their opinions about what people and organizations they thought were most able to defend the interests of their community. Members of Parliament came at the top of the list, followed by pressure groups and governments, who were even. Some respondents thought that no group or individual could help them. It should be emphasized that the interviewees acknowledged the help provided to Vietnamese refugees by political parties, the government, pressure groups and members of Parliament.

The Community and the Media

Our respondents said that, in their information role, the national media not only do not give enough coverage to the Vietnamese community but when they do cover it, help perpetuate prejudices because they choose to show what does not work. "Specifically, when the press covers crimes and delinquency issues, they rush quickly to identify the ethnic origin." On the other hand, some pointed out that there has been progress in recent years: "Twenty years ago, the newspapers essentially portrayed the Chinese and Vietnamese as restauranteurs." These same people emphasized that, today, there is more information and it is quite diversified, and attributed this progress to the efforts of Vietnamese youth: "Young Vietnamese are the cause of this change to the extent that our level of education enables us to select the tools we need to fight and exert pressure. It is our generation that is making changes in the Vietnamese community, and we get Canadians' attention whenever they look at our community."

Our interviewees in Quebec read mainly *La Presse* and *Le Devoir* and some bought the *Gazette*. In Toronto, the *Toronto Star* was the most popular, followed by the *Globe and Mail* and *Time* magazine. Five of our ten interviewees read Vietnamese newspapers. As for television broadcasts, they said they preferred public affairs programs.

CONSTANTS AND SIMILARITIES

The preceding analysis of the results of our inquiry shows the existence of an internal dynamic in each community. This dynamic is based on a series of cultural, religious, historical, generational and personal determinants. It can also be explained as much by the route each community took to reach this country as by their reception in Canada. Such a dynamic shows how risky it is to generalize about how visible minorities internalize Canadian political culture and participate in representative institutions.

Briefly, our analysis suggests caution and prevents us from drawing monolithic portraits of these communities' actions, opinions or behaviour.

Despite these reservations, it seemed possible to identify several constants that emerged from questions asked by this study. How do visible minorities perceive the Canadian political system? How do they perceive the electoral mechanisms, such as election law, balloting methods, the party system and financing, and the politicians who govern us?

This third section attempts to answer these questions from the results of our inquiry. We highlight the constants and similarities before proceeding to our recommendations.

Which Canada?

Our interviews clearly demonstrate how interested our respondents were in Canadian politics. Except for a few members of the Chinese and Vietnamese communities, almost all our interviewees demonstrated extensive knowledge of Canadian political issues and several said they were passionately interested in current political debates.

> I am very interested in Canadian and Quebec politics, and how could I be otherwise? This is a very special country, and that hit me in the face as soon as I arrived here ... The constitutional debate – really, I wouldn't miss it. (An interviewee of Haitian origin from Montreal.)

In fact, they were interested in politics, they said they wanted to participate and play a greater role, and at the same time they pointed out that it is extremely difficult for them to speak critically of what is going on here. Because they often come from countries that do not teach democracy or equality, they thought native-born Canadians deny them this possibility. Several of our interviewees felt this way, even those who had been in Canada for more than 10 years. They often developed this feeling after negative reactions from people very close to them, especially colleagues.

> The image of your country of origin also has an effect on their perception of you ... I think that the great prosperity of Japan results in more respect for Canadians of Japanese origin. (An interviewee of Indian origin from Montreal.)

> Whether you like it or not, the reputation of the country one comes from influences the perception in the host country. (An interviewee of Haitian origin from Montreal.)

Because they were interested in Canadian politics, our respondents were often very severe about Canada's foreign policy. They found our politicians ignorant of major international issues and unfamiliar with political problems in their countries of origin.

> I think that the Canadian government does not know enough about the international situation. (An interviewee of Lebanese origin from Montreal.)

Many of them said that Canada's foreign policy is a carbon copy of American foreign policy.

> One could say that Canada doesn't play a real role but a symbolic one. The Americans drag us along behind, and that is too bad ... I think we have the right to our own place in the sun, and we should be more involved at the international level. (An interviewee of Lebanese origin from Montreal.)

> Canada follows the United States; in any case, that is what many people think. Big brother does it, so we follow. We should have our own opinion; we shouldn't be following no matter what. (An interviewee of Vietnamese origin from Toronto.)

Our study shows that the communities we analysed have specific relationships with the Canadian political system, either directly or indirectly. Our research also shows that several of our interviewees saw themselves as social and political actors; they repeatedly said they are concerned for Canadian society and the issues it now faces. They wanted to be social and political actors and they rejected the idea that they belonged to communities that remain on the fringe of Canadian society. Unfortunately, they did not always find the openness that they would like to see in the society.

> It is a way of being Canadian, to have something to contribute; we are not here only to take but also to give; it is a way of enriching and promoting Canada's image in the eyes of the world, an image of an open society made up of different people who all contribute service. (An interviewee of Jamaican origin from Toronto.)

> In Vancouver, the Chinese play a very important role in economic, cultural, political and industrial planning! (An interviewee of Chinese origin from Vancouver.)

Moreover, the most politicized stressed that government decisions about national and international policy affect all Canadians, whether they like it or not, visible minorities as well as others.

> I think that the ethnic communities must make certain that they fully understand the system. All the laws enacted in the past affect ethnic groups ... Therefore, ethnic groups must pay attention to all laws because all laws affect them. (An interviewee of Jamaican origin from Toronto.)

Because they see themselves as "political actors" or political subjects, the communities in our analysis do not consider themselves as "foreign bodies." On the contrary, they demonstrate their interest in participating in Canadian politics by their stake in issues that are not always those of the two founding peoples.

> But the problem is that when nobody is interested in politics, who will defend our interests? We therefore must encourage visible minorities to be interested in politics. (An interviewee of Vietnamese origin from Montreal.)

It seems that these communities subscribe to an integration rationale peculiar to them that can, in some cases, be seen by the society as conflicting and opposing. The study of the communities illustrates this very well.

> The question we ask is: what type of democracy should we have in a multi-ethnic society? Will we build a democracy in which the majority will push the minority aside? (An interviewee of Indian origin from Montreal.)

At another level, our research shows that our interviewees' communities believe strongly in a democratic, free and egalitarian Canada. Although they often criticized politicians' decisions, they were proud to live in a country like Canada, which they saw as a land of asylum precisely because it is free.

> I am bored with [Canadian] politics, but I have always been interested in democracy ... Canada is a democracy: one can vote. There is a government and a prime minister that we have chosen. (An interviewee of Indian origin from Vancouver.)

> Most Chinese chose Canada because it has the reputation of being a
> peaceful and democratic country. (An interviewee of Chinese origin
> from Vancouver.)

> We Vietnamese will always remember the generosity of the Canadian
> government and its attitude toward the Boat People. I think we are in
> a democratic country and that everyone's interests are protected by
> the law. (An interviewee of Vietnamese origin from Toronto.)

Without making direct reference to the rule of law, our interviewees often turned to this concept for support when they spoke of Canada
and when they stressed its superiority on the international level.

> Look at democratic countries like Canada ... at least the system, the
> mechanisms allow you to make a change if you want it. You can exert
> pressure, you can fight, defend laws ... I love this system because it
> authorizes you to speak, that is the best thing. (An interviewee of
> Vietnamese origin from Toronto.)

> I reiterate my great respect for the parliamentary system. In spite of
> all the criticisms that can be made of it, it is the one I prefer. (An inter-
> viewee of Haitian origin from Montreal.)

> Native-born Canadians do not appreciate the value of the system
> under which they live. It takes immigrants to tell them. (An inter-
> viewee of Egyptian origin from Montreal.)

Their perception of Canada rests on their conviction that they live
in a free and democratic country. This image was very strong among
the interviewees in our study, who often came from regions in the grip
of dictatorial regimes or even torn by war. But our study shows that
many of them want Canadian democracy to change its expression, to
be reborn in different political and administrative institutions. They
want a multi-ethnic and multiracial democracy, since from their point
of view the system of two founding peoples no longer has any justifi-
cation. Although they do not reject this vision of Canada, they challenge it very strongly.

> There is a certain hierarchy here: at the top, the English who came
> from the United Kingdom; they have been part of the government
> structure for a long time. Then the French (in Quebec it may perhaps
> be different), then white Europeans, and at the bottom the other
> immigrants, with perhaps other hierarchies at this level too. It is the

fundamental characteristic of the system, a hierarchy based on race and language. (An interviewee of Indian origin from Montreal.)

I expect the system to be more representative of ethnic groups. (An interviewee of Vietnamese origin from Toronto.)

If you think of Canada in terms of its two founding peoples, then it is representative. But Canada is changing and ethnic groups are a reality. They absolutely must be represented. (An interviewee of Jamaican origin from Montreal.)

However, it is apparent that the strong sense of belonging to Canada demonstrated by our study respondents took on a negative tone when they spoke of the place reserved for immigrants. Immigrants often felt excluded and rejected; "I am an outsider," one of them told us in an interview.

From their point of view, Canadian democracy will continue to be a vague and imprecise concept if society continues to be unable to integrate visible minorities.

The Two Faces of Canada

The rate of assimilation of the communities in our study depends on their living and working conditions and on the social stratification within each community studied. It must also be noted that, within these communities, people's socio-economic status is often tied to their immigration and that, here again, it is difficult to generalize. Although, as the preceding analysis shows, the socio-economic status of most of our interviewees was higher than the Canadian average, our interviewees saw Canada as a country that does not treat all immigrants the same. From their point of view, there is a basic rank structure, which results in a difference between the treatment of native-born Canadians and those from communities that are not of French or British origin.

This distinction between native-born citizens and those of ethnic origin must not be perpetuated. They are citizens in both cases and as such they have the same rights and duties in Canadian society. (An interviewee of Moroccan origin from Montreal.)

In addition to this basic rank structure, there is another for visible minorities. Our interviewees made a clear distinction between white immigrants of European extraction (Italians, Greeks, Eastern Europeans) and themselves, immigrants from Asia and the Caribbean, North Africa and the Middle East – Arab, Asiatic or Black immigrants. Several interviewees felt discriminated against and excluded from society, either because of their culture of origin or because they are the "others," the foreigners.

> The fact that administratively we are called a visible minority labels us irreversibly as intruders because we are visible. From the start, they pretend the majority is invisible. But we who are visible, we will always be the "other" for someone. I cannot be totally Québécois because I belong to a subcategory. (An interviewee of Haitian origin from Montreal.)

> Many definitions of Canada have served particular needs at particular times, but this is no longer true. One definition that has survived, although it is no longer appropriate, is that of the duality of Canada, the concept of the two founding nations. I think that originally it was well considered; it may have been foolish, but in the context it had meaning. But saying that Canada was founded by two cultures, two groups, two races, immediately excludes ... the multiplicity of people of different cultures ... For a white society, francophone or anglophone, there is only one definition; if something is not included in this definition, then it is not a Canadian norm. (An interviewee of Jamaican origin from Toronto.)

> The oldest communities, such as the Jewish or French communities, today can claim their place. But later immigrants, such as the Indians, Chinese, Italians and Poles, are still in the first stage. I don't think there is a single Indian member of Parliament at either the federal or provincial level. (An interviewee of Indian origin from Toronto.)

> People from visible minorities, such as the Chinese, must fight to climb the social ladder at work or to obtain positions in the administration ... Many Chinese are also well-heeled businesspeople. But they don't have a place in the government, they are not in a position to be able to change policies. It is decidedly more difficult for Chinese professionals. I call this institutional racism and glass ceiling. (An interviewee of Chinese origin from Vancouver.)

In fact, each community we encountered thinks it is not treated as well as other communities in Canada; our Black interviewees were undoubtedly the most vigorous denouncers of the racism and discrimination they have experienced.

> A Greek or an Italian is not treated differently from a French Canadian or an English Canadian. But Blacks are; for example, if you present

yourself at the office of a government organization, they don't tell
you that you're not wanted. On the other hand, this is often what their
attitude says. Moreover, the police are often brutal with Blacks. People
speak harshly to you. (An interviewee of Jamaican origin from
Montreal.)

A member of the PQ with a Black skin can be a problem. When serious
matters are discussed, the network is closed. (An interviewee of Haitian
origin from Montreal.)

In several interviews, a feeling of disappointment was expressed.
In the communities in our study, there was a strong sense of the difference between rights obtained on becoming a Canadian citizen and the
real possibility of exercising those rights. Some individuals experienced
or were still experiencing feelings of rejection from the society, and
these feelings were more intense among persons who experienced a
sense of failure in their professional life.

I want to be treated as a Canadian. Otherwise, they can give me back
my visitor's visa. (An interviewee of Moroccan origin from Montreal.)

Right from the start, there is a difference between nationalities. Blacks
have more problems than whites, who can pass as immigrants from
Europe. The other thing is names. People are really resistant to names
that sound Moslem. (An interviewee of Moroccan origin from
Montreal.)

A Closed Political System and Utilitarian Political Parties

The political system must be democratic and open to any citizen, regardless of political leanings; such a system must be immune to financial
pressures, but also free of the ruling cliques that too often control political parties. Several political science studies show clearly the many
obstacles to the average citizen's understanding of this system and
especially to participation in it (see "Approach Taken in the Review"
under the section "Theoretical Approaches and Courses of Action").
How do new arrivals to Canada perceive this system and the role of
political parties? How do they see political institutions and electoral
processes? Our study revealed several characteristics.

In the political system, to be chosen as a candidate, you need support
from about 1 000 association members. Those groups are not free of
racism, and even if they were, they would think of their electorate,
and would tend to think that a candidate from the majority commu-

nity would have a better chance of winning. People are not racist because they want to be; it is mainly a question of ignorance. (An interviewee of Indian origin from Montreal.)

These views summarize the perceptions of the system in Canada. Of course, those who have been politically active, or are still, have a more complex understanding. Despite everything, people still feel they belong to communities that are excluded from the decision-making process.

All this support encourages me to become involved in various issues in a permanent way – as a Black person (though I detest this way of thinking). People say you can succeed in Canadian politics only if you are white. Myself, I want to show the opposite. (An interviewee of Haitian origin from Montreal.)

It is difficult to pick out all the criticisms of the system of representation. The examples in the interviews show that from the respondents' point of view the Canadian political system, though based on equality of rights, opportunity and status, is dominated by the white Anglo-Saxon majority.

I look at the House of Commons and as far as I am concerned, I see nothing but white men. Now, this country is not made up of white men only. (An interviewee of Jamaican origin from Toronto.)

While they believed deeply in equality of rights, opportunity and status, they noted that the Canadian political system perpetuates significant distortions by excluding people and communities that do not belong to majority groups. They denounced the system's lack of representativeness and how it is balanced to the disadvantage of communities that are not of British or French origin. Several talked about women, who they believed are doubly excluded.

There is no representation in politics. It is always the same people who have been there for years. It is always the same team. (An interviewee of Chinese origin from Montreal.)

Very few members of ethnic groups participate and are involved in politics. Even the first generation feels more Canadian than ethnic. I expect the system to be more representative of ethnic groups. (An interviewee of Vietnamese origin from Toronto.)

The assumption of power by the Anglo-Saxon establishment represents more or less the main obstacle to greater participation by ethnic groups in the Canadian political system. (An interviewee of Syrian origin from Toronto.)

What I call mental colonialism still exists. Being a man, I can tell you it is easy to accept women's equality, but when the time comes to grant this equality, to accept equality in fact, it is another matter altogether. It is the same thing for visible minorities, and racial equality is not yet a political reality in Canada. That will take time. (An interviewee of Indian origin from Montreal.)

In a democracy like Canada's, political parties are part of the state; they are at the heart of administration and decision making; they play an important role in political control. Although Canadian political parties have been forced to evolve over the course of history, the fact remains that they are the point of entry to the political system. The interviewees in our inquiry were well aware of the importance and significance of political parties in Canada. They knew that without the parties, they would find it impossible to participate fully in the political system. They also knew that political parties are influenced by networks from which ethnic minorities are excluded. Finally, they noted that their main obstacle was the lack of money.

Canadian politics is bound up with getting electoral support, and the power of money and of white Anglo-Saxon Protestant men. It is difficult for people without money to run for election, given the way election campaigns are financed … To be a candidate, you must belong to a political party; it is the law and you have no choice. But there are certain supporters that the political parties do not want. (An interviewee of Vietnamese origin from Montreal.)

That depends on communities' capacity to raise funds, to support the candidate financially. There is still no local apparatus. (An interviewee of Indian origin from Montreal.)

And I think it is because the parties' structure, anglophone or francophone, is mainly white. Some communities, such as the Italian community, have penetrated these structures. But I think this is not representative of the whole population because these groups are largely excluded. And I think it is a priority for the political parties themselves to attempt active recruitment of these people, at all levels of activity, including candidacies. How? By going into communities, by changing their attitudes toward grassroots organizations. They must not be satisfied with asking them to represent their community; they must ask them to nominate candidates, to volunteer for executive positions in the party, to work actively in the party committees on financing and development. They have to suggest opening the party's decision-making centre ... And they must structure their committees so these people are integrated into main committees such as financing, policy development and nomination committees, all the positions that really open the doors to power. That way, we will nominate candidates who reflect society and elect members of Parliament who reflect society. It is exclusion that prevents people from getting involved. (An interviewee of Jamaican origin from Toronto.)

Our inquiry shows that if a system is to be representative, it must integrate groups of all ethnic origins. Our research also shows the challenges that political parties must face if they want to be open, equitable and deserving of electors' confidence. The most politicized interviewees in our study sharply criticized what they called the utilitarian side of political parties, especially during election campaigns.

Nearly all parties have a short chapter in their program on intercultural relations, cultural communities – in the PQ as well as the Liberal party and the NDP. We are beginning to improve campaign rhetoric. Certain aspects have been built into their platforms because they sense which way the wind is blowing. There are no concrete results yet, however. (An interviewee of Haitian origin from Montreal.)

Ethnic candidates who drive around in Cadillacs and limousines have been parachuted in. But what is the difference? The name of the game is to buy members ... In principle, if you go by their structures, political parties are open to minorities ... I would like to see the parties that make a point of having ethnic candidates parachuted in realize that they would win if they had people who were integrated (and I use this word advisedly) into the system, so they can develop policy and membership, and not just put up signs and telephone people. (An interviewee of Chinese origin from Vancouver.)

In short, political parties have much to do to change their image among visible minorities. These minorities hesitate between self-exclusion – after all, matters would be decided with or without them – and the search for new political models. Our interviewees thought it would make it easier to defend their specific interests if the number of MPs from visible minorities was increased.

The election of more members of ethnic communities at all levels should be encouraged, since these people represent ideas. There are many highly educated people who could help the Canadian political system face the challenge posed by the integration of visible minorities. (An interviewee of Egyptian origin from Montreal.)

Most ethnic groups feel that no one really cares about them. They have begun to be more active in political parties and to choose people they think will meet their needs. (An interviewee of Indian origin from Toronto.)

Perhaps more ethnic candidates would help. At least they could speak to the Chinese in their own language. (An interviewee of Chinese origin from Vancouver.)

From Community Associations to Pressure Groups

The interviewees in our study participated actively in various community associations, both as volunteers and as permanent salaried employees. They told us that they saw these associations as opposite to political parties. From their point of view, these groups are most able to promote their specific community interests. Because they did not always want to involve themselves in the issues supported and debated by the leading political parties, they tended to use community associations and pressure groups as intermediaries between the political system and their communities.

If the interests of my community are ever defended at the political level, it is obviously by pressure groups. (An interviewee of Chinese origin from Montreal.)

We cannot function without pressure groups; they are a key element of the system. It is important that there be many pressure groups in a democracy like ours. They speak powerfully, they represent groups, elected representatives listen to them and find the best possible answer for them. (An interviewee of Jamaican origin from Toronto.)

The interests of my community are most often defended by the pressure groups. (An interviewee of Vietnamese origin from Montreal.)

Certainly, in Canada, not all political forces are necessarily grouped in political parties. Nevertheless, the parties play a primary role in the political sphere. Our study shows that visible minorities feel excluded from these traditional structures, which reject them. The minorities, therefore, turn to pressure groups and community associations whose mission is to defend them and promote their interests. From their point of view, political regulation or control should be carried out through these intermediaries when the interests of their communities are involved. An image is thus projected, developed from a dual process of political regulation that presents political parties as agents promoting and defending the interests of dominant groups, and community associations and pressure groups as agents promoting and defending the interests of minority groups.

> Pressure groups can produce changes in government, perhaps in areas like employment, social services and the public sector, to make the minorities part of the machinery. If I went to Revenue Canada and saw a person of Indian origin sitting there, I would feel that it was my government. (An interviewee of Indian origin from Montreal.)

Briefly, they want to be represented and be part of society. To feel included, they invest in community associations and seek models in all areas of social and political life.

> It took 10 years before a Chinese was elected in Vancouver … I had already been asked how to increase the number of Chinese in the police force. I answered that you must first have models. Also, if you look at the experience of the Chinese in Hong Kong, you will see that they cannot vote there, so they have no experience. (An interviewee of Chinese origin from Vancouver.)

Various Comments and Assertions of Identity

It appeared at first that the comments of interviewees in our study were very different, each remark referring to a very specific life history. However, after several interviews we could see a pattern of respondents' immigration history, their reasons for coming to Canada, their relations with the society and their plans for the future. Briefly, our first questions about relations between visible minorities and the Canadian political system opened the door to our interviewees expressing their way of seeing and understanding of Canadian society as a whole, seeing and understanding whether they feel accepted by this society, and finally, seeing and understanding how they experience integration. Four different types of comments can be identified, each type referring to the affirmation of identity particular to a group.

Members of the first and smallest group talked about their community of origin as outside observers. Their comments were mainly about their perceptions of the dynamic emerging between their community of origin and Canadian society. The interviewees of this first group felt increasingly separated from their community of origin and identified strongly with the society. For them, "the other" was their community of origin.

> I don't need the support of my community because I am well integrated. My brothers live bottled up in Vietnamese society, but not me. They shut themselves out of Quebec society and I criticize them for that; in turn, they criticize me for the opposite reason. (An interviewee of Vietnamese origin from Montreal.)

The second and third groups, including most of our interviewees, were deeply involved in community associations. However, they did not all have the same feelings about the society. Interviewees of the second group lived very close to their community but still considered themselves integrated into the society, accepting its faults and qualities. Those from the third group were very uncomfortable in the society because they had serious doubts that it could accept their community. Although interviewees of the second group were often severely critical, the third group wavered between defensive and aggressive attitudes, especially when asked to express the specific claims of their community.

> I would like real public consultation at the national level and an attempt to develop a vision of Canada concerning social, economic and other policies. (An interviewee of Chinese origin from Vancouver.)

> In a sense, it is the same for Indians; they are not very well treated! Once you have the habit of seeing a certain type of people in certain positions, it becomes like a law ... Like the police, why don't we see all sorts of faces? You always see only one type of police officer; it is not a good thing in our community, it gives rise to the idea of "them" and "us." (An interviewee of Jamaican origin from Toronto.)

The interviewees of the second group seemed to have a double sense of belonging (to the society of origin and to the new society), while those of the third group saw themselves as "others," "different," the "excluded" ones. How intensely they felt this exclusion depended on their level of professional integration. Those whose employment situation was precarious expressed this sentiment more strongly than others.

The fourth group was also small. The interviewees of this group said that they didn't feel concerned about what goes on here. They experienced the problems of their community acutely. They had the feeling that the society does not accept them.

Of course, we speak of integration but there is no room for these communities. The programs that have been set up do not give them a chance. (An interviewee of Haitian origin from Montreal.)

Finding out these different feelings about their identity enabled us to understand our interviewees' ambivalence about the best methods to adopt for increasing their participation and representation in the political system. They did not want special conditions. Nor did they want representation by quota. They feared the appearance of a ghetto; they feared its perverse effects over the middle and long term. Nevertheless, respondents to our inquiry who worked daily with members of their community were well aware that without special, specific measures, visible minorities would not be able to participate fully in the political process. Our analysis of the communities' responses to our questionnaire has fully demonstrated that there are many obstacles to this.

Change and the Future

Identifying strongly with Canada and the democratic system, the interviewees in our inquiry were disturbed about Canada's future, and disturbed about the status of Canadians who are not of British or French origin. Some viewed the present decade with apprehension, afraid that certain groups will use them as scapegoats.

It took a Laurier Institute study to show that the rise in real estate prices was not caused by the Vancouver Chinese but by Chinese who came from Toronto. Before, the police spoke of "Chinese youth gangs." It took time for them to begin talking about "youth in trouble with the law." (An interviewee of Chinese origin from Vancouver.)

The referendum has left a deep wound because many Haitians, because they were francophones, were active on behalf of an independent Quebec. In Haitian history, the question of independence is fundamental. When the "no" won, the people on the "yes" side said that it was the immigrants' fault. They put everyone in the same basket and for the Haitians that has been very hard to take ... We could very easily be seen as scapegoats. (An interviewee of Haitian origin from Montreal.)

Despite these statements, our inquiry shows that the major political debates that will mark the coming years were very interesting to our interviewees. Several of them talked about Canada's internal problems, particularly the constitutional question and the Quebec–Canada division. They said they could play an important role in this issue and they believed that Canada's internal dynamics could be changed by the presence and specific contribution of visible minorities. In brief, they saw themselves as bearers of change and solutions.

> This country is facing a challenge. In my opinion, minority groups have a role to play in re-establishing the concept of one Canada. (An interviewee of Indian origin from Montreal.)

> I see a large role [for ethnic groups] especially if one considers that in the next 20 years immigrants will represent a considerable propor- tion of the total Canadian population. They consider this country their new home. They must not be ignored. (An interviewee of Egyptian origin from Montreal.)

These constants and similarities are far from being the only percep- tions that stand out from our analysis. Although partial and general, these trends are nevertheless very useful in understanding visible minori- ties' modes of participation in Canadian society in general and in the political system in particular. They also reveal the capacity and desire of these communities to adapt to the Canadian political environment.

RECOMMENDATIONS

Our research brings out unequivocally the problems in all regions and communities of Canada, of underrepresentation of visible minorities and the lack of candidates of ethnic origin nominated and elected in electoral districts.

However, that statement reinforces a peculiarly Canadian charac- teristic: in this country the law recognizes, particularly in section 27 of the *Canadian Charter of Rights and Freedoms,* a multicultural heritage in a bilingual context (Canada, Parliament 1982). Democracy and equity underlie every concept of political participation and representation. Moreover, in Canada, perceptions of representation – a fundamental element of democracy – are increasingly broadened to include not only the two founding peoples, but also various visible minorities. With this in mind, we have established three main objectives – two short-term and one long-term – on which to base our recommendations to the Commission.

Objectives

First Objective (short-term)
To increase political participation by members of visible minorities.

Second Objective (short-term)
To increase the representation of visible minorities, by increasing the number of candidates of ethnic origin and the number of elected representatives who belong to visible minorities.

Third Objective (long-term)
To increase the political competence of members of visible minorities by ensuring that they are more knowledgeable about the Canadian political system and understand issues better.

Moreover, the research, which consisted of a review of articles and monographs as well as interviews, produced three general observations, and these served as a starting point for our recommendations.

Observations

First Observation
Members of visible minorities see themselves as actors and agents of change.

Second Observation
In Canada, political parties are extremely important agents of political control and they must continue to play this role.

Third Observation
Community associations are a fundamental link between the society and members of visible minorities.

Recommendations
These are not surprising as the objectives and observations are so closely linked and always interrelated. However, for clarity, we grouped the following recommendations under the three main objectives.

First objective: to increase political participation by members of visible minorities.
As shown previously, extending the right to vote to landed immigrants tends to create more interest in politics and encourage new candidates. Similarly, many of our respondents said they think it only natural that residents who contribute to the country's economy and pay taxes should also have the right to participate fully in Canada's political life. Without that right, immigrants feel like second-class citizens. The right to vote and eligibility to do so therefore seem to be crucial elements in political participation.

As a result, **we recommend**:

1. **That in Canada all landed immigrants be allowed to vote; and that they also be eligible to vote in federal elections (***Canada Elections Act***, sections 50 and 53).**

The right to vote and eligibility are necessary but not sufficient to ensure that members of visible minorities will increase their exercise of this right. Indeed, as revealed in the articles and monographs and in the course of our interviews, several obstacles also stand in the way of their participation in political life.

The language barrier is not the least of these obstacles. It must be stressed that there is no magic solution to this problem. Many of our respondents thought that translating ballots and election information was one of the best solutions, but this does raise several questions, mainly practical ones. Must we systematically translate all information where numbers warrant? Could this create interethnic or interracial tensions? Do we not risk building a new Tower of Babel by translating everything for everybody? Would we translate material into Cantonese or Mandarin, for example, or into Punjabi or Hindi, or into all of these?

The *Canada Elections Act* (in sections 135 and 136, among others) already provides certain measures to help illiterate, visually handicapped or physically incapacitated voters on polling day. The Act also requires deputy returning officers to help voters who request assistance, to allow friends or relatives to accompany them into voting booths (section 135) and to appoint interpreters if voters speak unfamiliar languages (section 136). We think it would be worthwhile to strengthen these measures.

As a result, **we recommend**:

2. **That measures relating to rights of voters experiencing language difficulties, and the associated procedures, be publicized before voting day, particularly in the ethnic media and on posters.**
3. **That pictographs be added to help identify both candidates and political parties on the ballot and on posters at the entrances of polling stations in ridings where numbers of immigrants warrant.**

Many of the people interviewed during our study believed that something should be done about enumeration, one of the most crucial parts of the electoral process. On one hand, language seems to present a real barrier to many foreign-born voters, and not just those who are seniors. On the other hand, this language barrier is added to by what might be called a culture barrier: many members of certain communities shrink from the idea of door-to-door enumeration. Their hours of work are also often inconvenient.

In its current form, therefore, enumeration seems to represent an obstacle to political participation by members of visible minorities.

As a result, **we recommend**:

4.   **That a permanent voters list be established.**

Anyone could register at any time. New arrivals could register as soon as they obtained landed immigrant status (provided the *Canada Elections Act* was amended accordingly) or Canadian citizenship.

The establishment of a permanent list would, of course, have to be consistent with the *Canadian Charter of Rights and Freedoms*. If the option of a permanent voters list is rejected, we have other suggestions for measures to encourage participation by voters with language problems.

As a result, **we recommend**:

5.   **That at least one of the two enumerators be able to communicate in the language spoken and understood by the voter, and that in cases where neither enumerator can communicate with a voter or the voter's representative, arrangements be made for the voter to be enumerated later in his or her own language.**
6.   **That returning officers be required to encourage the recruitment of members of visible minorities in all ridings, especially in ridings where numbers warrant.**

Second objective: to increase the representation of visible minorities, by increasing the number of candidates of ethnic origin and the number of elected representatives who belong to visible minorities.
It is both curious and interesting to note, when considering representation of visible minorities, the similarity between many of the analyses and ideas raised in our research and those presented during the symposium organized under the auspices of the Commission on the active participation of women in politics (Erickson 1991).[9]

There is no doubt that one of the main obstacles to greater political representation in both cases is the tendency of the three leading political parties to protect incumbent members against competition within local associations. The period before nomination appears to be crucial. Some think the New Democratic Party is more open and more inclined to open its ranks to female and ethnic candidates. Certainly everyone agrees that political parties are important in expanding representation of visible minorities.

As a result, we recommend:

7. That the *Canada Elections Act* establish a maximum of two consecutive terms in office to encourage a turnover in elected representatives in ridings.
8. That the chief electoral officer set up financial incentive programs to encourage political parties to adopt measures that eliminate obstacles and discriminatory practices[10] relating to members of visible minorities.
9. That the chief electoral officer encourage political parties to set up a national ethnic committee charged with identifying and supporting potential candidates of ethnic origin.
10. That the chief electoral officer encourage parties, before drawing up their final lists of candidates, to establish banks of candidates of ethnic origin to be put forward at nomination meetings and others for management positions.
11. That the chief electoral officer encourage the organization of regional workshops for potential candidates of ethnic origin under the control of national party organizations, to familiarize potential candidates with nomination procedures.
12. That parties run visible minority candidates in "safe" ridings as well as in "ordinary" ridings, since candidates of ethnic origin must be seen as representing all inhabitants of their ridings, not only those of their own communities.
13. That political parties follow up progress made in encouraging greater participation by members of visible minorities in all their party organizations.
14. That the minimum age of delegates to leadership conventions of Canadian political parties be raised to 18 from the current 14.

The question of visible minority representation is also closely linked to political financing, which has been aptly called the "sinews of war." Erickson (1991) eloquently demonstrated that, in the case of female candidates, competition for nomination was fiercest in ridings where there was no sitting member, which meant candidates had to spend more money to win their party's nomination. Some of the comments we noted indicate that the situation is no different for candidates of ethnic origin.

As a result, **we recommend**:

15. That federal campaigns be financed from public funds raised from public donations, as is currently the case in Quebec.
16. That centralized party funds for nomination campaigns be made available to ethnic candidates before nomination.
17. That expenditure for nomination, election and leadership campaigns be capped and regulated by the *Canada Elections Act.*

Third objective: to increase the political competence of members of visible minorities by ensuring that they are more knowledgeable about the Canadian political system and understand issues better.
Encouraging people to vote does not necessarily make them feel justified in doing so or sufficiently interested in the Canadian political system or political issues. Long-term efforts are required to educate and make people more aware, which include the need for a continuous flow of information, not just spurts during election campaigns.

Several of the authors we reviewed stressed the extent to which the (non-ethnic) mass media transmit simplistic images of the political system and convey stereotypes. Most of our respondents confirmed the underrepresentation of ethnic communities in the media and the widespread existence of stereotypes, as did the Caplan-Sauvageau Task Force (Canada, Task Force 1986) and the Canadian Radio-television and Telecommunications Commission (CRTC 1985). At the same time, everyone agrees that the media are necessary.

However, if the ethnic media have not been clearly shown to be effective, the extent of their presence in Canada is undeniable. Lacroix (1988) recently compiled a list of no fewer than 324 ethnic periodicals, located for the most part in the major cities such as Vancouver, Montreal and Toronto. In all, more than 80 ethnic groups publish newspapers, newsletters and magazines in almost 50 languages. There are eleven daily newspapers, including two in Korean and eight in Chinese. Our interviewees confirmed the fundamental importance of the ethnic media and of ethnic community associations, many of which are undeniable sources of information and education.

As a result, **we recommend**:

18. That the chief electoral officer continue not only to disseminate information through the mass media but also to use the ethnic media.

19. That the chief electoral officer work with the authorities, departments and institutions concerned to set up incentive schemes to encourage newspapers, radio and television to inform visible minorities better about the Canadian political system.

20. That the chief electoral officer set up incentive programs, which would complement existing programs, to encourage ethnic community associations to educate their members and clients about the Canadian political system.

Obviously, these measures could not be effectively implemented without close cooperation and an overall vision of political participation by visible minorities. Community associations play an indispensable role in the integration of new arrivals, but they have neither the mandate nor the resources to encourage participation in political life adequately and efficiently. However, because they mediate for and integrate immigrants, they are integral to the process of educating newcomers about the Canadian political system. We recommend linking community associations and elected representatives through organizations similar to the district initiative and advisory committees of Paris.

As a result, **we recommend:**

21. That a visible minorities action committee be created under the responsibility of the chief electoral officer.

The mandate of this committee, which would be composed of elected representatives and delegates from ethnic federations, would be research, translation and development of financial incentive schemes for political parties, ethnic media and community associations designed to increase the political participation, representation and "political competence" of members of visible minorities.

Other Irritants in the Canada Elections Act

We would also like to draw the Commissioners' attention to certain points in the current Act that are not the subject of specific recommendations but that are nevertheless likely to be inconsistent with our fundamental objectives.

- Section 66, which states that the returning officer sends each voter a notice of enumeration. In light of the language barrier for many foreign-born voters, this notice should be written in the voter's mother tongue, especially in ridings where numbers warrant.

- Section 74, which states that the returning officer must send post-masters a proclamation stating where the votes will be counted the morning after polling day. In ridings or regions where the number of immigrants warrants, a translated version of this proclamation should be put up in the post offices.

- Section 79, which states the election day (with certain exceptions, a Monday). Out of respect for visible minorities in Canada, we think that polling should not be done during important religious festivals of certain communities, such as the Moslems and Jews.

APPENDIX A
INTERVIEWEE FACT SHEET

Name _____

Address _____

Tel. no. _____

Original and Current Nationality

Canadian citizen since _____

Civil status _____ Sex _____ Religion _____

Age _____ Income _____

Geographic Origin

Length of stay in Canada_____

Migratory itinerary_____

Level of education _____

Languages spoken _____

Original/Canadian profession _____

Militancy – association_____

Notes on the Inquiry

QUESTIONNAIRE

1. Are you a member of a political party?

2. If so, at what level?

   Municipal
   Provincial
   Federal

3. Have you ever contributed to the financing of an electoral campaign?

   At what level?
   Municipal
   Provincial
   Federal

4. Have you ever contributed to the financing of a political party?

   Municipal
   Provincial
   Federal

5. Did you vote in the last election?

   Municipal
   Provincial
   Federal

   If not, why not?

6. Do you intend to vote in the next elections?

7. Since your arrival in Canada, have you changed your political allegiance?

   At the provincial level?
   At the federal level?

   If so, why?
   If not, why not?

8. Have you ever been actively involved in politics?

9. If so, please give details of your experience.

10. Do you have the intention of being actively involved in politics in the future?

11. In your opinion, what would be the profile of a good MP?

    Of a good prime minister?

12. What is your view of Canadian politicians?

    Do you find them representative?

13. Are you interested in Canadian politics?

    If so, state main fields of interest.

    If not, why not?

14. What do you expect from Canadian politics?

15. What do you think of the system of political representation as it exists in Canada?

16. Do you consider this system representative of all members of Canadian society?

    If not, why not?

17. Does politics as practised in Canada have room for members of different ethnic groups?

18. In your opinion, what are the main obstacles to greater involvement in politics on the part of members of ethnic groups?

19. Do you see a particular role for ethnic groups in politics?

20. If you had to choose between a candidate from an ethnic group and one of French or British origin, which would you choose?

    Why?

21. Between a candidate from your own community and another candidate?

    Why?

22. Does the ethnic background of a candidate play a decisive role when you cast your vote?

    The religious background?

23. In an election, how do you make your choice?

    Put in order of importance:
    • Candidate's party
    • Sex of candidate
    • Candidate's ethnic origin
    • Election platform
    • Candidate's personality

24. What suggestions do you have for increasing the participation of the various ethnic communities in the Canadian political system?

25. What do you see as the future of that participation?

26. Do you think you are treated differently by the political system because of your ... origins?

27. Do you see differences according to nationality?

28. Since arriving in Canada, have you become more interested in politics?

29. Do you have a better understanding of problems facing Canadian society?

30. Do you consider that the interests of your community are protected in Canada?

    • by the political parties?
    • by the government?
    • by lobby groups?
    • by MPs?

31. In your dealings with political people and institutions, what do you prefer?

    • to be treated as a Canadian?
    • to be treated as a member of the community to which you belong?

32. Have you ever lobbied governments?

    If so, on what occasions? What did you do?

    If not, why not?

33. Do you sometimes talk about Canadian politics with friends, relations, work colleagues?

34. Are you personally acquainted with members of your community who have active political experience?

35. Do you play an active role in any associations?

    Which ones, and what do you do?

36. Do you consider that the mass media talk about members of your community enough?

37. Do you consider that the mass media present a positive image of your community?

38. Which newspapers do you read regularly?

39. Which television programs do you watch and which radio programs do you listen to regularly?

APPENDIX B

Table 3.B1
Composition of some ethnic categories, 1986 census

	Single origin	Multiple origin*
Arab origin (103 550)	72 315	31 230
Egyptian	11 850	4 135
Lebanese	29 345	15 685
Palestinian	1 070	525
Syrian	3 045	4 135
Arab, n.i.e.	27 275	10 230
South Asian origin (314 035)	266 800	47 235
Bengali	390	200
Singhalese	745	335
Gujarati	690	555
Punjabi	10 865	4 680
Tamil	1 275	925
Bangladeshi, n.i.e.	1 480	185
East Indian	220 630	40 805
Pakistani, n.i.e.	24 880	6 775
Sri Lankan, n.i.e.	5 830	1 455
East and South East Asian origin (688 485)	600 530	87 690
Burmese	600	810
Cambodian	10 365	1 430
Chinese	360 320	53 720
Filipino	93 280	13 775
Indonesian	1 265	2 265
Japanese	40 245	14 260
Korean	27 680	2 020
Laotian	9 575	1 510
Malay	815	1 565
Thai	1 230	1 700
Vietnamese	53 015	9 980
Other Asian, n.i.e.	2 145	935
Caribbean origin (81 160)	48 475	32 685
Cuban	410	775
Haitian	10 865	6 140
Jamaican	11 210	8 510
Puerto Rican	375	720
Other Caribbean, n.i.e.	950	1 380
Other West Indian	24 670	15 620
Black origin (260 335)	174 970	85 360
Black	170 340	83 775
African black	4 630	4 120

*The total of single and multiple responses will be greater than the total population for the region shown due to reporting of multiple ethnic responses for each group. For example, a respondent giving the origin "French and Italian" will be shown in the multiple French group and in the multiple Italian group.**

**[Translator's note: The French paraphrases the original note in the Census data source; I have used the English note from the original source (Statistics Canada Catalogue no. 93-109).]

n.i.e. = not included elsewhere.

APPENDIX C

Table 3.C1
Composition of some ethnic categories, 1986 census

	Male	Female	Total
Arab origin, n.i.e.	56 085	47 465	103 550
Nova Scotia	2 350	2 090	4 440
Quebec	18 425	15 410	33 835
Ontario	23 315	20 040	43 355
Alberta	6 460	5 360	11 820
British Columbia	2 495	1 965	4 455
Montreal	15 905	13 630	29 530
Toronto	11 050	9 415	20 465
Vancouver	1 765	1 440	3 205
South Asian origin	159 195	154 840	314 035
Nova Scotia	1 245	1 205	2 450
Quebec	11 665	9 820	21 485
Ontario	81 425	79 975	161 395
Manitoba	4 465	4 385	8 855
Saskatchewan	2 205	1 955	4 165
Alberta	17 530	17 115	34 645
British Columbia	39 520	39 290	78 810
Montreal	11 240	9 405	20 645
Toronto	62 955	62 435	125 380
Vancouver	26 095	25 880	51 975
East and South East Asian origin	339 645	348 845	688 485
Quebec	30 925	30 725	61 645
Ontario	146 290	152 560	298 845
Alberta	46 850	45 880	92 730
British Columbia	87 895	92 320	180 215
Montreal	27 005	27 140	54 140
Toronto	112 680	117 675	230 355
Vancouver	74 045	78 400	152 445
Caribbean origin	38 175	42 990	81 160
Quebec	9 635	11 170	20 805
Ontario	22 970	26 225	49 195
Alberta	2 390	2 360	4 750
British Columbia	1 565	1 380	2 945
Montreal	8 795	10 455	19 255
Toronto	18 190	21 685	39 875
Vancouver	1 160	1 040	2 200

APPENDIX C

Table 3.C1 (cont'd)
Composition of some ethnic categories, 1986 census

	Male	Female	Total
Black origin	123 245	137 085	260 335
Nova Scotia	6 275	6 730	13 005
Quebec	24 555	27 710	52 265
Ontario	72 945	85 195	158 140
Alberta	7 575	6 885	14 460
British Columbia	5 680	4 965	10 645
Montreal	22 870	26 165	49 035
Toronto	55 940	67 765	123 705
Vancouver	3 975	3 570	7 545
Arab, n.i.e.	21 100	16 395	37 500
Quebec	7 390	5 400	12 790
Ontario	9 325	7 625	16 950
Alberta	2 340	1 840	4 180
British Columbia	1 100	835	1 940
Montreal	6 390	4 925	11 315
Toronto	5 805	4 810	10 605
Vancouver	860	695	1 550
East Indian, n.i.e.	131 640	129 795	261 430
Nova Scotia	1 085	1 045	2 130
Quebec	7 910	7 165	15 075
Ontario	67 630	67 250	134 880
Manitoba	3 620	3 630	7 255
Alberta	14 385	14 030	28 145
British Columbia	34 210	34 070	68 280
Montreal	7 590	6 845	14 435
Toronto	52 365	52 560	104 930
Vancouver	22 505	22 435	44 935
Pakistani, n.i.e.	16 135	15 520	31 650
Quebec	1 930	1 555	3 480
Ontario	9 545	9 340	18 885
Alberta	2 050	1 940	3 995
British Columbia	1 650	1 740	3 445
Montreal	1 875	1 470	3 340
Toronto	7 220	7 350	14 570
Vancouver	1 415	1 520	2 935

Table 3.C1 (cont'd)
Composition of some ethnic categories, 1986 census

	Male	Female	Total
Chinese	205 940	208 100	414 040
Quebec	13 285	13 475	26 755
Ontario	89 480	91 480	180 960
Alberta	28 785	27 975	56 760
British Columbia	61 850	63 675	125 530
Montreal	11 970	12 215	24 185
Toronto	70 690	72 550	143 240
Vancouver	53 605	55 770	109 370
Vietnamese	34 440	28 555	62 990
Quebec	9 305	8 120	17 425
Ontario	11 660	9 705	21 365
Alberta	6 490	5 150	11 640
British Columbia	3 905	3 180	7 095
Montreal	8 175	7 200	15 370
Toronto	7 225	5 840	13 060
Vancouver	2 925	2 465	5 385
Haitian			
Quebec	7 565	8 530	16 095
Montreal	6 930	7 985	14 915
Jamaican	9 575	10 140	19 720
Quebec	450	565	1 010
Ontario	7 545	8 115	15 665
Alberta	830	755	1 590
Montreal	440	540	980
Toronto	6 090	6 830	12 915
Vancouver	340	310	645

n.i.e. = not included elsewhere.

ABBREVIATIONS

c.   chapter

R.S.C.   Revised Statutes of Canada

s(s).   section(s)

NOTES

In addition to Carolle Simard, who was in charge of the research, the following people participated in one or several stages of the work: Sylvie Bélanger, PhD student, Université du Québec à Montréal; Nathalie Lavoie, PhD student, Université de Montréal; Anne-Lise Polo, PhD student, Université du Québec à Montréal; Normand Rossignol, MA student, Université du Québec à Montréal; Serge Turmel, MA student, Université du Québec à Montréal; and Zhang Hang

Wei, PhD student, Université du Québec à Montréal. The research was done between 10 September 1990 and 15 February 1991.

In this study, quoted material that originated in French has been translated into English.

1. On this subject, we should mention several articles on Montreal neighbourhoods, such as Côte-des-Neiges (Blanc 1986), Chinatown (Chan 1986) and the anglophone West Indian community (Labelle et al. 1983), and on the Canadian Constitution, etc. (Woehrling 1986). Among monographs on the subject, we should point out *Minorités et État* by Guillaume et al.

2. Here we would like to make a distinction based on the fact that some of our respondents said they intervene even when this does not involve their countries of origin.

3. It should be remembered that one of our respondents had always lived in Canada; his interests and understanding of Canadian problems could not therefore be contrasted with his past experiences.

4. This could be coincidental because when we conducted our interviews, municipal elections had just been held in Vancouver and several of the candidates were of Chinese origin. Three of our four respondents who were members of municipal political parties lived in Vancouver.

5. If we identify the geographical origin of our respondents from the languages they speak (of which we have listed only the most significant; other Indian languages they mentioned were Tamil, Urdu, Marathi and Malayalam), we can speculate that perhaps as many as five of our ten respondents came from the Punjab and the rest came from various other Indian states.

6. See the preceding note.

7. These are problems faced by people of Indian origin who bring spouses from India. Most of these cases involve arranged marriages; it is a southern Asian tradition that parents choose their children's spouses.

8. Note that two Jamaicans were elected in the September 1990 Ontario provincial election: Alvin Curling (Liberal) and Zanana Akande (New Democratic Party). Most of our respondents mentioned personal connections to one of these two MLAs. The interviews held in Toronto indicated that participation in an election by a member of the ethnic community was a mobilizing factor.

9. Moreover, some of our recommendations were inspired by that study's conclusions.

10. The recommendations in Judge Rosalie Abella's 1984 report on employment equity were made in the same spirit (Canada, Commission 1984).

BIBLIOGRAPHY

Anderson, Alan B., and James S. Frideres. 1981. *Ethnicity in Canada: Theoretical Perspectives.* Toronto: Butterworths.

Anwar, M. 1986. *Race and Politics – Ethnic Minorities and the British Political System.* London: Tavistock.

Blanc, Bernadette. 1986. "Problématique de la localisation des nouveaux immigrants à Montréal." *Canadian Ethnic Studies* 18 (1): 89–107.

Breton, Raymond. 1983. "La communauté ethnique, communauté politique." *Sociologie et Sociétés* 15 (2): 23–37.

Canada. *Canada Elections Act,* R.S.C. 1985, c. E-2.

———. *Canadian Charter of Rights and Freedoms,* ss. 2, 5, Part I of the *Constitution Act, 1982,* being Schedule B of the *Canada Act 1982* (U.K.), 1982, c. 11.

Canada. Commission on Equality in Employment. 1984. *Report.* Ottawa: Minister of Supply and Services Canada.

Canada. Parliament. 1982. *The Constitution and You.* Ottawa: Minister of Supply and Services Canada.

Canada. Task Force on Broadcasting Policy. 1986. *Report.* Ottawa: Minister of Supply and Services Canada.

Canadian Radio-television and Telecommunications Commission. 1985. "A Broadcasting Policy Reflecting Canada's Linguistic and Cultural Diversity." Public Notice 1985-139. Ottawa: CRTC.

Chan, Kwok B. 1986. "Ethnic Urban Space, Urban Displacement and Forced Relocation: The Case of Chinatown in Montreal." *Canadian Ethnic Studies* 18 (2): 65–78.

Chan, Kwok B., and Lawrence Lam. 1983. "Resettlement of Vietnamese-Chinese Refugees in Montreal, Canada: Some Socio-psychological Problems and Dilemmas." *Canadian Ethnic Studies* 15 (1): 2–15.

Courtois, Stéphane, and Gilles Kepel. 1988. "Musulmans et prolétaires." In *Les Musulmans dans la société française,* ed. Rémy Leveau and Gilles Kepel. Paris: Presses de la Fondation nationale des sciences politiques.

Dahlie, J., and T. Fernando, ed. 1981. *Ethnicity, Power and Politics in Canada.* Canadian Ethnic Studies Association, Vol. 8. Toronto: Methuen.

D'Arcy, François. 1985. *La représentation.* Paris: Economica, Collection Politique comparée.

De Marchi, Bruna, and Anna Maria Boileau. 1982. *Boundaries and Minorities in Western Europe.* Milan: Franco Angeli.

Dias, Manuel. 1986. "La vie culturelle et associative des immigrés." *Projet* 199:61–66.

Ehrlich, Stanislaw, and Graham Wootton, ed. 1980. *Three Faces of Pluralism: Political, Ethnic and Religious.* Westmead: Gower.

Enloe, Cynthia H. 1986. *Ethnic Conflicts and Political Development.* New York: University Press of America.

Entzinger, Han. 1984. "Les Pays-Bas: Entre une stratégie pluraliste et une stratégie intégrationniste." In *Diversité culturelle, société industrielle, État national: Actes du colloque,* ed. Gilles Verbunt. Paris: Éditions Harmattan.

Erickson, Lynda. 1991. "Women and Candidacies for the House of Commons." In *Women in Canadian Politics: Toward Equity in Representation,* ed. Kathy Megyery. Vol. 6 of the research studies of the Royal Commission on Electoral Reform and Party Financing. Ottawa and Toronto: RCERPF/Dundurn.

Forrest, James. 1988. "Social Status, Urbanization and the Ethnic Dimension on Voting Behavior in Australia." *Ethnic and Racial Studies* 11 (4): 489–505.

Fried, C., ed. 1983. *Minorities: Community and Identity.* A report of the Dahlem Workshop *Minorities: Community and Identity,* presented at Berlin, 28 November–3 December 1982. Berlin: Springer Verlag.

Fugita, Stephen S., and David J. O'Brien. 1985. "Structural Assimilation, Ethnic Group Membership, and Political Participation among Japanese Americans: A Research Note." *Social Forces* 63 (4): 986–95.

Guillaume, Pierre, Jean-Michel Lacroix, Réjean Pelletier and Jacques Zylberberg, ed. 1986. *Minorités et État.* Talence: Presses universitaires de Bordeaux and Quebec: Presses de l'université Laval.

Hawkins, Freda. 1982. "Multiculturalism in Two Countries: The Canadian and Australian Experience." *Review of Canadian Studies* 17 (1): 64–80.

Isajiw, Wsevolod W. 1983. "Multiculturalism and the Integration of the Canadian Community: Perspectives/Opinions." *Canadian Ethnic Studies* 15 (2): 107–17.

Jazouli, Adil. 1986. "Les maghrébins de France, objets et sujets du politique." *Projet* 199:23–28.

Juteau, Danielle. 1986. "L'État et les immigrés: de l'immigration aux communautés culturelles." In *Minorités et État,* ed. Pierre Guillaume et al. Talence: Presses universitaires de Bordeaux and Quebec: Presses de l'université Laval.

Kim, Wong Yong. 1986. *Mass Media Use and Political Participation of Ethnic Minorities.* (UMI Dissertation Information Service.) Austin: University of Texas.

Labelle, Micheline, Serge Larose and Victor Piché. 1983. "Politique d'immigration et immigration en provenance de la Caraïbe anglophone au Canada et au Québec, 1900–1979." *Canadian Ethnic Studies* 15 (2): 2–23.

Lacroix, Jean-Michel. 1988. *Anatomie de la presse ethnique au Canada*. Talence: Presses universitaires de Bordeaux.

Lacroix, Jean-Michel, and Stanislav Kirschbaum. 1986. "Les Slovaques à Toronto pendant l'ère Trudeau." In *Minorités et État*, ed. Pierre Guillaume et al. Talence: Presses universitaires de Bordeaux and Quebec: Presses de l'université Laval.

Laferrière, Michel. 1984. "Le cas du Canada." In *Diversité culturelle, société industrielle, État national: Actes du colloque*, ed. Gilles Verbunt. Paris: Éditions Harmattan.

Lecompte, Monique, and Claudine Thomas. 1983. *Le facteur ethnique aux États-Unis et au Canada*. Lille: Presses de l'Université de Lille III.

Leithner, Christian. 1988. "Immigrants and Political Involvement in Canada: The Role of the Ethnic Media." *Canadian Ethnic Studies* 20 (1): 1–19.

Le Lohé, Michel. 1979. "The Effects of the Presence of Immigrants upon the Local Political System in Bradford, 1945–77." In *Racism and Political Action in Britain*, ed. Robert Miles and Annie Phizacklea. London: Routledge and Kegan Paul.

Lemieux, Vincent. 1986. "Les Minorités et l'État: quelques propositions générales." In *Minorités et État*, ed. Pierre Guillaume et al. Talence: Presses universitaires de Bordeaux and Quebec: Presses de l'université Laval.

Leveau, R., and G. Kepel. 1988. *Les musulmans dans la société française*. Paris: Presses de la Fondation nationale des sciences politiques.

Loo, Chalsa M. 1985. "The Biliterate Ballot Controversy: Language Acquisition and Cultural Shift among Immigrants." *International Migration Review* 19 (3): 483–515.

Magnusson, Warren, and Andrew Sancton, ed. 1983. *City Politics in Canada*. Toronto: University of Toronto Press.

Miles, Robert, and Annie Phizacklea, ed. 1979. *Racism and Political Action in Britain*. London: Routledge and Kegan Paul.

Mohl, Raymond A. 1986. "The Politics of Ethnicity in Contemporary Miami." *Migration World* 19 (3): 7–11.

Moodley, Kogila. 1981. "Canadian Ethnicity in Comparative Perspective: Issues in the Literature." In *Ethnicity, Power and Politics in Canada*, ed. J. Dahlie and T. Fernando. Canadian Ethnic Studies Association, Vol. 8. Toronto: Methuen.

Olsen, Marvin E. 1982. *Participatory Pluralism: Political Participation and Influence in the United States and Sweden*. Chicago: Prentice-Hall.

Parry, Geraint. 1980. "Pluralism, Participation and Knowledge." In *Three Faces of Pluralism*, ed. Stanislaw Ehrlich and Graham Wootton. Westmead: Gower.

Peter, Karl. 1981. "The Myth of Multiculturalism and Other Political Fables." In *Ethnicity, Power and Politics in Canada*, ed. J. Dahlie and T. Fernando. Canadian Ethnic Studies Association, Vol. 8. Toronto: Methuen.

Portes, Alejandro, and Rafael Mozo. 1985. "The Political Adaptation Process of Cubans and Other Ethnic Minorities in the United States: A Preliminary Analysis." *International Migration Review* 19 (1): 35–63.

Rath, Jan. 1983. "Political Participation of Ethnic Minorities in the Netherlands." *International Migration Review* 17 (3): 445–69.

———. 1988. "La participation des immigrés aux élections locales aux Pays-Bas." *Revue européenne des migrations internationales* 4 (3): 23–33.

Raub, Patricia. 1988. "The *National Geographic Magazine*'s Portrayal of Ethnicity – The Celebration of Cultural Pluralism and the Promise of Social Mobility." *Journal of Urban History* 14 (3): 346–71.

Richmond, Anthony. 1984. "Le Canada et l'Australie." In *Diversité culturelle, société industrielle, État national: Actes du colloque*, ed. Gilles Verbunt. Paris: Éditions Harmattan.

Thernstrom, S. 1983. "Ethnic Pluralism: The U.S. Model." In *Minorities: Community and Identity*, ed. C. Fried. Berlin: Springer-Verlag.

Toinet, Marie-France. 1983. "L'accès des groupes ethniques aux médias." In *Le facteur ethnique aux États-Unis et au Canada*, ed. M. Lecompte and C. Thomas. Lille: Presses de l'Université de Lille III.

Tramier, Sylviane. 1990. "En France, le difficile passage de l'individuel au collectif." *Le Devoir*, 11 December.

Verba, Sydney, Bashiruddin Ahmed and Amil Bhatt. 1971. *Caste, Race and Politics: A Comparative Study of India and the United States*. Beverly Hills: Sage Publications.

Verba, Sydney, N.H. Nie and Jae-On Kim. 1978. *Participation and Political Equality: A Seven Nation Comparison*. Cambridge: Cambridge University Press.

Verbunt, G., ed. 1984. *Diversité culturelle, société industrielle et État national: Actes du colloque*. Paris: Éditions Harmattan.

Woehrling, José. 1986. "La Constitution canadienne et la protection des minorités ethniques." *Les Cahiers de Droit* 27 (1): 171–88.

Wolfinger, Raymond E., and Steven J. Rosenstone. 1980. *Who Votes*. New Haven: Yale University Press.

Wood, John R. 1981. "A Visible Minority Votes: East Indian Electoral Behaviour in the Vancouver South Provincial and Federal Elections of 1979." In *Ethnicity, Power and Politics in Canada*, ed. J. Dahlie and T. Fernando. Canadian Ethnic Studies Association, Vol. 8. Toronto: Methuen.

Zylberberg, Jacques. 1986. "La régulation étatique des minorités religieuses."
   In *Minorités et État*, ed. Pierre Guillaume et al. Talence: Presses
   universitaires de Bordeaux and Quebec: Presses de l'université Laval.

CONTRIBUTORS TO VOLUME 7

Yasmeen Abu-Laban   Carleton University
Alain Pelletier   Research Analyst, RCERPF
Carolle Simard   Université du Québec à Montréal
Daiva K. Stasiulis   Carleton University

ACKNOWLEDGEMENTS

The Royal Commission on Electoral Reform and Party Financing and the publishers wish to acknowledge with gratitude the permission of the following to reprint and translate material:

Harvard University Press; Danielle Juteau.

Care has been taken to trace the ownership of copyright material used in the text, including the tables and figures. The authors and publishers welcome any information enabling them to rectify any reference or credit in subsequent editions.

Consistent with the Commission's objective of promoting full participation in the electoral system by all segments of Canadian society, gender neutrality has been used wherever possible in the editing of the research studies.

THE COLLECTED RESEARCH STUDIES*

---

* The titles of studies may not be final in all cases.

COMMISSION ORGANIZATION

CHAIRMAN
Pierre Lortie

COMMISSIONERS
Pierre Fortier
Robert Gabor
William Knight
Lucie Pépin

SENIOR OFFICERS

Executive Director
Guy Goulard

Director of Research
Peter Aucoin

Special Adviser to the Chairman
Jean-Marc Hamel

Research
F. Leslie Seidle,
   Senior Research Coordinator

Legislation
Jules Brière, Senior Adviser
Gérard Bertrand
Patrick Orr

Coordinators
Herman Bakvis
Michael Cassidy
Frederick J. Fletcher
Janet Hiebert
Kathy Megyery
Robert A. Milen
David Small

Communications and Publishing
Richard Rochefort, Director
Hélène Papineau, Assistant
   Director
Paul Morisset, Editor
Kathryn Randle, Editor

Assistant Coordinators
David Mac Donald
Cheryl D. Mitchell

Finance and Administration
Maurice R. Lacasse, Director

Contracts and Personnel
Thérèse Lacasse, Chief

Editorial, Design and Production Services

Royal Commission on Electoral Reform and Party Financing

Editors Denis Bastien, Susan Becker Davidson, Ginette Bertrand, Louis Bilodeau, Claude Brabant, Louis Chabot, Danielle Chaput, Norman Dahl, Carlos del Burgo, Julie Desgagners, Chantal Granger, Volker Junginger, Denis Landry, André LaRose, Paul Morisset, Christine O'Meara, Mario Pelletier, Marie-Noël Pichelin, Kathryn Randle, Georges Royer, Eve Valiquette, Dominique Vincent.

Le Centre de Documentation Juridique du Québec Inc.

Hubert Reid, *President*

Claire Grégoire, *Comptroller*

Lucie Poirier, *Production Manager*
Gisèle Gingras, *Special Project Assistant*

Translators Pierre-Yves de la Garde, Richard Lapointe, Marie-Josée Turcotte.

Technical Editors Stéphane Côté Coulombe, *Coordinator;*
Josée Chabot, Danielle Morin.

Copy Editors Martine Germain, Lise Larochelle, Elisabeth Reid, Carole St-Louis, Isabelle Tousignant, Charles Tremblay, Sébastien Viau.

Word Processing André Vallée.

Formatting Typoform, Claude Audet; Linda Goudreau, *Formatting Coordinator.*

Wilson & Lafleur Ltée

Claude Wilson, *President*

Printed and bound in Canada by
Best Gagné Book Manufacturers